the internet made painless

THIS IS A CARLTON BOOK

CLD 21567
This edition published in 1999 for Colour Library Direct, Godalming Business Centre,
Woolsack Way, Godalming, Surrey GU7 1XW. Printed and bound in Italy

1 3 5 7 9 8 6 4 2

A CIP Catalogue for this book is available from the British Library

ISBN 1 85868 891 4

Executive Editor: Tim Dedopulos
Production: Alexia Turner

Notice of Liability
Every effort has been made to ensure that this book contains accurate and current information. However, the Publisher and the author shall not be liable for any loss or damage suffered by readers as a result of any information contained herein.

Trademarks
Microsoft® and Windows® are registered trademarks of Microsoft Corporation. All other trademarks are acknowledged as belonging to their respective companies.

Printed and bound in Italy

the internet made painless

Terry Burrows

Colour Library Direct

CONTENTS

WHAT IS THE INTERNET, REALLY?

Unless you've just returned from a lengthy stay on a distant planet you can't fail to have heard about the Internet. You'll have noticed terms like "information superhighway" being uttered enthusiastically on your TV by serious-looking young men, and seen those mysterious "www" codes popping up everywhere. But what IS the Internet? And what use is it to YOU?

WHAT DOES THE INTERNET DO?

If you link a number of computers together it creates what is known as a "network". The Internet is the mother of all networks. Indeed, it is a massive network of networks connected by fibre optic cables, satellite and microwave links and telephone lines. When your home computer is connected to the Internet you can communicate and exchange information with other computers linked up to the network. And there is a lot of information out there. Indeed, the Internet is the greatest repository of information ever to have been assembled AND IT'S THERE AT YOUR FINGERTIPS. If that hasn't captured your imagination, let's look at some of the things you can do when you're connected.

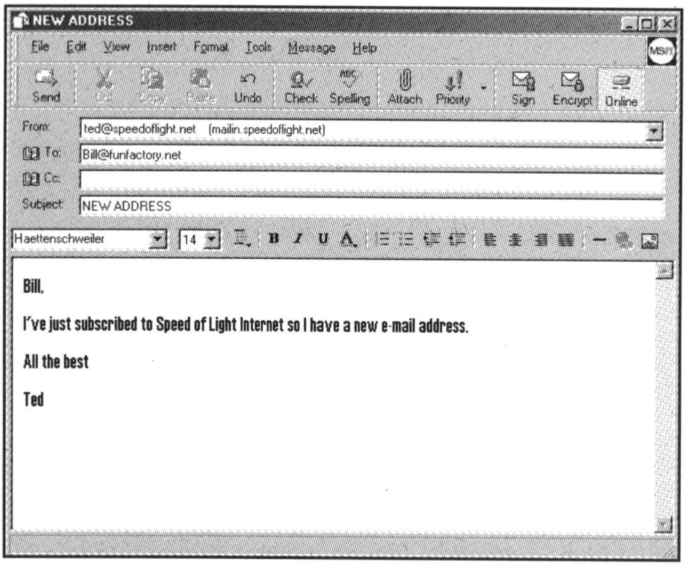

SEND AND RECEIVE E-MAILS

Instead of putting your letters in an envelope, buying a stamp at the post office, putting the stamp on the envelope and putting it in the postbox, you can simply type a message into your computer, connect to the Internet and press the "send" button. It should arrive at its destination anywhere in the world within a few minutes. And it should also cost you less than a two-minute local telephone call. Of course, the recipient also has to have an e-mail address!

THE WORLD WIDE WEB

This is the most thrilling part of the Internet. At its best, the Web can seem like one big multimedia program. Using a piece of software called a "browser" you can read pages of text, listen to music, look at images and watch video clips. You can even interact with some pages, playing games or controlling three-dimensional views. Most of the content you'll find on the Web is put there by other ordinary Internet users – although it's the "official" sites that are usually the most impressive in their use of the newest techniques in Web page design.

Web sites can typically be advertisements for new products, online stores where you can buy products with your credit card, fan sites devoted to bands, sports or hobbies, or they might simply consist of a few pages about the author.

Web sites are also fairly easy to set up for yourself, so if you have a particular hobby or interest, you can share it with other like-minded users all over the world.

WHERE DID THE INTERNET COME FROM?

Although most of us have only known about the Internet since the mid-1990s, it's actually a good deal older. It sprang to life in 1969 largely as a result of Cold War paranoia. The US Department of Defense commissioned the Advanced Research Project Agency to create a massive military computer network which would be known as ARPANET. The idea was that if one of their bases was disabled by a nuclear strike, the network of computers would not be broken – the remaining bases would still be able to communicate with one another online. The system that ARPA devised involved breaking information down into small "packets" of data which could move around the network to be reassembled at their destination. If one of the computers in the network failed to work, the packets would simply find alternative routes. In 1982, the US military abandoned ARPANET. What remained became known as the Internet and was taken up by American universities and scientific foundations. Gradually more and more computers joined the Internet. By the late 1980s, commercial organizations linked to the Internet began to sell their own connections to the public. These companies, usually called ISPs (Internet Service Providers) are connected to the Internet via high-speed routing links known as "backbones". So when we think of ourselves as being "connected" to the Internet we are, in fact, linked to a computer system (maintained by our ISP) that passes and receives messages to and from the Internet.

NEWSGROUPS

Sometimes referred to as USENET, the tens of thousands of newsgroups around the world are Internet-based forums for open discussion. Each newsgroup is rather like a public notice board on which messages can be posted, read and responded to. Many of the thousands of different newsgroups on the Internet cover VERY specific subjects. For example, if you collect stamps, you may want to join the newsgroup alt.collecting.stamps, in which philatelists can get together and do their thing. If this proves too general for some, newsgroups often break down into more specific groups. For example, alt.collecting.stamps.us is for discussion about American stamps and nothing else.

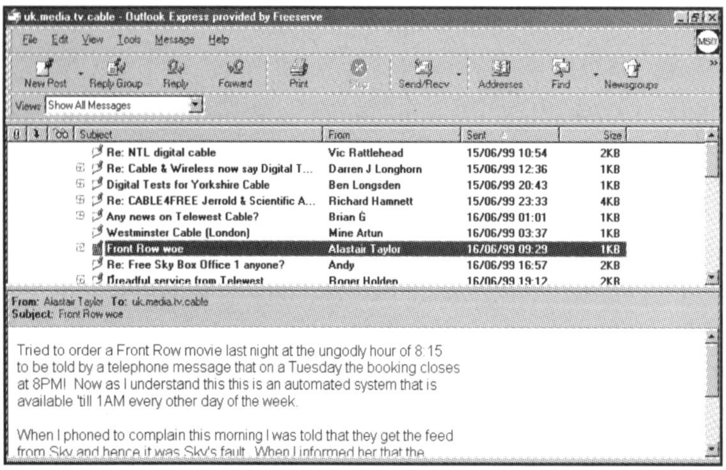

INTERNET CHAT LINES

The problem of communicating through e-mail or newsgroups is that conversations can lack a sense of immediacy. There is no guarantee that the person you are "talking" to is online at the same time as you. You may have to wait until they next log on to get a reply. Conversations, therefore, can become rather stilted affairs. One way in which it's possible to enjoy real-time communication with others is by using an online chat system such as Internet Relay Chat (IRC). The IRC software simulates a room full of people, with different channels (still usually called "rooms") often devoted to special interests. Each time you type a message at the bottom of the screen the other people in the room (those who are connected to that IRC channel at that moment) will immediately see the message and can respond.

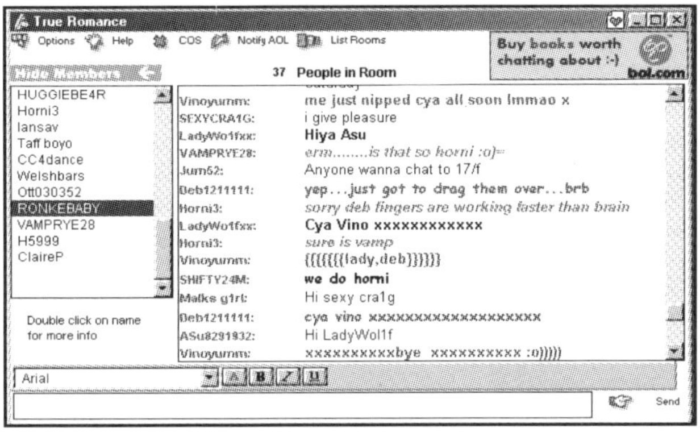

The future of one-to-one chatting also looks assured as it becomes increasingly more straightforward to hold voice conversations over the Internet – this allows you to have global conversations for the cost of a local call. If you have compatible video equipment you can also establish video phone links in the same way.

DOWNLOADING FILES

The Internet can be viewed as a massive archive from which you can obtain new software for your computer. You'll find hundreds of thousands of programs out there just waiting for you to press a "download" button. And this is all generally legal. Program designers often make their software available for free – they just do it as a hobby. Others allow you to give their programs a trial run – if you like it you can buy it. As far as the expensive commercial programs go, sometimes you can download updates or bug fixes which will only work if you have an authorised copy running on your machine. Downloads usually take place from Web sites, although, as you will see, there are other ways.

There are many other useful downloads you can make. For example, photographic and video images, sound files, or even copyright-lapsed literature.

INTERNET GAMING

If playing games on your PC is your thing, then the Internet can increase your pleasure exponentially. Famous PC games such as Quake and Doom (which can be played by more than one user when computers are linked) can, if your service provider caters for it, be played across the Internet with anyone, any time, anywhere in the world.

BUT ISN'T IT FOR GEEKS?

The Internet has had some bad press in the past. It's sometimes easy to get the impression that Net surfers are sad, friendless nerds who would be better off turning their attention to getting a life. Nothing could be further from the truth. The Internet has something to offer EVERYONE, irrespective of their age, sex, level of education or interests. And the good news is that, not only is it getting bigger and better all the time, but it's getting cheaper and easier to use. There has never been a better time to start taking part in the greatest communications revolution since the advent of television.

A LOOK INTO THE FUTURE?

There can be no question that very quickly the Internet has changed the way in which we live, work and communicate. A new breed of employee – the "teleworker" – has already emerged. With work-places increasingly reliant on computers, there is no need for some to commute to an office when their work can be done at home and "dialled-in" over the Internet. For kids, the Internet is fast becoming an indispensible education tool, with much typical school library reference material available from sources on the Internet. The multimedia side of the Internet continues to progress by the day. Some have predicted that in the not-so-distant future there will be no need for us to buy CDs or videos. We'll simply use the Internet as an on-line juke box. As for shopping, already the big supermarket chains allow us to shop for groceries on the World Wide Web and then have them delivered for a small charge. All of this is likely to mean some pretty fundamental changes to society. One problem that has already emerged is that of "data overload". Simply put, there is SO MUCH out there on the Internet that we're finding it increasingly difficult to see through the fog and reach the information we want.

1 GETTING STARTED

Taking your first tentative steps into cyberspace can be a rather daunting prospect. And it's rather unfortunate that the most elementary steps – like getting your basic Internet connection worked out and your computer configured – are arguably the most taxing. With a bit of luck, the tips you'll find over the next few pages should be enough to get you started without too much hassle. After this, everything else is a breeze.

WHAT YOU NEED

Here is a checklist of all the items you need at your disposal to access the Internet. If you don't have them right now, we'll tell you how to get hold of them.

BASIC REQUIREMENTS

Getting connected to the Internet is a pretty straightforward business. All you really need is a personal computer, a modem, a standard telephone line and an account with a service provider (for access to the Internet). You will also need some suitable software, although in nearly all cases the bare essentials will come as a part of the basic starter pack from your service provider. When you get connected you can download other useful programs from the Internet.

Your computer connects to a regular domestic telephone line through a piece of hardware called a modem. This links you via your service provider to the Internet and so effectively becomes your gateway to cyberspace.

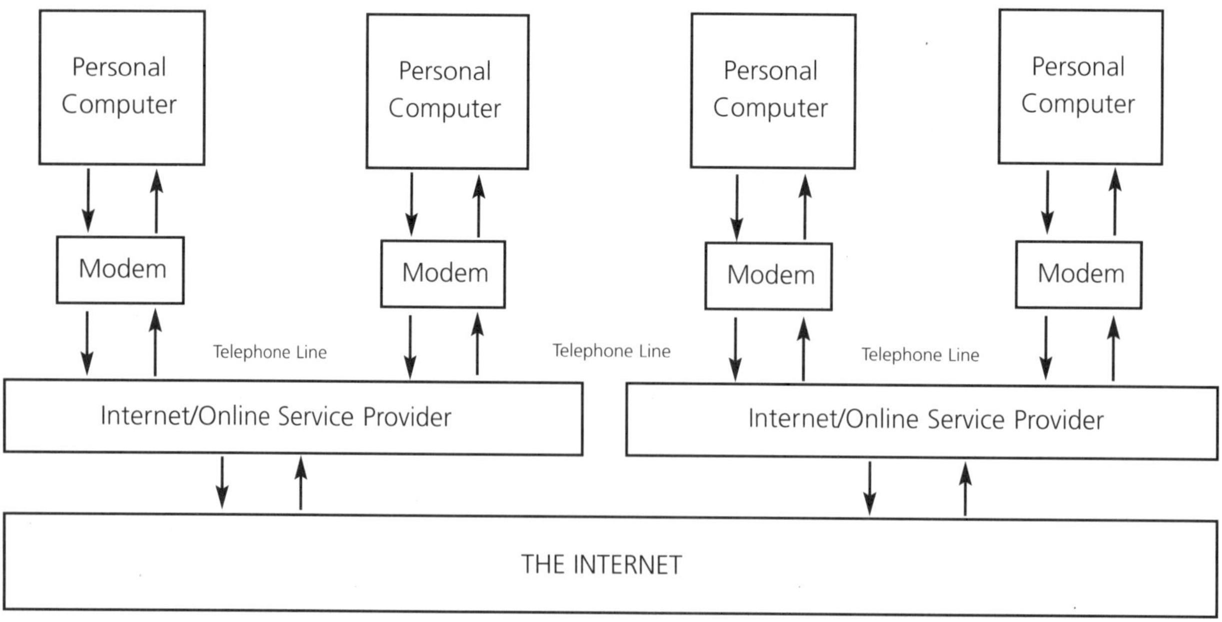

HOW MUCH KNOWLEDGE DO I NEED?

For the purposes of this book, we'll make three assumptions: that you already own a home computer, that you are familiar with basic operating functions like running programs and manipulating a mouse, and that you have a telephone line. Nearly all of the software examples shown throughout feature programs running on a PC under Windows 98. Don't worry if you prefer a different type of computer – an Apple iMac or G3, for example – the basic principles remain the same, although you may occasionally notice that some of the menu-bar options within the software look different.

WHAT'S A MODEM?

A modem – technically a "Modulator/Demodulator" – is a piece of hardware that connects to your computer and turns digital signals into a format that can be passed along a telephone line. It can also convert them back to their original form. If you have bought a new computer over the past year or so, there's a good chance that you already have a modem fitted. Modems come in two distinct forms. It will either be a physical box that connects between your computer and the telephone socket or a piece of electronic circuitry that slots neatly inside the computer's casing. Both types of modem work equally well.

SPEED ISSUES

The most important aspect to consider when choosing a modem is the speed at which it can transmit and read data. This speed is measured in "bits per second". The fastest standard modem that most Internet service providers can deal with is 56K (56,000 bits per second) – don't bother with anything slower. This speed is sometimes referred to as "V.90". Standard modem speeds have increased four-fold during the last five years, but we now seem to have reached the uppermost limit of what is possibile through an ordinary telephone line – for the time being, at least.

Other features you might want to look out for when you buy a modem are fax and voice support. Many allow you to transmit and receive faxes on your computer, and some will even double up as telephone answering machines.

SERVICE PROVIDERS

Once you've got all your hardware sorted out, the final component of your Internet armoury is the service provider. This is the company that gives you access to the facilities of the Internet. A list of service providers can be found on pages 170-173.

WHAT TYPE OF PROVIDER?

Companies selling or giving Internet access can be categorized as Internet Service Providers (ISPs) or Online Service Providers (OSPs). An ISP simply gives you a means of connecting to the Internet. This should include at least one unique e-mail address as well as space for you to create your own Web pages. OSPs also give these features but present the Internet through their own entry menus. The advantage of the OSP approach is that it makes the initial Internet experience much more organized and straightforward for beginners. Furthermore, each OSP has its own specialized services with unique databases covering the likes of news, travel, weather and other special interests accessible only to their subscribers.

The downside of OSPs is that the amount of money you pay each month usually depends on the length of time you have been connected to the Internet service, so for heavy users it can be a very expensive business. Most ISPs simply charge a sign-on fee and a fixed monthly charge, irrespective of online time. A recent development has been the birth of "free" ISPs. These companies make their money through advertising or deals with telecommunications companies – the only charges made to the consumer are for technical support.

As always, different people have different needs, so before you subscribe to any service you should understand exactly what you'll be getting – especially where you have to pay.

YOUR ISP/OSP CHECKLIST

Technically speaking, there is very little to choose between most of the current leading ISPs and OSPs since most of them offer broadly similar services. Consequently, there's no reason at all to stay with an ISP if you are not happy with the service you get. It's a good idea to take up free trial offers – you should be able to figure out within a month whether an ISP provides you with good day-to-day access. Here is a checklist of points that you should consider before you sign up. Don't worry if you don't understand some of the terms right now – they'll be explained later.

COSTS

1. Is there a charge for registration?
2. If there is a monthly fee, does it provide unlimited access to the Internet?
3. If cost is based around usage, how much is it per hour?
4. Do you have to sign up for a minimum period?
5. Can you cancel at any time?
6. Are there free trials?

CONNECTION

7. Is the connection local? If not, your telephone bills are liable to go through the roof.
8. What is the speed of access? You should be to connect at modem speeds of 56K.
9. What is the ratio of ISP/OSP modems to subscribers?If it's more than 15:1 you could have problems getting connected in some cases.
10. How much unscheduled downtime has there been over the last year? This means how often has the ISP/OSP been offline to its subscribers.

SOFTWARE

11. Does the ISP/OSP provide its own software? If so does it run on your type of computer?
12. What software is provided free of charge?

SUPPORT

13. Is there a technical support line?
14. Is there a charge for technical support?
15. Does support cover your type of computer?

FEATURES

16. Are e-mail accounts POP3 or SMTP? (both should be supported).
17. How many e-mail addresses will be allocated to you?
18. How will your e-mail addresses appear?
19. How much free Web space is provided? You should expect at least 10MB.
20. How much does Web space cost beyond the basic allowance?
21. Are MP3 files or RealAudio streams allowed from your Web page?
22. Which Usenet newsgroups are held on the server?
23. Can "alias" domain names be supported?

SETTING UP AN ACCOUNT

To show you how easy it can be to set up an Internet account, we'll create one using the FreeServe ISP. We'll also show an example of the online service provider America OnLine for comparison.

GETTING READY FOR ACTION

To get started you need the FreeServe access CD, which can be picked up in some electrical stores or ordered over by telephone (see pages 170-173). This contains all the information you need to configure your computer, a Web browser and software for reading and writing e-mails. Begin by putting the CD into your CD drive.

1 Click on the FreeServe icon in the CD drive. Click on INSTALL FREESERVE in the welcome screen.

2 Install Internet Explorer. Follow the steps, each time clicking on NEXT until installation is done. Clicking on FINISH will cause your computer to restart.

3 When your computer restarts, you should automatically go into FreeServe's set-up screen. Click on CONTINUE to start up the INTERNET CONNECTION WIZARD. This connects you to the Internet.

Your computer "calls" Freeserve's dial-up number which was automatically installed with Internet Explorer.

4 If the connection was successful, you will see the ONLINE SIGNUP SCREEN. To get to the next stage, click on REGISTER FOR A NEW ACCOUNT.

5 Before you work out your account details, you are asked to fill in some personal details about yourself and your interests.

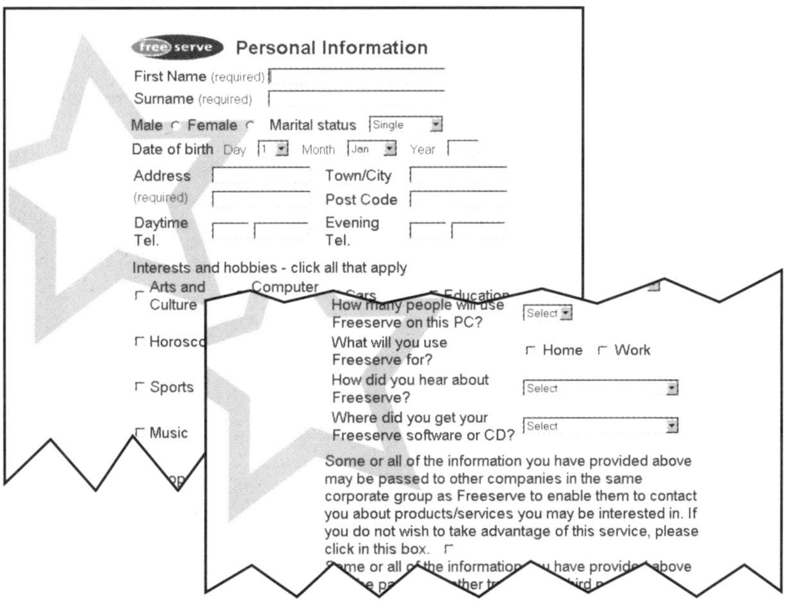

6 With formalities out of the way, specify your e-mail address and password. You will be asked to enter this twice to confirm it. Make a note of address and password. You will need it in future.

A valid e-mail address may be fred@bloggs.freeserve.co.uk. You can read more about e-mail addresses in chapter 3.

7 If your e-mail address and password are both valid, click on FINISHED. You now have an Internet account with FreeServe as your ISP.

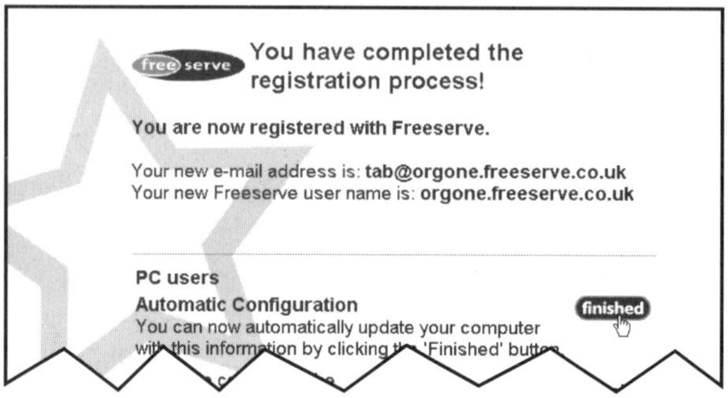

8 Whilst you are still connected, try your first experience of life on the Internet by clicking on the FREESERVE INTERNET shortcut which was installed on your desktop. If things have worked correctly you will see the FreeServe home page.

Don't worry that the home page on your own screen doesn't match the one shown here – it changes every day.

ONLINE SERVICE PROVIDER

AOL (America OnLine) are now the world's largest OSP. Their service is more all-encompassing than the regular ISPs in that much of its content is available only to subscribers and not to other Internet users. Although it isn't free, AOL is a good bet for the beginner simply because its set-up and operation is so straightforward. To make AOL work you need its free client program, which is loaded onto your computer just like any other software. When you start up the program you have the option of setting up an account or entering your identity code and password. Thereafter, the AOL program can perform all of your standard Internet tasks.

One of the benefits of using an OSP is access to the subscriber services – referred to as "AOL channels". Whether you find them useful will determine your attitude to online service providers such as AOL. You can see some examples of AOL's channels shown below.

1 Click on AOL CHANNELS and select ENTERTAINMENT from the drop-down menu.

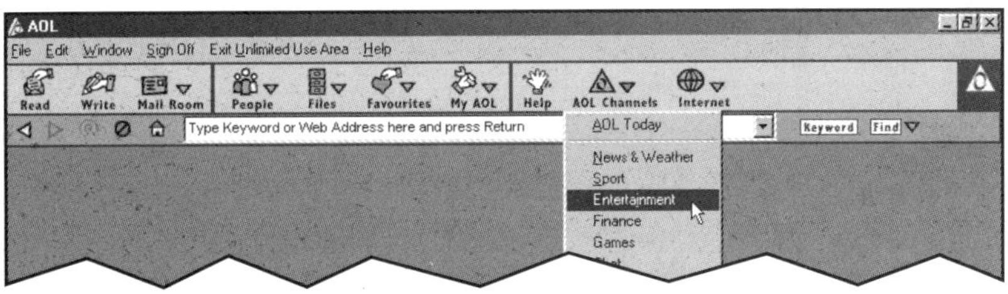

2 In the AOL ENTERTAINMENT page click on MUSIC.

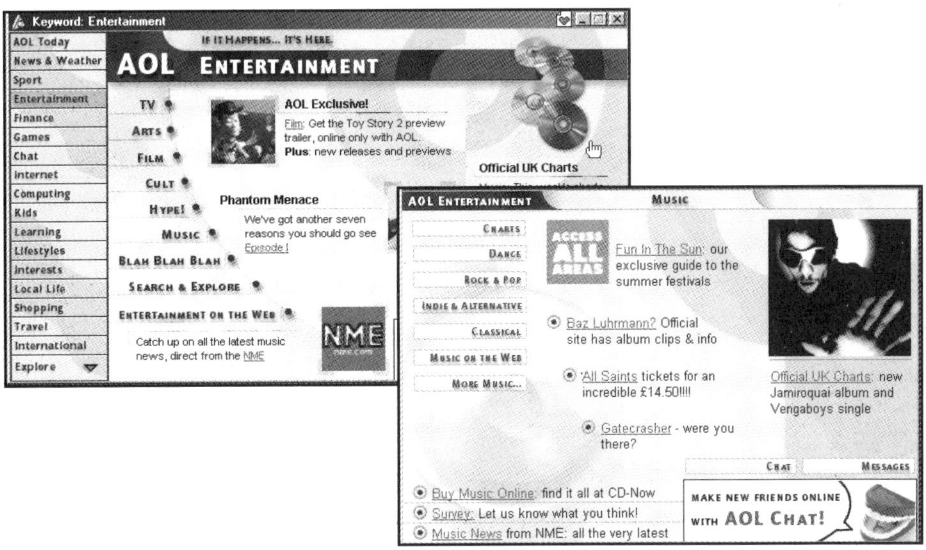

IF YOU MUST...

The approach you've just seen to getting connected (i.e. when an ISP or OSP "holds your hand" during the sign-on procedure) is increasingly the norm. It's great because it masks the complexities of configuring your computer. However, it is possible (and sometimes necessary) to go through this process manually, although this can allow plenty of potential to make errors along the way.

NUMBERS AT THE READY

If you need to make a manual connection, there are a number of pieces of information that you need to get from your ISP.

- **Local access telephone number**
- **Your ID**
- **Your password**
- **IP Address**
- **Domain name server address(es)**
- **Your domain name**
- **SMTP server**
- **POP server**
- **POP3 password**
- **News server**
- **E-mail address**

1 Click on the START pop-up menu. From the PROGRAM folder hierarchy select ACCESSORIES, COMMUNICATIONS and finally INTERNET CONNECTION WIZARD.

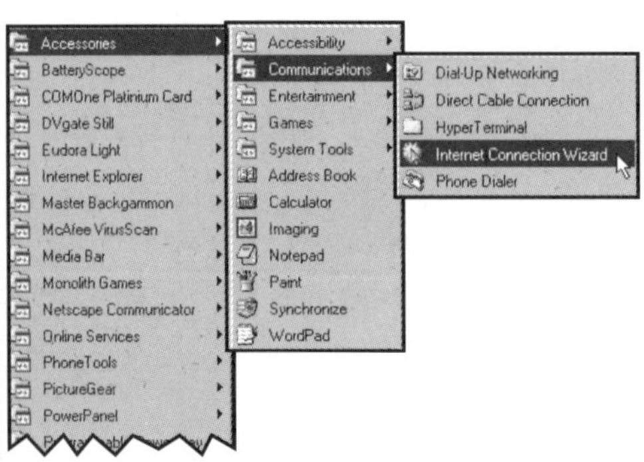

2 In the welcome page for the INTERNET CONNECTION WIZARD click on the third option to create a manual connection. Click on NEXT.

If you get into difficulty, the INTERNET CONNECTION WIZARD's online tutorial may be able to help you.

3 On the next page select the option for connection through a phone line and modem. Click on NEXT.

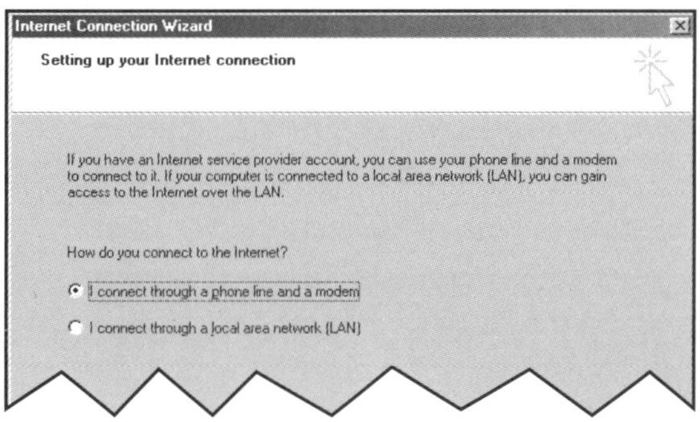

4 Enter the local access phone number that connects to your ISP. Click on ADVANCED.

5 In the ADVANCED CONNECTION PROPERTIES dialog box select the ADDRESSES tab. Enter the IP ADDRESS and the DNS ADDRESSES. Click on OK.

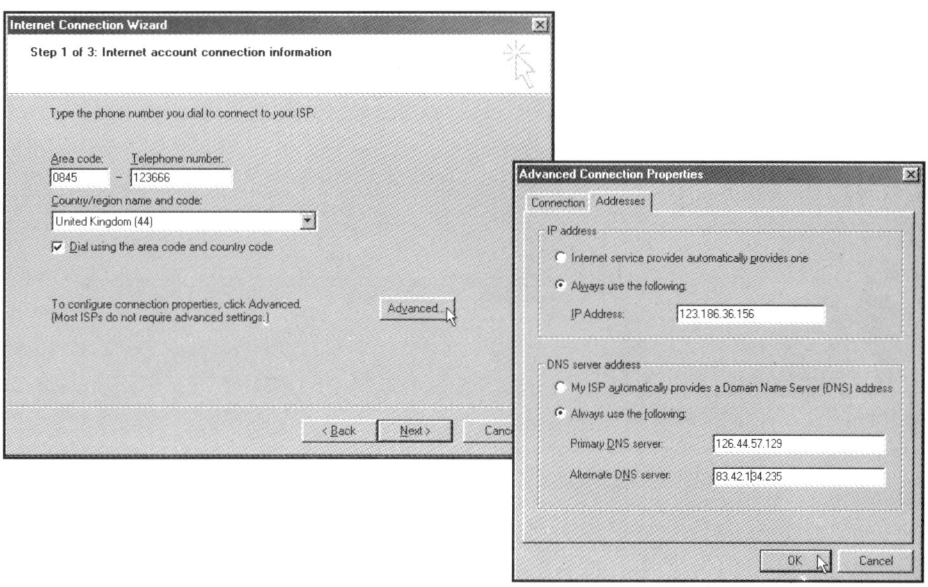

6 Type in your USER NAME and PASSWORD. Click on Next.

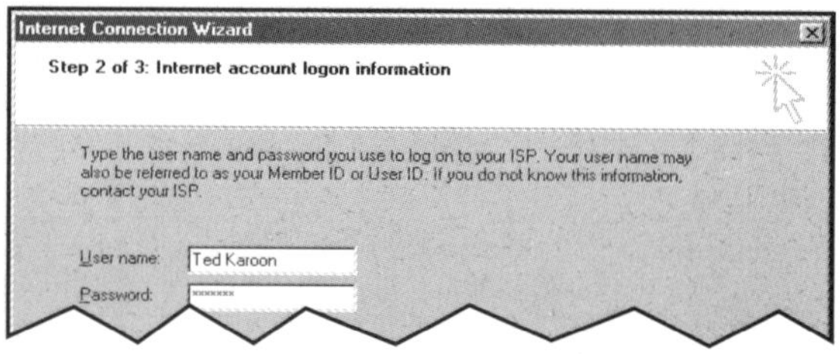

7 Type in the identity you want to give to the connection. It makes sense to call it by the ISP's name. Click on NEXT.

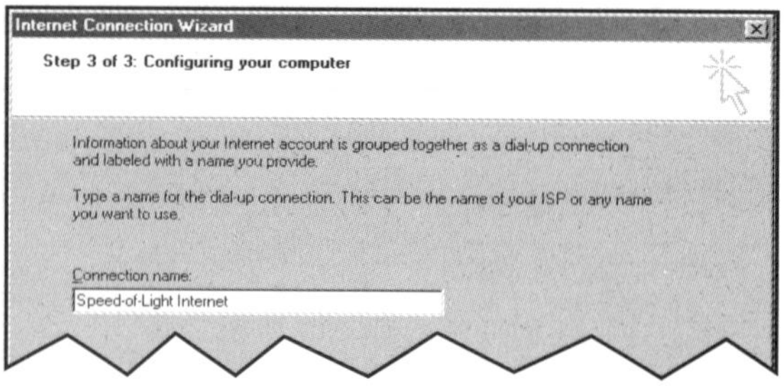

8 You are now asked if you want to set up your mail details. Click on YES and then on NEXT.

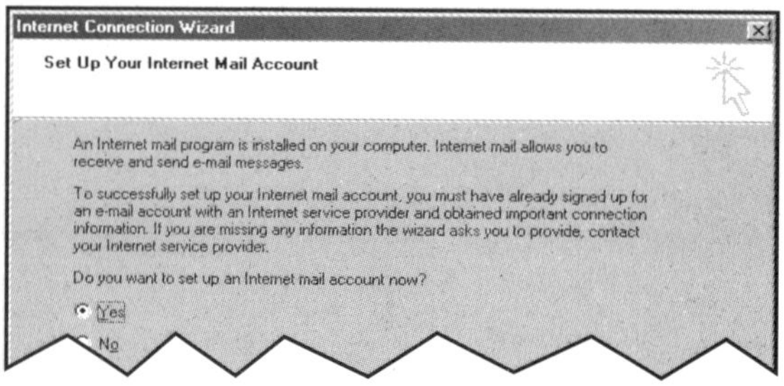

9 Type in the name that you want to appear on your outgoing e-mails. Click on NEXT.

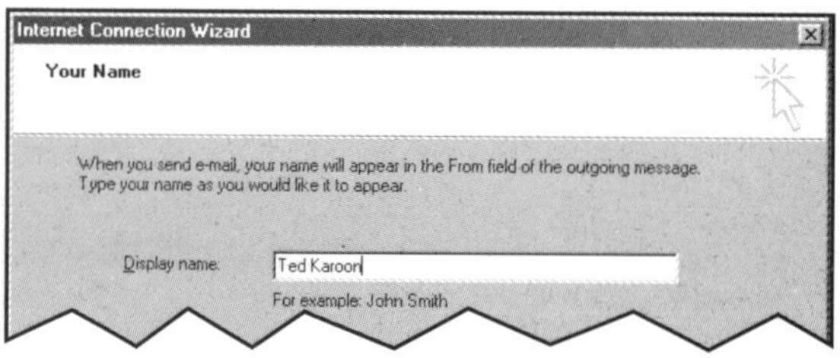

10 Type in your the e-mail address you've agreed with your ISP. Click on NEXT.

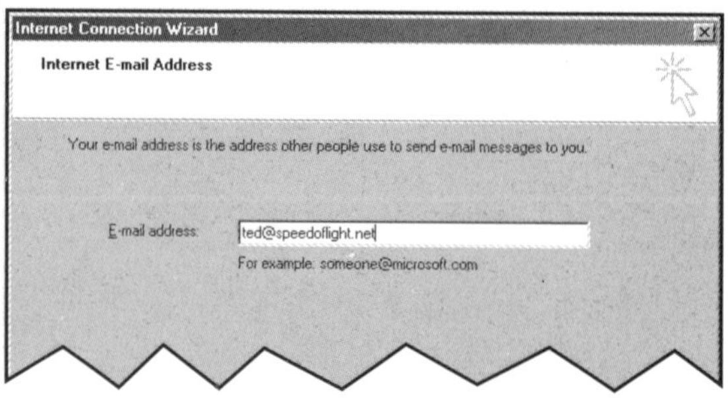

11 Select the type of server on which the incoming mail will be held (this is usually POP3). Type in the names of both the incoming and outgoing mail servers. Click on NEXT.

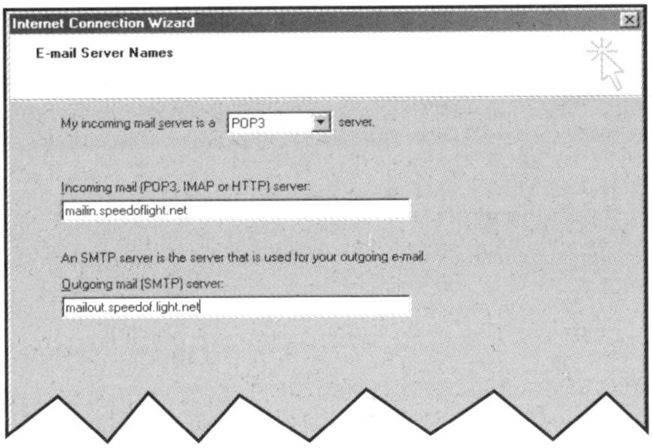

12 The process is now complete. Click on FINISH.

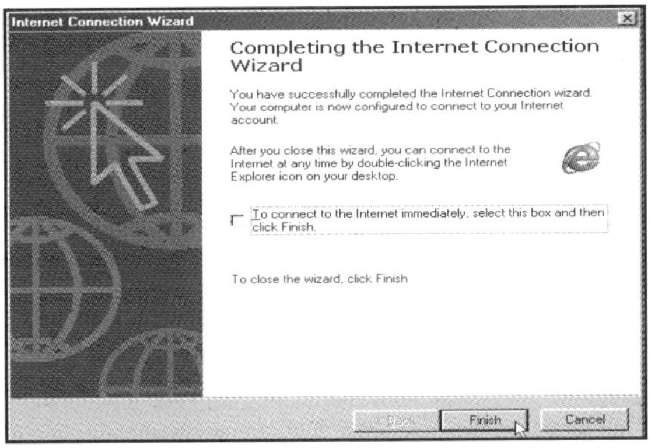

TEST YOUR NEW CONNECTION

You can tell if your new connection has worked by running a Web browser. When the program has loaded, the DIAL-UP CONNECTION dialog box should appear with the connection details that you've just set up. Click on CONNECT and your modem should burst into action.

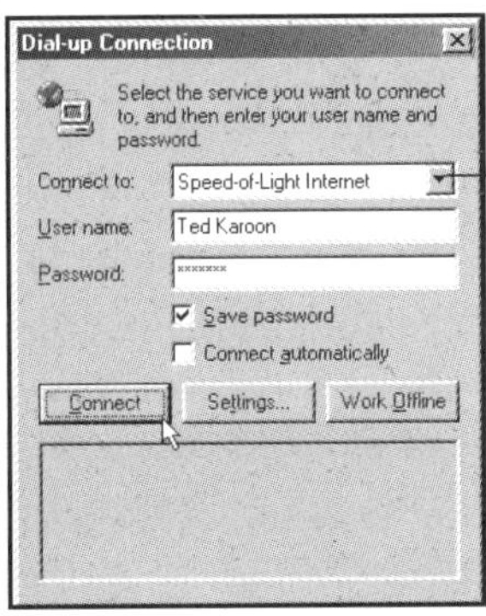

If you have more than one ISP account you can select the one you want to use by clicking on the arrow and choosing from the drop-down menu.

NO CONNECTION?

If you've got this far without any trouble, then well done! For those less lucky, here are a few ideas that might help out.

- Is your telephone line working? Plug in a phone and listen out for a dialling tone.
- If you are using an external modem, is it switched on?
- Is your modem connected to the telephone socket?
- If you are using an external modem, is it s it connected to your computer with the correct cables?
- Look inside the Windows CONTROL PANEL and click on MODEMS to ensure that the correct model is specified.
- If your modem has a volume control, turn it up and listen for the characteristic high-pitched buzzing sound when you dial out. If you don't hear anything the problem is between your computer and the modem. If you do, it will probably be a configuration problem.
- If your modem doesn't have a loudspeaker, you can perform the experiment by running DIALLER in the ACCESSORIES folder and entering a friend's phone number. When they answer the phone they should hear the buzzing sound.
- If all of this works, make sure that the local access phone number of your ISP is set up correctly in your Dial-In box.
- If the modem signal reaches your ISP but still doesn't get you online, there is likely to be a problem with your ID or password. Check that the spelling you have used is correct, and also if the case of the letters matches.
- If your connection is accepted but you can't seem to get anywhere on the Internet, check that the DNS addresses have been correctly entered. If the problem is with mail or news groups, check the naming of the mail and news servers. Contact your ISP if you don't know the correct names.
- OK, the only other option is to throw your hands up in the air and admit defeat – it's time to hand matters over to your ISP's technical support line.

2

THE WORLD WIDE WEB

The World Wide Web is the most fascinating aspect of the Internet. There's more information packed into the millions of Web sites than in every library in the world put together. It is the ultimate repository of information and it's getting more and more vast by the minute. This section will see you through the basics of life on the Web, from how to view pages, to finding your way through this incredible maze of information.

WHAT IS THE WORLD WIDE WEB?

Imagine that everyone in the world was given a blank piece of paper on which they could write or draw anything they wanted. It could be a description or picture of themselves or information about their work and hobbies – absolutely anything. Now imagine that there was some way in which anyone could look at any of those pieces of paper from anywhere in the world at the press of a button. This is in essence what the World Wide Web is all about, but instead of pieces of paper they are electronic documents that you can view on your computer screen.

HYPERWHAT?

These electronic documents – usually described as "Web pages" – are far more sophisticated than simply static information on a page. It's possible to manoeuvre around the Web by clicking the mouse over specially designed "hot" areas of the page. You can tell where these are because the text is shown underlined or in a different colour and the cursor changes its appearance from a pointer to a finger icon. These hot areas are sometimes known as "hyperlinks". The author of the page creates these hyperlinks to help you more quickly to different sections of the document. This is useful because although it's called a Web "page", it could have the equivalent of 50 pages worth of content. These longer pages are navigated using a scroll bar at the side of the

HOW DO HYPERLINKS WORK?

Web pages are written in a very simple computer language called HTML – indeed, it's so simple that by the end of this book you'll be able to write it for yourself. HTML stands for HyperText Markup Language, which was developed by a British particle physicist named Tim Berners-Lee. A series of instruction "tags" are inserted into pieces of ordinary text to control the way the page looks and behaves when viewed in a Web browser. Tags can determine the typeface used or act as instructions to display an image file or play a sound file. And, of course, they can also be used to link you up to other Web pages.

page, but it is usually easier to move around the document by clicking on a link. Hyperlinks can also be used to connect you to a different Web page altogether. You can see a good example of how this can work by looking at a "signpost" page which acts as an index to other Web sites. In these cases you don't need to know the addresses of the Web pages to access them; you simply click on the hyperlink and it takes you straight there.

1 Clicking on any one of the underlined hyperlinks connects you to the relevant Web site.

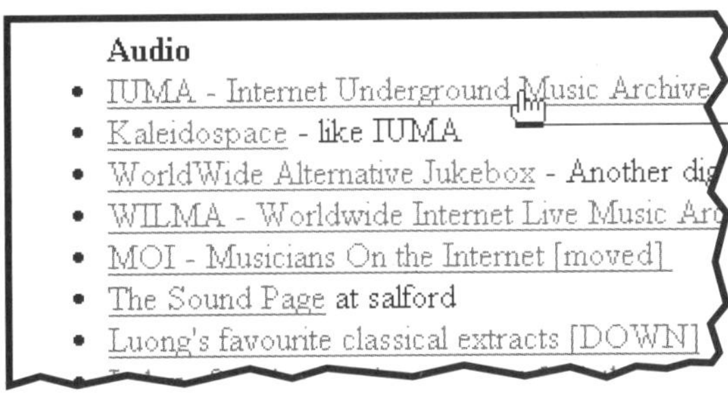

The cursor becomes a finger icon when above a hyperlink.

2 The main page for the Internet Underground Music Archive – the link selected above.

WEB ADDRESSES

Just as there would be no point in posting a letter if you didn't write an address on the envelope, you wouldn't be able find a Web site unless it had some means of identification. As it happens, every single one of the millions of Web pages on the Internet has its own unique address. Sometimes, as we saw on the previous page, where a hyperlink exists you may not be aware of the linked page, but it's there none the less. A Web address is known as a URL.

HOW WEB ADDRESSES WORK

Even before you first ventured onto the Internet, you can't have failed to notice those mysterious little codes beginning with http://www that invariably now appear at the foot of billboard adverts or company letterheads. For reasons we don't need to know, these codes are called "Uniform Resource Locators". Most people simply know them as URLs.

Let's look at a real example of a URL to see how they work. The page http://www.parliament.uk/parliament/index.htm is the official A to Z index of the British Parliament.

COMPONENTS OF THE URL

A URL is made up of three different components: the protocol; the domain; and the page (which may include a file path).

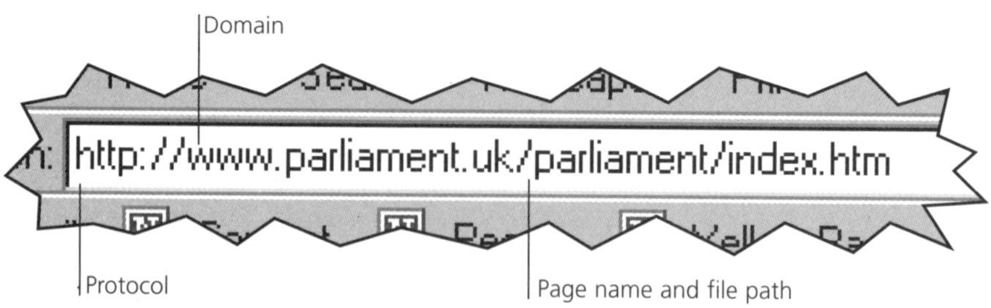

UPPER OR LOWER CASE?

Generally speaking, Web addresses are case sensitive. This means that the capital letters and their equivalent lower-case letters are treated as separate letters entirely. Although the vast majority of URLs are lower case, from time to time you may come across a Web site that uses capital letters in its URL. You MUST enter the letters as shown or you will not be able to connect to the site. For example, you won't find the Web page http://www.fredsmithwengineering/New_Products if you type in the URL http://www.fredsmithwengineering/new_products. A good rule to bear in mind is to always use lower-case letters unless told otherwise. You won't go far wrong if you stick to this principle.

PROTOCOL

The first part of a Web page's URL will always begin with the letters http followed by a colon and two forward slashes. It is this code that tells the Internet that it is a Web page. Later you will see another type of URL protocol that uses the prefix ftp:// ("file transfer protocol").

Since the protocol for Web sites is ALWAYS the same, the http:// part is often left out to simplify matters when Web addresses are printed. These are the Web addresses that seem to begin with the letters "www". To make them work, however, you still have to insert the http:// protocol at the front.

DOMAIN

The second part of the URL is the domain name. In our example it is www.parliament.uk/. At its simplest, the domain tells you on whose computer the Web site is stored. In this case, it is evidently the British Parliament that runs the computer or server which connects to the Internet. Personal web pages generally use the domain names for e-mail addresses with "www" inserted at the front. These are usually a combination of the ISP's name and the user's own unique "node" name. For example, if your ISP's domain is myserver.net and you've chosen the name smithengineering, your home page would probably have a URL of http://www.smithengineering.myserver.net.

PAGE NAMES

The third part of the URL is the page name. In our example it is parliament/index.htm. Because the text is separated by slashes, we know that the page we're looking for is buried in a hierarchy of folders and subfolders. If we don't specify a page name at all, and just type in http://www.parliament.uk it will probably take us to the "home page" – the top layer, if you like. Typing in http://www.parliament.uk/parliament will take us a layer down. Finally, http://www.parliament.uk/parliament/index.htm brings us to the desired page.

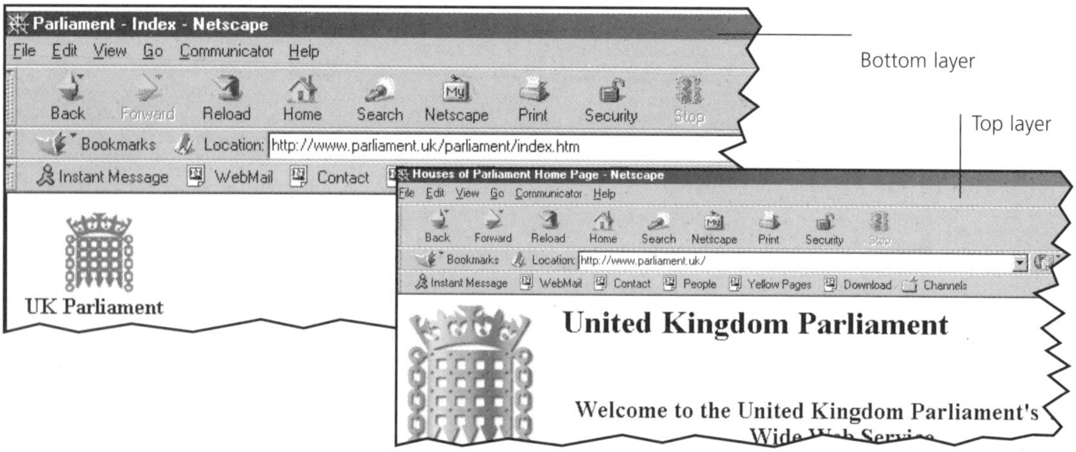

DOMAIN NAMING STANDARDS

With so many people around the world coming online, the Internet industry has valiantly battled in an attempt to get some sensible naming standards in place. This theoretically enables Internet users to know a little about the owners of the site. The approach has been to use a series of suffixes separated by "dots" which aim to tell us something about the owner's organization and from which country they come. Here is a list of the most commonly used organization abbreviations:

.ac	Academic body, school or college
.co	Business
.com	Commerical organization (usually American)
.edu	US academic institution
.gov	Government agency
.net	Internet Service Provider
.org	Organization

The national suffixes are also easy to work out. Britain is .uk, Germany is .de, France is .fr, Italy is .it, Japan is .jp and Finland is .fi. If you see a domain name without a national suffix it is likely to be American company or an international business.

To give you some examples: www.bbc.co.uk is the domain name for the British Broadcasting Corporation. Similarly, www.virgin.net is the domain name for the VirginNet Internet Service Provider.

These domain naming standards only represent guidelines and are not exactly rigorously adhered to – you will find plenty of anomalies as you work your way through the Web.

DOMAIN COPYRIGHT

Finally, with "e-commerce" taking off, as more and more well-established businesses begin trading on the Internet, the issue of copyrighting domain names becomes increasingly important. When international domain copyrighting came into being in the mid-1990s, some smart individuals were very fast off the mark to stake their claims on some of the most famous business names in the world. When these businesses finally went online they sometimes found they had to pay out large amounts of money for the right to trade in cyberspace under their own brand names.

CAN YOU NAME YOUR OWN DOMAIN?

For most people, getting a URL for their Web pages means having a domain that includes the name of the Internet Service Provider. But if you're an up-and-coming (but poverty-stricken) business, trading via the Internet with clients from around the world, such names can seem unprofessional – it's a bit like driving a Ferrari with the name of the car hire company emblazened along the side. So how do you go about getting a succinct domain that consists purely of your own name? There are two main options, but both work on the same principle. For a premium, most ISPs will set up a domain service for you, but this can cost you hundreds or even thousands of pounds a year. A cheaper option is to use an intermediary who will register your domain name and keep it stored on their own server. This then "points" incoming traffic to the web site on your ISP's server. In this way, you can call yourself www.internationalfinance.com on your headed notepaper and adverts (if that name hadn't already been registered), but every time someone tries to connect to this name, it would in fact reach plain old www.fredsmith.freeinternetservice.co.uk. These deals usually also include e-mail forwarding to any ISP you choose.

WEB BROWSERS

To survey the undoubted wonders of the World Wide Web you need just one piece of software – a "web browser". The good news is that this software won't cost you a penny. Indeed, you only have to buy one of the numerous monthly Internet magazines to get the latest version of the two main programs – Microsoft's Internet Explorer and Netscape's Navigator (which is part of their Communicator package).

WHAT IS A BROWSER?

At its simplest, a browser is a piece of software that lets you view the pages of the World Wide Web. However, in the few years since they were first developed, browsers have changed their function to encompass all aspects of life on the Internet, such as sending and reading e-mails, posting to newsgroups and downloading files from archives. Although a Web browser may not be able to perform some of these functions as elegantly as specialized software, it is absolutely essential for getting the most out of the Internet.

USING A BROWSER

To surf the World Wide Web all you need besides a browser is a valid account with an internet service provider (or an online service provider) and the address of the Web site with which you want to connect.

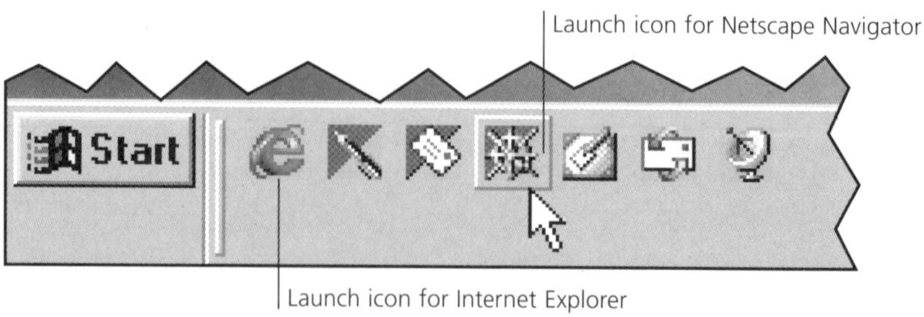

When you launch your browser program it looks to see whether or not you are online. If you aren't already connected to the Internet the browser will automatically prompt you with your computer's dial-up window. If you choose to make the connection, the browser will attempt to connect to its default home page. Unless you specify otherwise, this will be the home page specified by Netscape or Microsoft. Both of them are good starting points for Web novices as they contain lots of useful hyperlinks to other sites; so if you really want, you can start on the World Wide Web without knowing a single URL.

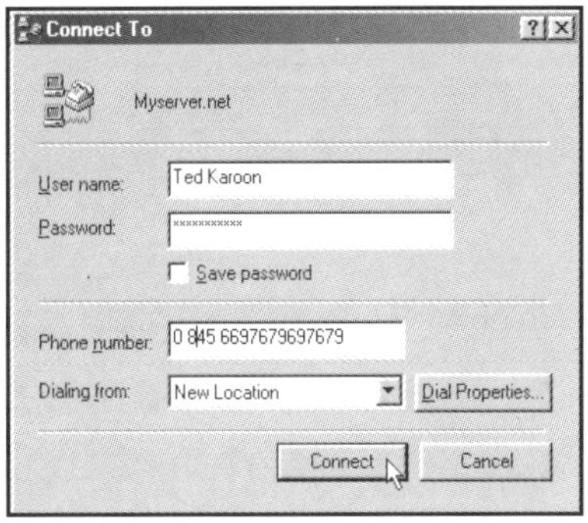

Specifying a Web address is really straightforward, though. All you do is position the cursor in the address location box, type over the existing URL and press the ENTER key. That's really all there is to it.

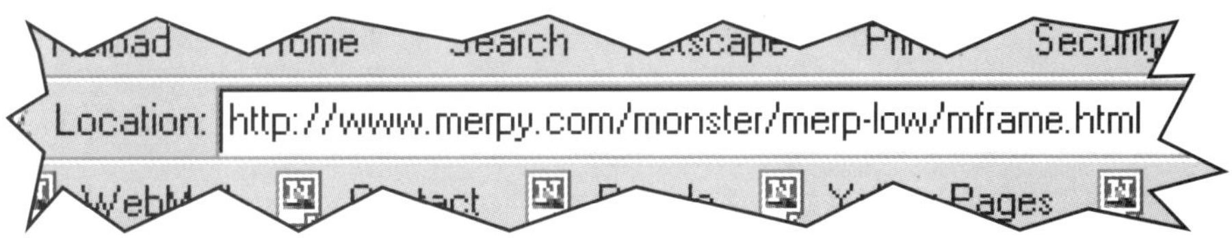

WHERE DID BROWSERS COME FROM?

The single most influential figure in the development of the Web browser was a young American computer (and business) wizard named Marc Andreesen. In 1993, he led a team that developed Mosaic, the forerunner of all Web browsers. Mosaic was the first browser able to deal not only with text but also images. Shortly afterwards, while still in his late twenties, Andreesen jointly founded the Netscape Corporation and produced Navigator, which quickly turned him into a multi-millionaire. For several years Navigator was the clear market leader until Bill Gates and Microsoft inevitably joined the challenge with Internet Explorer. Although both browsers have been broadly comparable since then, Microsoft pulled level with Netscape when they began introducing Explorer as a standard part of the Windows operating systems. Nowadays, almost every new PC arrives with a copy of Internet Explorer ready loaded. In 1998, Andreesen sold Netscape to the international Online Service Provider America OnLine (AOL). Navigator now comes as a part of the Netscape Communicator package.

NETSCAPE NAVIGATOR

Below you can see how a typical Web page looks using the Netscape Navigator Web browser. Across the page some of the features and drop-down menus are described, although in many instances you will find that their functions are quite self-evident.

THE MAIN SCREEN

Netscape Navigator's main screen is made up from of a series of drop-down menus and navigational tools. Only the active area changes when you connecet to a new web page.

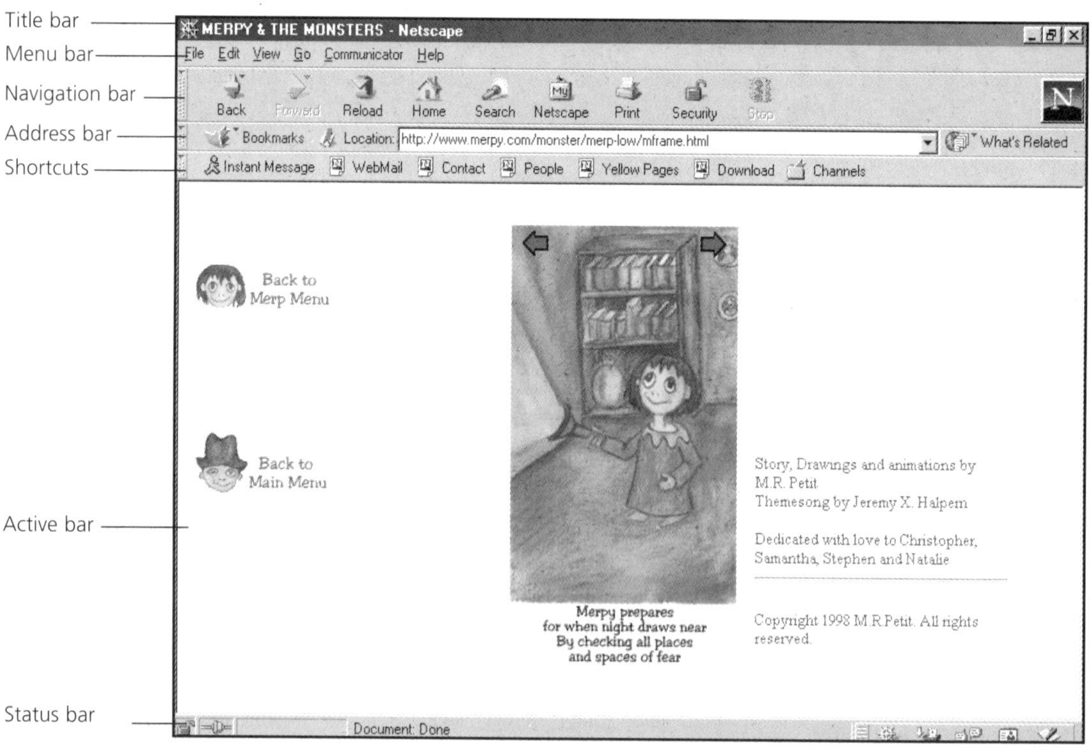

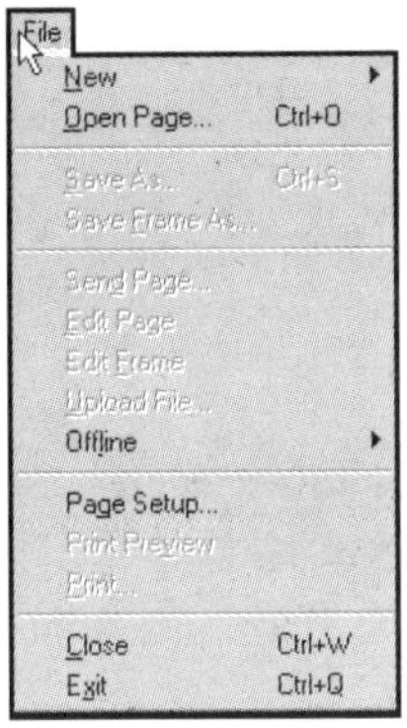

File menu

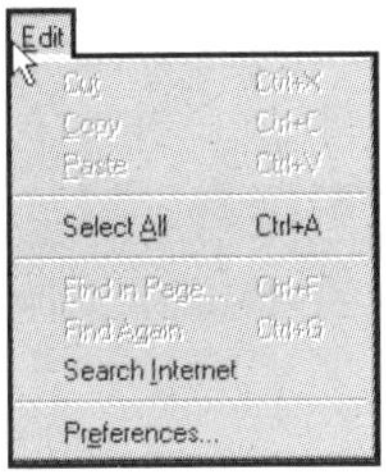

Edit menu

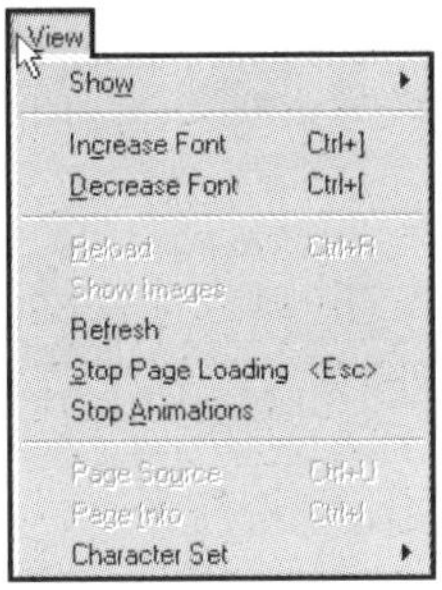

View menu

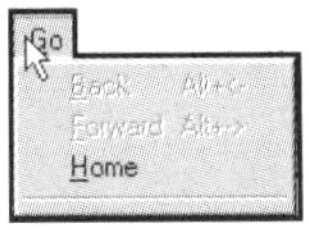

Go menu

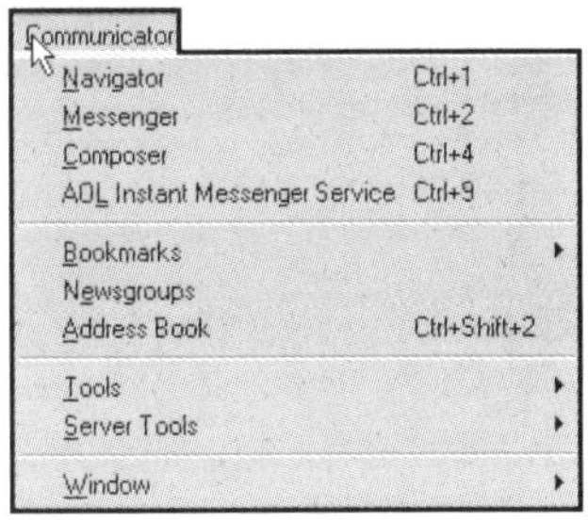

Communication menu

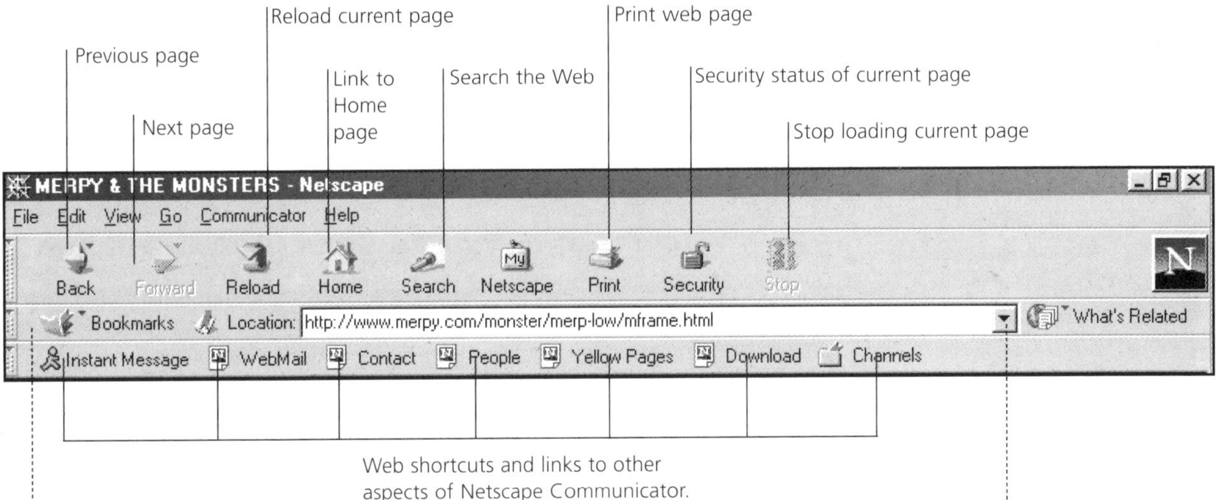

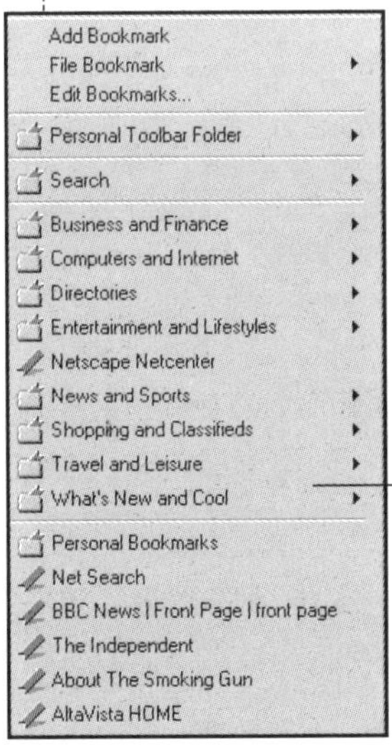

Bookmarks menu shows all the Web sites you have chosen to "bookmark". Both browsers come preloaded with many useful bookmarks.

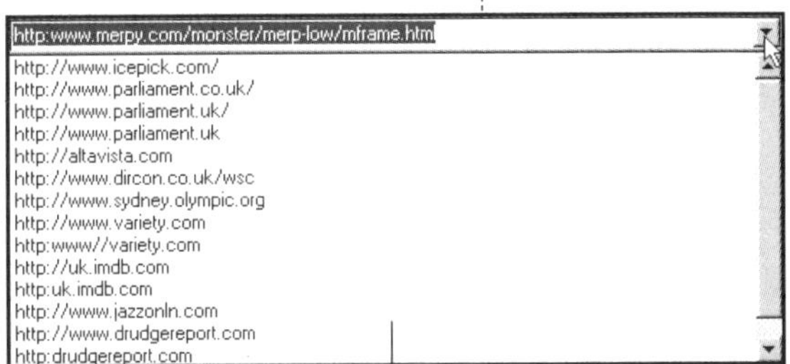

Location menu shows the previous sites you've visited. Click on any URL to connect to any one of these sites.

INTERNET EXPLORER

Here are the basic features of Microsoft's Internet Explorer. If you compare it to its Netscape equivalent you will see that there is very little basic difference between the two. Even if you become used to working with one of them, you will have no trouble in making the other one operate with equal success.

HOME PAGE

The basic Internet Explorer screen can be split into six parts. The Title Bar tells you the name of the current web site. The Menu Bar is made up of six drop-down menus that control the program's functionality. The Navigation Bar contains options that govern your movements around the Web. The Address Bar shows the URL of the current web site. The main area of the

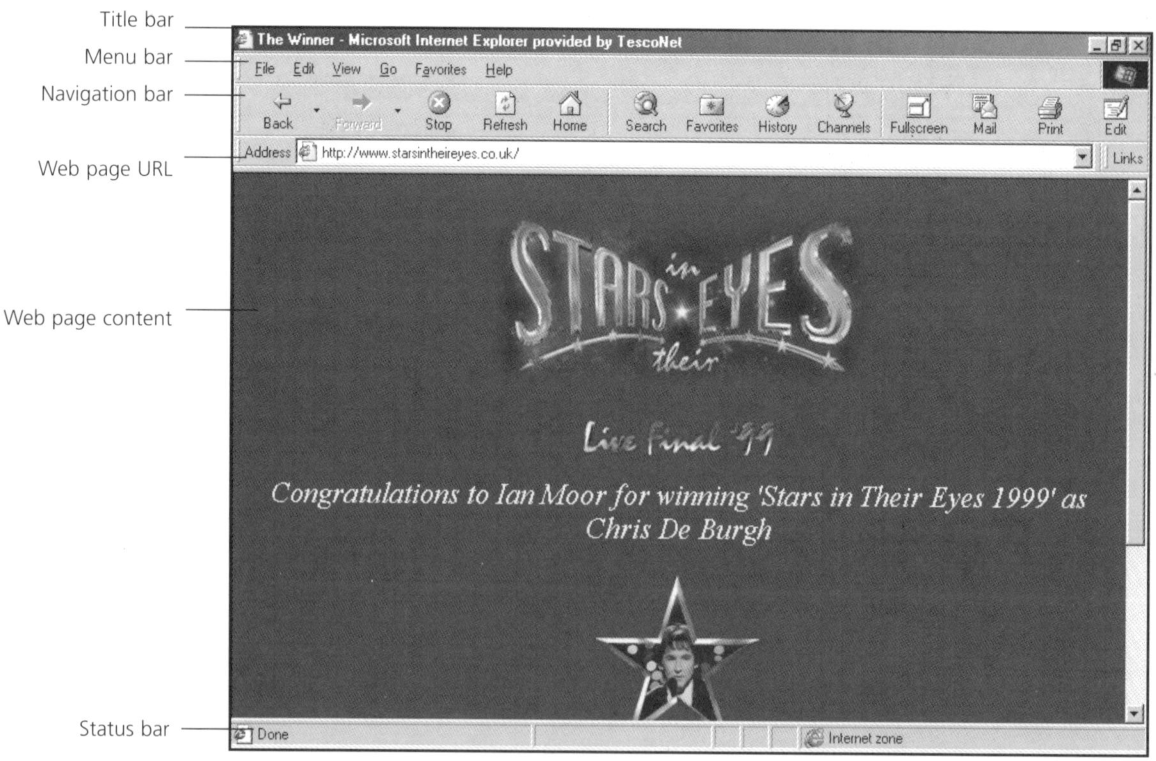

screen displays the Web page content. Finally, the Status Bar at the foot of the screen indicates how much of a website has been loaded – a percentage figure is displayed until complete when the Status Bar reads "Done".

Below you can find detailed descriptions of the contents of each drop-down menu and of the Navigation Bar and Address Bar. Each of these bars can be switched off by double-clicking on the vertical stripe at the far left of each bar. You can further maximize page space in Internet Explorer by pressing the "F11" key.

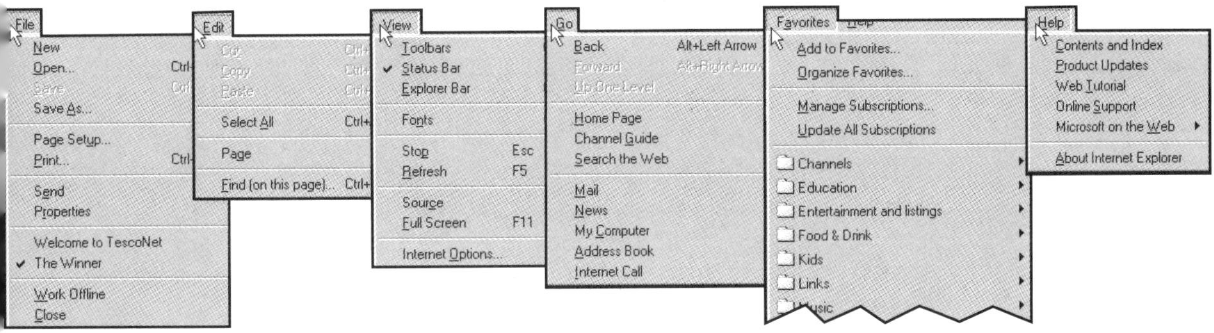

File menu   Edit menu   View menu   Go menu   Favorites menu   Help menu

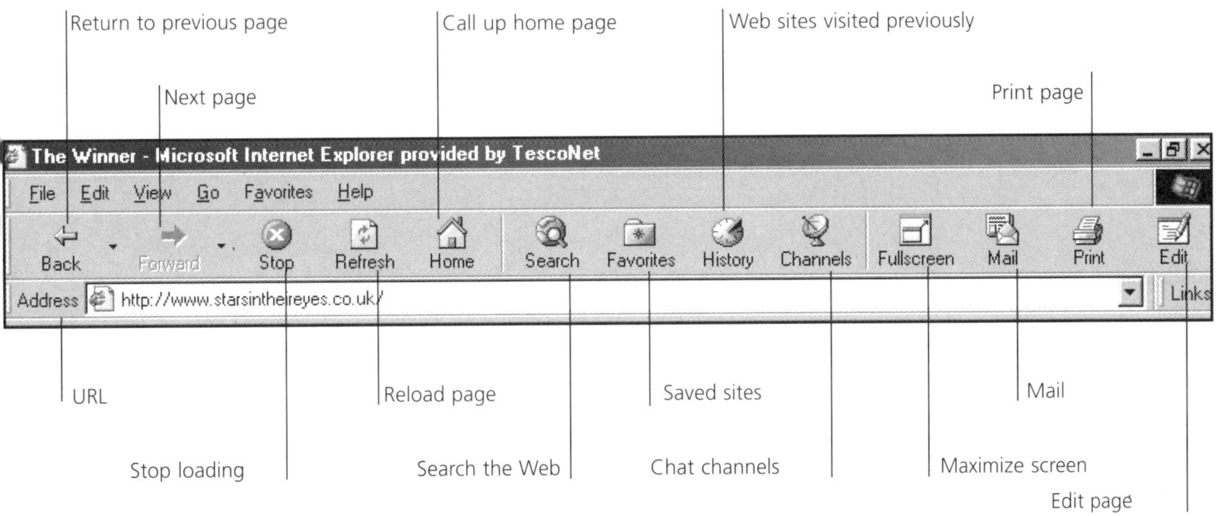

INSTALLING YOUR BROWSER

Installing a web browser is a very straightforward – the most time you'll spend is in customizing the settings so that you get them just right for your system. If you've bought a recent PC with Windows 98 already installed then you won't necessarily need to do anything at all – you'll find that Internet Explorer is pre-installed with it. However, new versions appear all the time, so the one you have installed on your hard disk may not be the most recent one.

WHERE DO YOU GET THE SOFTWARE?

First thing's first. In the current hyper-competitive climate, you shouldn't ever have to buy a Web browser. This situation may change in the future, but for the moment the software is all free. So if you can't buy a copy, where does it come from? There are three possibilities. Firstly, when you sign up with an ISP, you usually get the software as a part of the startup package. You can also obtain a copy of any free ISP's installation CD and usually just download the browser without even having subscribe. Secondly, the free CDs that are given away with PC and Internet magazines often have the most recent versions of the main two browsers. These are the simplest options.

There is a third option, however. If you want to get your hands on new releases of the software as soon as they become available, you can download it from the Netscape or the Microsoft home pages. Be warned, however, that these files are usually at least 8Mb in size, and even with a speedy modem they will still take you a considerable while to download. The disadvantage of using "hot-off-the-press" software is that sometimes certain minor program errors (called "bugs") may not yet have been discovered.

INSTALLING FROM A CD

Even for a complete beginner, installing a browser from a CD is simplicity itself. You double-click on the "setup.exe" file and just follow the instructions in the dialog boxes. You will usually be given the option of making a "custom" installation. It's best to leave these to the more experienced users – by and large you will have nothing to lose by going for a full installation every time. If you are kicking off the installer from a CD that came free with a magazine the process may be even more transparent – you may simply have an option on a menu to install the browser. In such cases you just double-click on the icon and follow the dialog boxes.

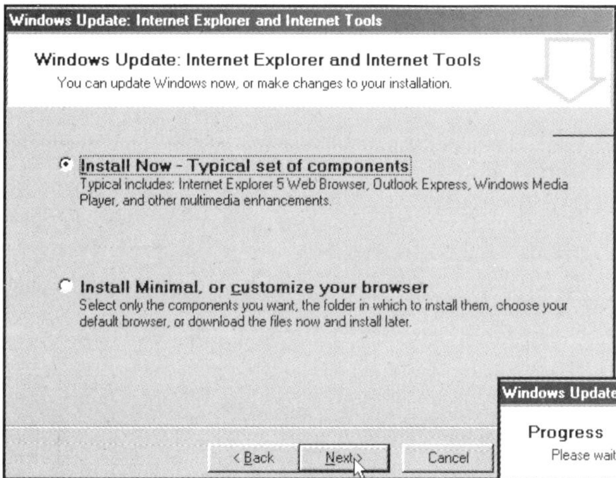

Installation start screen

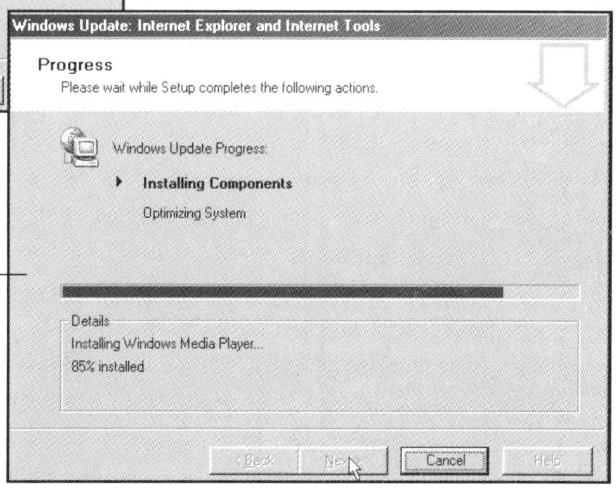

Installation in progress

CONFIGURING YOUR BROWSER

Don't panic! All this means is understanding how to customize the browser's settings to suit your own personal preferences. For example, most of the raw text that appears on a Web site has an undefined font – the way in which it appears on your screen will depend on the settings you have chosen. There are many ways in which you can customize your browser. The coming pages show how to make changes to Internet Explorer.

SETTING THE TOOLBARS

Like most examples of good contemporary software design, Microsoft's Internet Explorer provides you with many different ways of performing the same task. As such, you might find that some of the toolbar options are not neccessary. We can fix this by switching off any of the toolbars that we don't want to appear on the screen. This allows a greater area of the Web page to be displayed.

1 Click on the VIEW menu and select TOOLBARS. A tick alongside any of the options in the drop-down menu shows that these toolbars are currently being displayed.

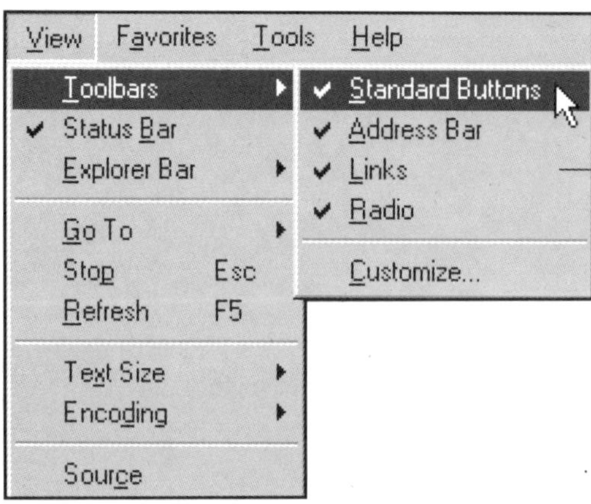

A tick against a menu option acts as a switch. Click on a ticked option to turn it off; click on an unticked option to turn it back on.

MAXIMUM SCREEN

In Internet Explorer you can maximize the screen area devoted to the Web page by pressing the F11 key. This immediately loses the title bar, menu bar, all of the toolbars except the standard option and the status bar beneath the page. This is by far the easiest way to customize your viewing of the World Wide Web. To make things even easier, F11 acts as a toggle switch – press it again and the options revert back to their original settings.

INTERNET OPTIONS

The possibilities for configuring the way in which your browser interacts with the World Wide Wide can be found in the TOOLS menu. Clicking on INTERNET OPTIONS produces a dialog box. Each of the six tabs at the top of the box contain a page of configuration options. The most useful choices can be found on the top page, marked GENERAL.

1 Click on the TOOLS menu and select INTERNET OPTIONS. The INTERNET OPTIONS dialog box appears.

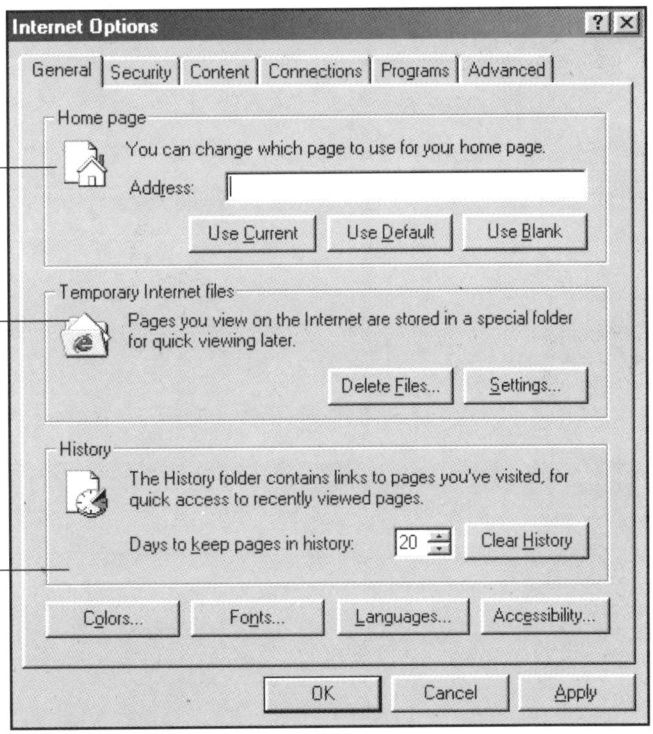

Type the URL for the page which you want to open each time you start the browser.

Settings for the folder that stores information from Web pages you have visited previously.

Storage of links that have been visited.

SETTING THE FONTS

You can also use the GENERAL screen of the INTERNET OPTIONS dialog box to change the way Web pages look in your browser. There are two kinds of font that you can alter. The WEB PAGE font governs how web pages that have formatted text but no specified font will appear; the PLAIN TEXT font controls the display of unformatted text.

1 Click on the FONTS button in the GENERAL page of the INTERNET OPTIONS dialog box.

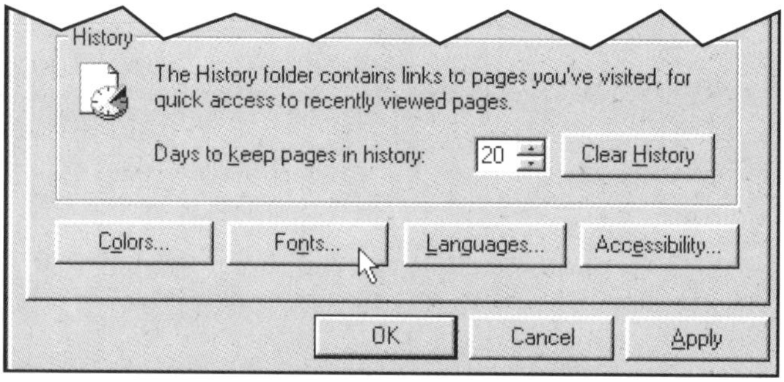

2 Select the desired WEB PAGE font or PLAIN TEXT font from the options offered. Click OK to confirm your choice.

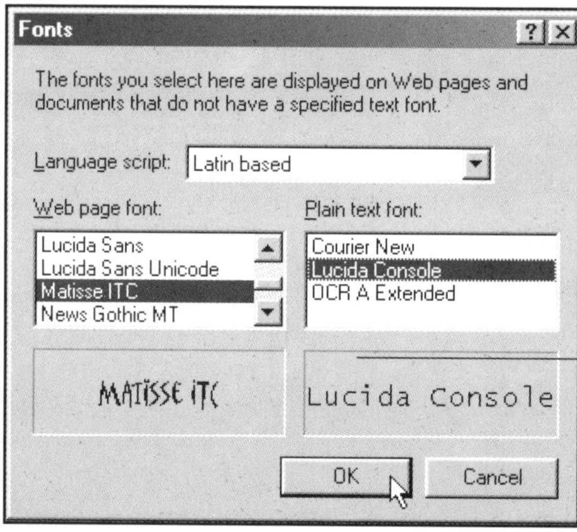

New fonts are displayed beneath their menus.

WHAT ABOUT NETSCAPE?

The same kind of configuration changes can also be achieved in Netscape Navigator. If you click on the EDIT menu, the final entry on the drop-down list that appears is PREFERENCES. Clicking on this option generates a dialog box which contains exactly the same kind of options as Internet Explorer. The PREFERENCES dialog box also contains the configuration options for Netscape's newsgroup, e-mail and web page composition features.

OTHER INTERNET OPTIONS

The remainder of the tabs in the INTERNET OPTIONS dialog box are for slightly more obscure uses that are perhaps best left until you've found your feet on the Web.

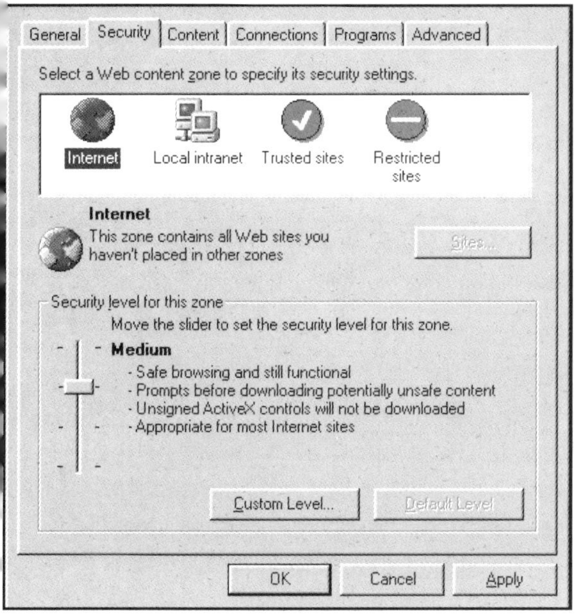

SECURITY

This doesn't refer to the actual content of the Web pages, but the kind of sites that your browser will accept: for example, "active" pages with embedded programs.

CONTENT

A very crude filtering system. If you switch it on it will vastly limit the number of sites that you can see.

CONNECTION

Features for Internet users who are part of a local network, such as those in a typical office, or those who have set up their own dial-up networking connections.

PROGRAMS

Allows you to specify the default programs for other services such as e-mail and newsgroups.

ADVANCED

A check-list that allows you to specify functions that you DON'T want to happen: for example the automatic playing of video clips which in some cases can slow browsing down to a tortuous level.

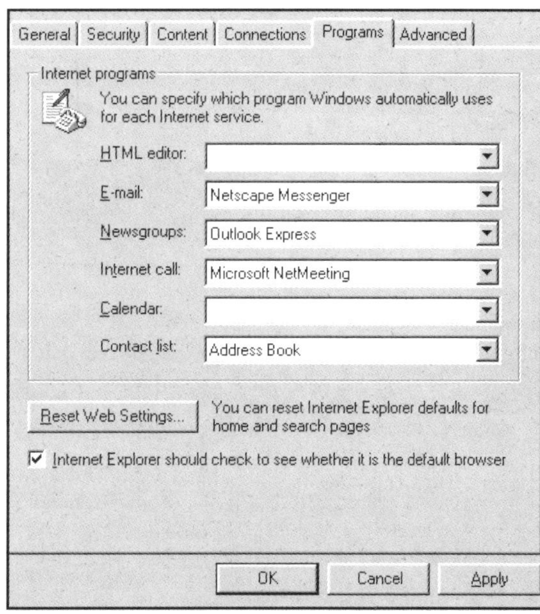

LET'S GO SURFING!

With your Internet connection and browser properly configured, it's time to get you out there on the World Wide Web. In no time at all you'll be surfing some of the many millions of fascinating sites.

CHOOSE YOUR BROWSER

In this example we'll use Netscape Navigator to look at Netscape's default site – this is the page that Navigator will automatically connect to unless it's told otherwise. We'll also test out some of the hyperlinks built into the page. If you don't have Navigator or would prefer to use Internet Explorer, you will automatically be logged on to Microsoft's default page. To see the Netscape site from here you must type http://www.netscape.com into the location window.

1 Run Netscape Navigator.

Launch icons are shown along the bottom of the Windows 98 screen. You can also run the programs by choosing from the START MENU options or double-clicking on a desk-top icon.

2 If you are not online you'll be prompted with the CONNECT TO box. Otherwise, go to the DIAL-UP NETWORKING folder and launch the connection from there.

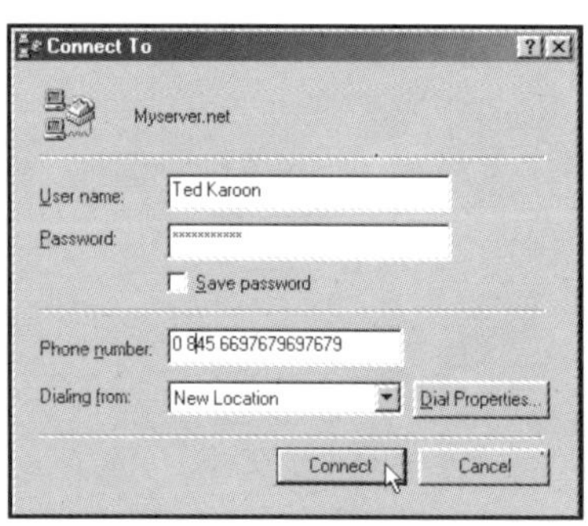

3 The first site to load will be the NETSCAPE NET CENTER. This has numerous hyperlinks to other sites. Click on ABCNEWS.COM to find out the day's main news stories.

Link to the ABCNEWS.COM Web site.

4 The front page lists an index of the news stories. Click on the main headline.

5 The next page you see is the full story behind the headline on the previous page.

FINDING SITES

Clicking on hyperlinks is an entertaining way of navigating around the World Wide Web and will often lead you down some of the more unexpected avenues of cyberspace. But what if you want to find more specific information? The answer comes in the form of "search engines". These are Web sites that allow you type in a keyword which it will use to provide you with a list of relevant sites.

USING A SEARCH ENGINE

To see a search engine in action let's go back to the Netscape home page (http://www.netscape.com).

1 Click on the SEARCH THE WEB options menu and select EXCITE.

All the options on the list are different search engines.

2 Enter your search topic and click on SEARCH.

This web search aims to finds sites related to the film *Reservoir Dogs*.

3 The EXCITE main page lists the results of your search.

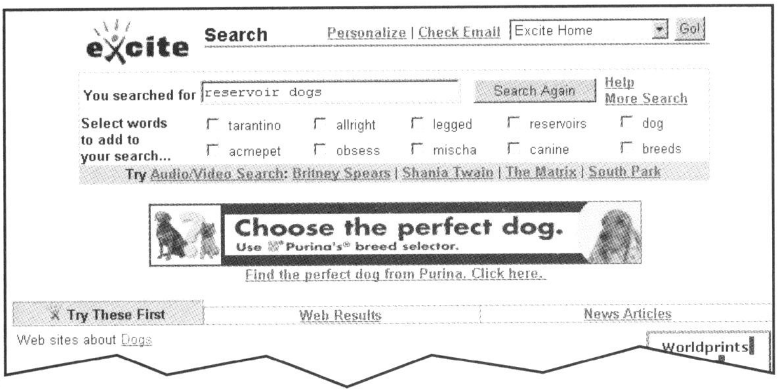

4 Click on any of the hyperlinks in the list to get connected to the website.

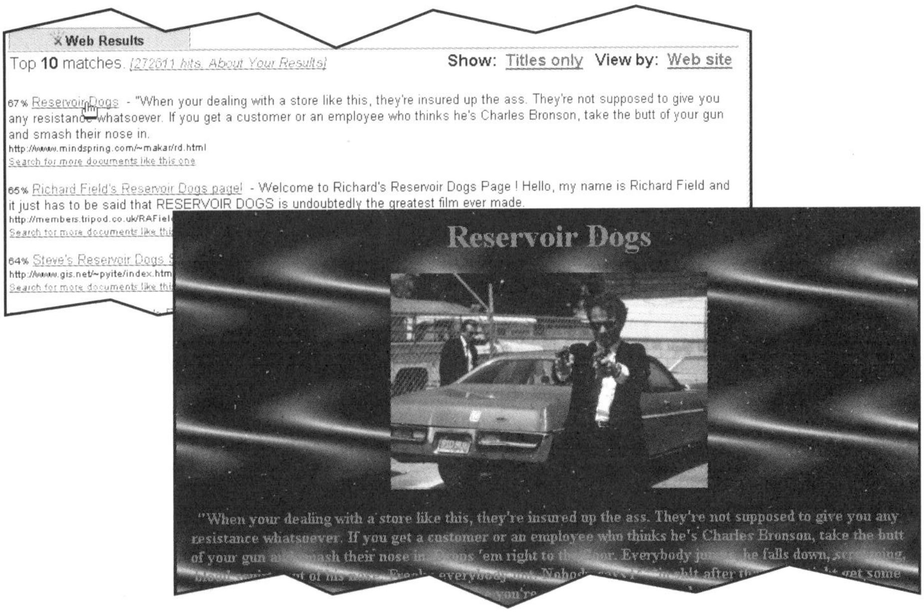

REFINING YOUR SEARCHES

If you look at the top of the second cutaway screen above, you will see that EXCITE found almost 300,000 Web sites that had some kind of match to your search criteria. If you look at the top screen, however, you can see the way in which EXCITE has interpreted your search. Not only is the search engine looking for sites related to the Tarantino film, it also wants to bring your attention to all the other sites relating to dogs or reservoirs! One of the arts of using a search engine is in refining your criteria. The most effective way of avoiding the above problem is to present your search as a single phrase. If instead of **Reservoir Dogs** you had typed in **"Reservoir Dogs"** or **Reservoir+Dogs**, Excite would only have found references to the two words used together. Over the page you will find out how to make even more sophisticated searches of the World Wide Web.

ADVANCED SEARCHES

Some search engines allow you to make even more refined selections than those suggested on the previous page. In this example we'll use AltaVista, which is one of the Web's most powerful search tools. Its ADVANCED page allows you to run "Boolean" searches using words like "AND" "OR" and "NOT".

1 Type in the URL which will take you to AltaVista's home page – http://www.altavista.com.

2 On the AltaVista home page click on ADVANCED in the top right-hand corner.

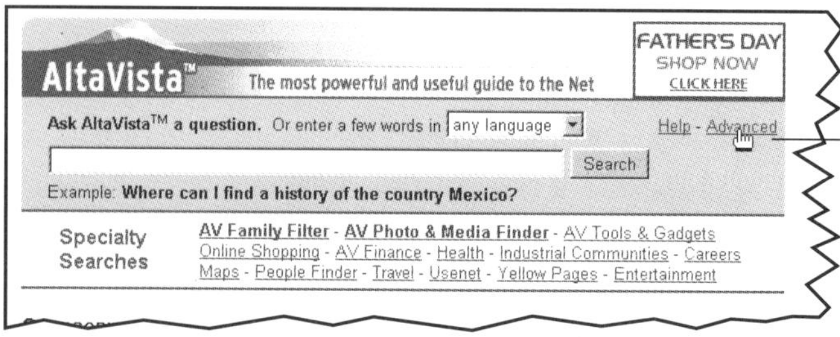

Link to AltaVista's advanced search page.

3 Enter advanced search criteria and click on SEARCH.

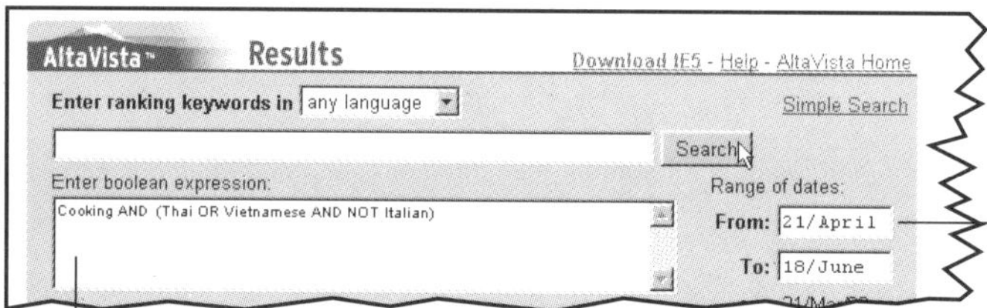

You can also enter date ranges.

This search looks for all "Thai" "cooking" and "Vietnamese" "cooking" sites, but blocks all "Italian" "cooking" sites.

BOOLEAN SEARCHES

AltaVista's "advanced" feature make use of Boolean algebra. Don't worry, you don't need to be good at maths to understand this. The main Boolean "operators" are the words AND, OR, NOT and NEAR. For example, FISH AND CHIPS would seek documents that used the words "fish" or "chips"; FISH OR CHIPS would seek documents that used either or both words; FISH AND NOT CHIPS ("FISH NOT CHIPS" is not a valid Boolean sentence), would seek only documents using the word "fish", but precluding them if they used the word "chips". FISH NEAR CHIPS looks for documents that uses both words as long as they are no more than 10 words apart.

OTHER SEARCH SITES

EXCITE and ALTAVISTA are only two of the many search engines that can be used to find specific Web sites (or in some cases newsgroups). Many of the original search engine designers were research students in the US when they developed their ideas during the early 1990s. Some of these young men are now multi-millionaires. Search engines are free for us to use as often as we want. For the privilege we have to put up with the intrusive advertizing banners that fund these businesses, which although rather tedious represents a fair exchange.

There are two distinct types of search site. The traditional search engine has "robot" programs that constantly scour cyberspace, collecting names, locations and details about Web sites they find. These are formed into a great database to which you connect when you make a search. The alternative is a Web directory which is a manually created list of pages sorted into categories. The main difference between the two is that although search engines delve deeper into cyberspace and should be more up-to-date, directories offer you a far more focussed search. If you search for "cocktail recipes" in a directory, all of the websites you find will be directly relevant; if you use a search engine you will turn up sites that happen to contain the words "cocktail and "recipe". A list of the most popular search engines and directories is shown below. Because they all work in slightly different ways, it's a good idea to vary your usage among the different sites.

ALTAVISTA	**http://www.altavista.com**	**EXCITE**	**http://excite.com**
FREEPAGES	**http://www.freepages.co.uk**	**GOTO**	**http://www.goto.com**
HOTBOT	**http://www.hotbot.com**	**INFOSEEK**	**http://www.infoseek.com**
LOOKSMART	**http://www.looksmart.com**	**LYCOS**	**http://www.lycos.com**
SNAP	**http://www.snap.com**	**WEBCRAWLER**	**http://www.webcrawler.com**
YAHOO!	**http://www.yahoo.com**	**YELL**	**http://www.yell.com**

4 AltaVista has completed its search. Click on any of the hyperlinks to get connected to the Web site.

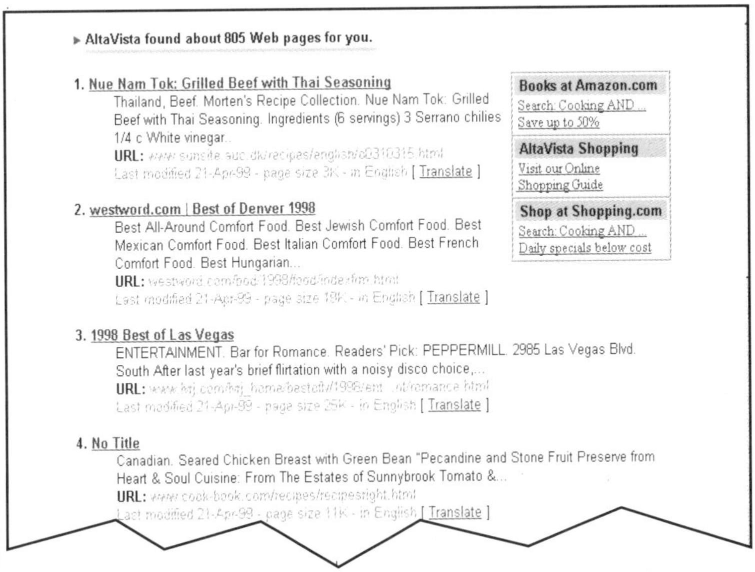

STORING YOUR FAVOURITES

As you surf the Web you will quickly come across sites that you want to return to again and again. Rather than keeping a note of the URL and retyping it each time you want to gain access, both Internet Explorer and Netscape Navigator allow you to "bookmark" your favourite sites so that you can connect to them at the click of a button.

BOOKMARKING IN NETSCAPE

You can access your bookmarked sites by clicking on the BOOKMARKS icon and selecting the site from the drop-down list. Netscape automatically creates common category folders in which you can store your favourite sites in a more organized manner. Bookmarking a site is simplicity itself.

1 Click on the BOOKMARKS icon.

2 From the drop-down menu, click on ADD BOOKMARK. The page will be added to the foot of the list.

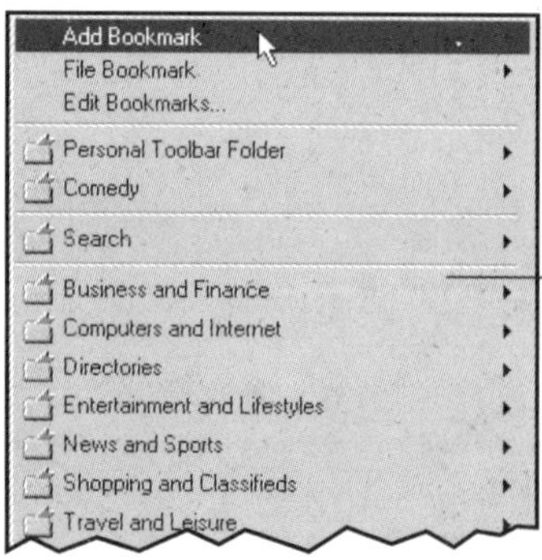

Category folder

ACCESSING A BOOKMARKED SITE

As long as you are online, visiting a bookmarked site can be achieved with a couple of clicks of the mouse. Begin by clicking on the BOOKMARKS icon.

1 Click on the chosen site from the drop-down list or from within the category folders.

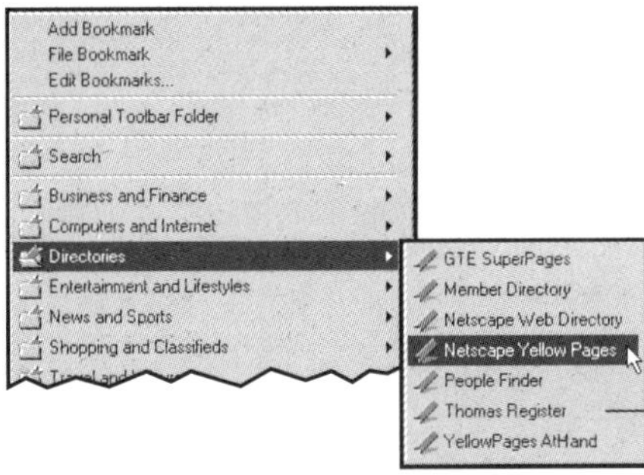

ORGANIZING YOUR BOOKMARKS

Each time you bookmark a site it gets stored at the bottom of the drop-down list. This can quickly grow to the point where it becomes difficult to use. To avoid this, you can store favourite sites either in the category folders provided, or in newly created folders of your own. Click on the BOOKMARKS icon.

1 Choose EDIT BOOKMARKS from the drop-down list.

2 Select the site that you want to move from the BOOKMARKS window. Drag-and-drop into the category folder of your choice.

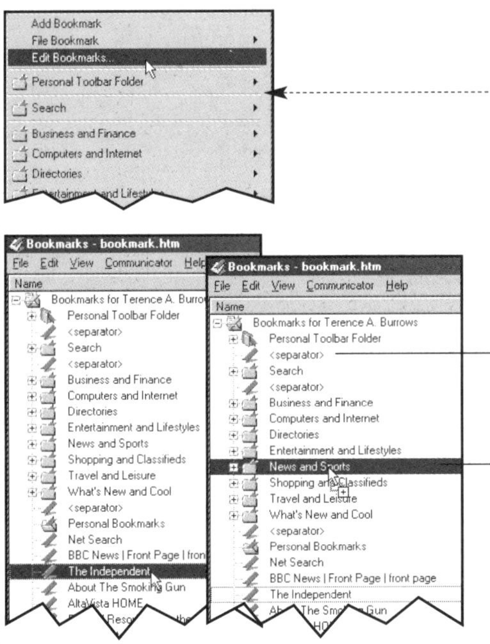

"Separator" creates a segregating line in the BOOKMARKS list.

The INDEPENDENT bookmarked site is now stored in the NEWS AND SPORTS folder.

CREATING A NEW CATEGORY

Of course, you don't have to go with the folder categories that Netscape automatically provides: you can easily set up and name new categories according to your needs. Once again, begin by clicking on the BOOKMARKS icon.

1 Click on EDIT BOOKMARKS. In the BOOKMARKS window, click on NEW FOLDER.

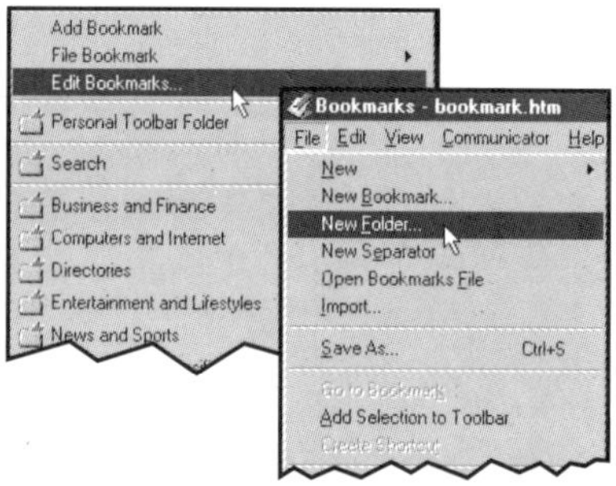

2 The BOOKMARK PROPERTIES box appears. Enter the name of the new folder and, if you feel inclined, a description. Click on OK.

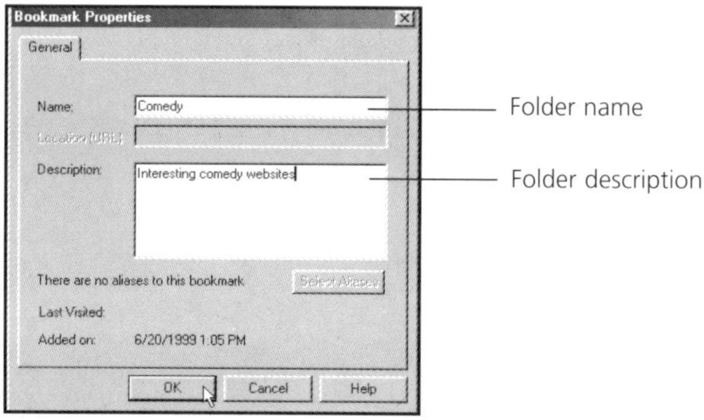

3 The new category folder appears in the list in the BOOKMARKS window and drop-down menu.

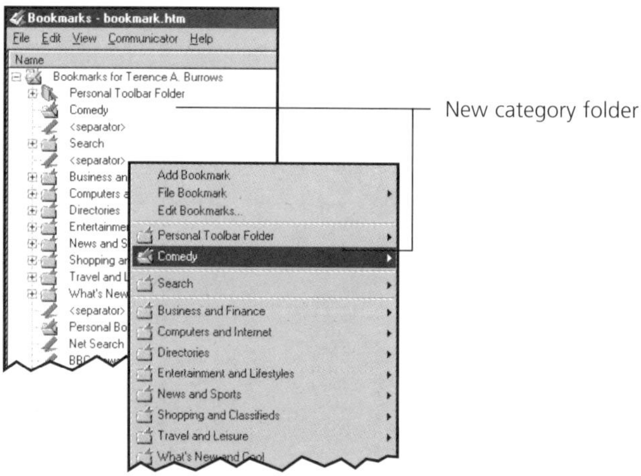

THE MICROSOFT METHOD

Most of the bookmarking features you have seen shown for Netscape Navigator are also available using Microsoft's Internet Explorer. The main difference is one of terminology: what Netscape calls "bookmarks", Microsoft refers to as "favorites".

1 Click on the FAVORITES icon in Internet Explorer's main toolbar. Select your chosen site from the drop-down menu or from within the category folders.

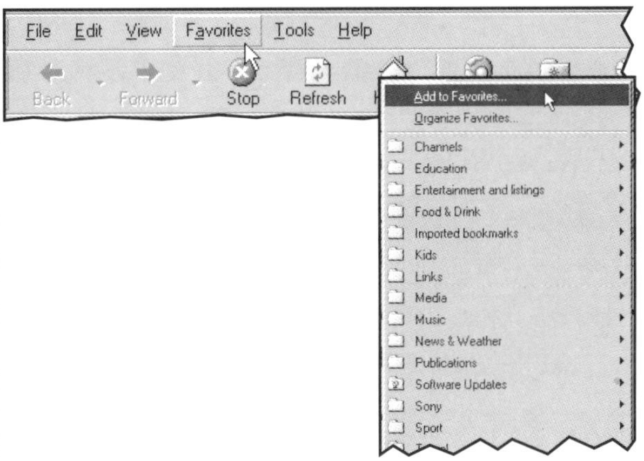

EDITING AND ORGANIZING FAVORITES

The organization of category folders also works in much the same way as Netscape Navigator.

1 Select ORGANIZE FAVORITES from the browser's FAVORITES menu.

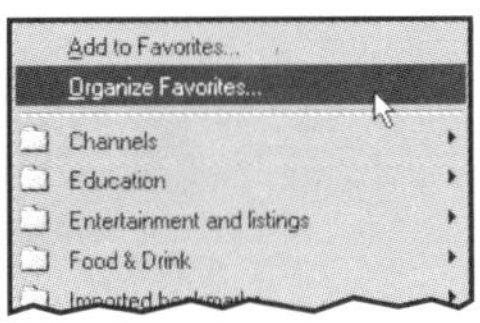

2 The ORGANIZE FAVORITES dialog box provides a variety of options. Select a site and click on MOVE TO FOLDER. Choose the destination from the BROWSE FOR FOLDER dialog box.

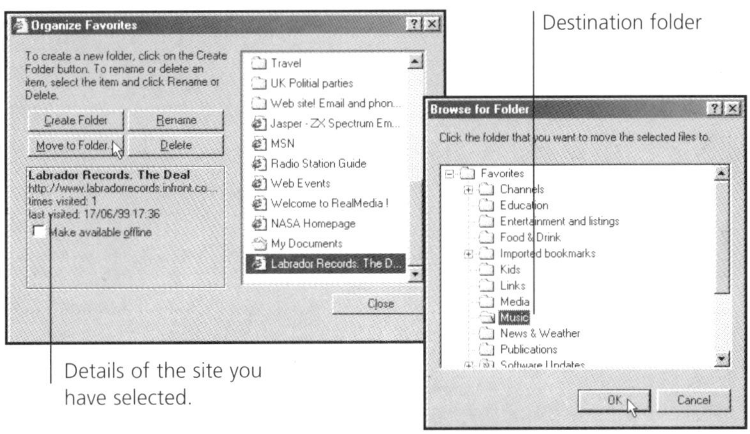

SUPERCHARGED BROWSING

When you think about it, the "big two" Web browsers are both excellent pieces of software in the breadth of the functions they fulfil. But the Internet continues to develop at a rapid pace, and sometimes a Web site is just so futuristic that your browser can't deal with it without a helping hand. This usually comes in the form of what is called a "plug-in".

WHAT ARE PLUG-INS AND HOW DO THEY WORK?

Plug-ins are tiny programs that add functionality to your Web browser. They are usually needed when you come across a site that offers more than a standard display of text and images; for example, it may play sounds and videos in real-time, or display animations or three-dimensional models.

How do you know in advance if a Web site needs a plug-in before you make that connection? You don't need to worry about this since Web browsers are very good at asking you for help if they can't do something. Quite simply, if you need a plug-in, your browser will tell you. In most cases, it will also open a hyperlink connection to a Web site from which you can download that plug-in.

The final good news is that plug-ins are also free – all you pay for is the time it takes to download, which in most cases won't be more than a few minutes.

Hundreds of plug-ins exist, but very few of them take off in a big way. If – like Macromedia's ShockWave and Flash, for example – a plug-in looks set to become significant to the future development of the World Wide Web, then new releases of each browser usually arrive with the latest version of that plug-in already in place.

PLUG-INS OR VIEWERS?

Although they tend to be lumped together under the general term "plug-in", there are two distinct types of add-on software for your browser. A true plug-in enables a sound or image to be displayed within the browser's own window. A different type of add-on (sometimes called a "viewer") is an entirely separate program that opens its own window to play or display sounds and images. These programs can function independtly from the browser, but are usually automatically "kick-started" by an instruction from the Web site. One of the most useful viewers is RealPlayer, a program that can play streamed audio and video from the Web.

REALAUDIO

Only a few years ago getting decent sounds from the Web was a tall order. If you wanted high fidelity you had to download a hefty sound file and needed some decent software to play it back. This changed with audio streaming systems like RealAudio, which allows you to play sounds as they are being downloaded. To play RealAudio files you need to download the RealPlayer software from http://www.realaudio.com, which also acts as a video streaming system. Although the sound quality is not yet comparable to a CD, it improves with each new release.

MP3

The most recent buzz in the Internet music world is MP3. This is a new format in which near-CD-quality music can be downloaded from the Internet. In itself, this isn't anything new except for an incredible degree of data compression that can reduce a three-minute stereo pop song to around three megabytes of data. Where once it might have taken an hour or more to download such a file, it should now take less than ten minutes using a fast modem (although the most popular MP3 sites are so heavily used at the moment that congestion is common).

Such is the hype surrounding MP3 that some have suggested that in future we may all be downloading our music from the Internet in this way. This has also thrown the music industry into a panic since numerous MP3 sites have already sprung up across the globe from which music can be illegally downloaded. Unlike RealAudio files, MP3s have to be downloaded before they can be played, although after downloading them you should find that the sound you hear is close to CD quality.

To play MP3 files you need an MP3 player. One of the most popular players is Winamp, which is shown below. Not only can this play MP3 files, but numerous other audio formats. It can be downloaded from http://www.winamp.com.

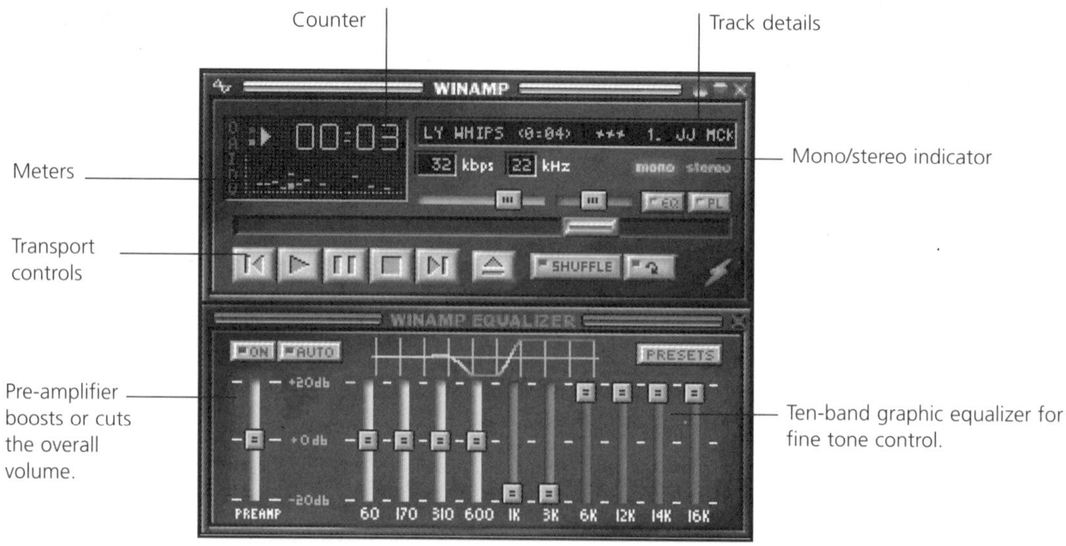

VIDEO FORMATS

The main impediment to making the most sophisticated plug-ins do their business as intended is the speed at which our computers are connected to the Internet. This is especially true of video formats where even if you have a 56K modem, download times are long and streamed video is at best a little jerky. For offline playback, you can expect a one-minute video clip to be around three megabytes in length and will take at least ten minutes to download.

There are three commonly used file formats that can be found on Web sites. The most common is MPEG; files in this format can be recognized by the extensions .mpeg, .mpg or .mpe. The QuickTime format was created by Apple for their Macintosh computers, although this format can now be played on all types of computer. QuickTime files usually have the extensions .mov and .qt. The third format, which is less common on the Web, is Video For Windows, which uses the file extension .avi.

To see and hear a video file you need a software player that can work with the appropriate format. ActiveMovie, which is loaded with Internet Explorer, is both a browser plug-in and an independent viewer. Although this software can read all three formats listed above, it is only completely reliable for the playback of .avi files. For PC users, a better alternative is to download a shareware program called Net Toob, which can not only read numerous video and audio formats but also provide streaming for MPEG movies (http://www.nettoob.com). You can download the program on a 30-day free trial period.

Net Toob Controller

Net Toob Screen

QUICKTIME

There are a variety of different types of QuickTime format, as well as several viewers and plug-ins. QuicktimePlayer can cope with pretty well any video format.

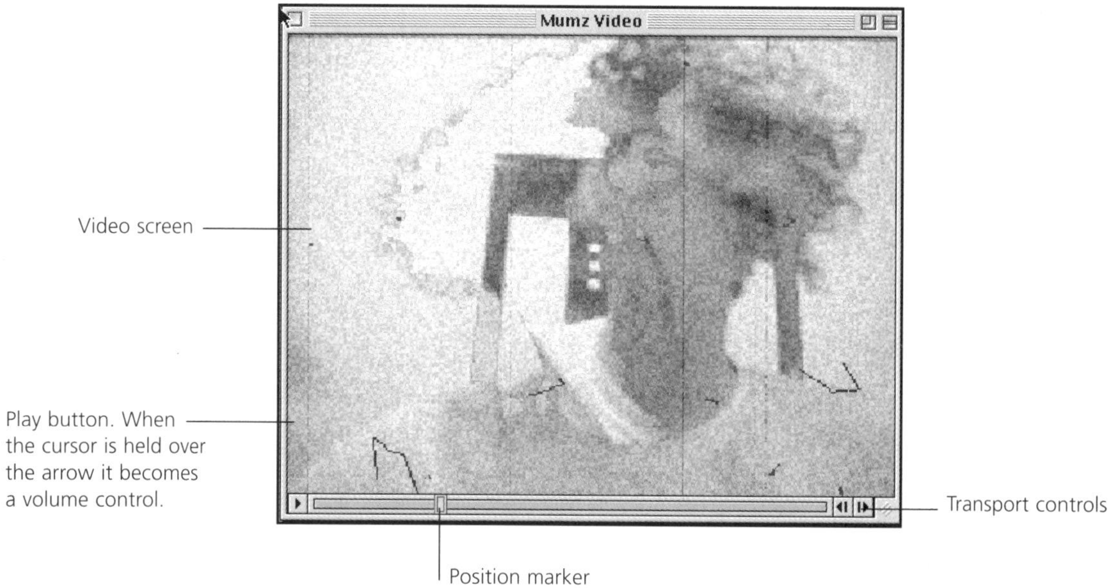

ANIMATION

The recent explosion of animation on the Web has brought about some of the most successful developments for working around the limitations of download times. Two plug-ins – Macromedia's ShockWave and Flash have led the way. ShockWave allows browsers to view Web sites that feature highly sophisticated animations which have been created using Macromedia Director – one of the most widely used multimedia programs in the world. Director can integrate images, videos and text to create superb animations. Flash is a simpler plug-in which is also used to create simple movement. Both of these excellent plug-ins can be obtained from Macromedia's Web site (http://www.macromedia.com).

If you want to include ShockWave features on your own Web site, you need to get hold of Macromedia Director – although as an industry-standard product, this software is not only pretty expensive, but demanding to use. The Flash software is much simpler to operate and has the benefit of being downloadable for a trial period.

If you want to see some interesting uses of Flash and ShockWave, Macromedia run a special site devoted to showing off the full potential of these plug-ins, as well as providing technical advice for new designers. If you are interested, log on to http://www.shockwave.com.

Each button creates a new animation in the centre screen.

JAVA AND ACTIVEX

Two names that you are certain to come across in relation to multimedia on the Web are "Java" and "ActiveX". JAVA is a programming language developed by Sun computers which enables Web pages to contain special in-built programs called "applets". These programs can make static Web pages more lively or interactive. The beauty of JAVA is that it is "machine independent"; that means it will run on every type of computer. In recent times, both Netscape Navigator and Internet Explorer have been updated so that they can run any JAVA applet.

Microsoft's own ActiveX adds the same kind of functinality to Internet Explorer (although not Netscape Navigator). ActiveX was designed to work as an extension of the Windows operating system. If you encounter a Web site that contains an ActiveX program you will usually be given a warning with an option not to download.

ActiveX programs can be recognized as having the suffix **.ocx**; JAVA programs end in **.class**. JAVA also has a scripting language that can be written into Web page constructions. Called "JAVASCRIPT", these routines are much slower than the applets. Since they can be downloaded and run automatically, some people are suspicious of JAVA and ActiveX programs. Consequently, both Navigator and Internet Explorer allow users to switch off support for either one.

THE THIRD DIMENSION

Virtual Reality Modelling Languages (VRML) are incredible plug-ins that allow you to see the same image from different angles either by moving the cursor around on the screen or by clicking on a control panel. Imagine, for example, that you see an image of a room from a perspective as if you had just walked through the door. By dragging the mouse to the top of the picture the image may slowly pan upwards to the ceiling, or you may start to "move" into the room, with the perspective shifting as you move the mouse.

VRML plug-ins are usually given the suffix .wrl. Two examples are WIRL (downloadable from http://www.platinum.com) and Superscape's Viscape (http://www.superscape.com). The latter can be seen in the example below which shows four views of the same car taken at different points in its rotation.

TROUBLESHOOTING

We'll finish this section on the World Wide Web with a look at what to do when your surfing activities seem to have been brought to an unexpected halt.

I CAN'T GET CONNECTED TO A SITE...

• Check that you have a valid Internet connection. If you don't then use your dial-in software to make the connection to your ISP. If this still doesn't work check all of the connections between your computer, modem and telephone line. If you have an external modem and you don't hear it bleeping away at connection, it's likely that you are not properly connected.

I HAVE A VALID INTERNET CONNECTION BUT STILL CAN'T GET CONNECTED TO A SITE...

• A good starting point is to click on your browser's STOP button and then try to connect again.
• Check the URL you typed into the location window is correct.
• If it's a popular site, the problem may simply be due to Internet congestion – if it happens persistently, break off and try again later.

EVERYTHING SEEMS TO TAKE SO LONG...

• The Internet is just like any other highway – if there's a lot of traffic it will take time to move from one place to another. (No wonder that some wags have christened it the "World Wide Wait"). You'll find things go much more quickly if you do your surfing outside of peak hours.
• There could be something amiss with your ISP's server. Call them to see if there's a problem. Beware, though, if your ISP charges for technical support you might have to pay to ask!
• Maybe it's time to box up that old 14.4K modem and join the modern world! If you have a faster model (56K is the norm now), check the modem's initialization settings to ensure that they haven't inadvertently been set to operate at a lower speed.

THE WRITING ON THE SCREEN IS TOO SMALL – IT'S DIFFICULT TO READ

• Both Internet Explorer and Netscape Navigator can be altered to display most of the text you see on a Web page. Not only can you alter the size of the text, you can use a totally different font. Check page 44 to see how this is done.

I KEEP GETTING THESE STRANGE "ERROR CODES"

• Don't worry - this is probably not your fault at all. Certain error codes are sent out by a server when it can't interpret your request. If you encounter "NOT FOUND 404", this usually means that the Web site can no longer be located at that URL. If you have had to enter a path of subfolders in the URL, try moving up a level. Do this by removing the text that follows the last forward slash in the URL; this may give you a clue as to any new name. If you were connecting to the site via a hyperlink it might be possible that the link was wrongly named. Other faults include "UNAUTHORIZED 401", "FORBIDDEN 403" and "SERVICE TEMPORARILY OVERLOADED 502". In all cases, if you are desperate to make the connection you should contact the Webmaster for the ISP who owns the server – error code screens often give you this option in any case.

I CAN'T USE MY BROWSER TO READ A NEWSGROUP

• Check the configuration preferences to ensure that your ISP's news server has been correctly named. If you have multiple accounts it can be easy to connect to one ISP while at the same time specifying a different ISP's news server in the browser.

• Not all ISPs carry all of the possible newsgroups. As a matter of policy, some of them block certain of the "alt.sex…" and "alt.binaries…" groups. In other cases, a call to your ISP will usually be enough to procure future access.

I CAN'T USE MY BROWSER TO SEND/READ MY MAIL

• As above, check the configuration preferences to ensure that your ISP's mail servers have been correctly named. You will usually need the name of the incoming and outgoing mail servers, your POP3 user identity and password.

3 E-MAIL

Once upon a time, if you wanted to send a letter you had to visit a post office, buy a stamp, write your message down on paper, put an address and stamp on the envelope and put it in the post box. If you were lucky, a few days later it would be delivered. This has all changed with the development of "e-mail". A letter sent via the Internet could be delivered anywhere in the world within a few minutes. And all for the price of a local telephone call.

THE BASICS

Before the World Wide Web exploded into the public arena, e-mail was far and away the main reason that most people subscribed to a service provider. But even now, e-mail still accounts for the vast majority of Internet usage.

HOW DOES E-MAIL WORK?

There really is a close analogy between sending an e-mail and an ordinary letter using the regular postal system (or "snail mail" as Netheads like to call it). Using a special e-mail program (your browser will have one built in), you type your "letter", enter an e-mail address, and press a button to send it. You also use the same program to read e-mails that have been sent to you. What happens, though, if the person you are writing to doesn't happen to be online when you send your message? You'll be relieved to know that it ISN'T like sending a fax to someone whose machine is turned off – e-mails just sit there waiting for you. The message is held on your ISP's mail server – a computer that functions rather like an electronic sorting office. Each time you run your e-mail software it sends a message to the mail server to ask "is there any mail for me?". If there is then it is downloaded onto your computer. It's as simple as that.

E-MAIL ADDRESSES

When you first subscribe to an ISP you will be given at least one e-mail address. This address will single you out from the many millions of other Internet users throughout the world. Internet addresses are formed from three components: the username, the "@" symbol and the domain name.

tedkaroon@myserver.net

Username — Domain name

The domain name is the address of your ISP. In this example it is "myserver.net". The username – "tedkaroon" – is unique within the subscribers to that service provider.

Some ISPs allow for the user name to become a part of the domain name. In such cases, a so-called "node" name is prefixed to the existing domain name and separated by a dot. This allows more than one e-mail address to be set up for a single subscriber. If we assume that in our example the user name was derived from the subscriber's first name and surname, a new alternative address might be ted@karoon.myserver.net (where "karoon" is the node name). This could mean that other family members could have their own addresses, for example janice@karoon.myserver.net. In such cases, the node name must be unique rather than the letters preceding the "@" symbol.

WHICH SOFTWARE?

As with all essential Internet software, you will find that many of the most effective dedicated e-mail programs can be acquired either as freeware or shareware. Additionally, you can also send and receive e-mails using the standard Web browser packages Internet Explorer and Netscape Communicator. Some of the most popular examples are listed below. You can find out how to download files and software from remote sites in chapter 4.

Outlook Express Made by Microsoft, Outlook Express is the most commonly used e-mail program simply because it comes as a part of the Internet Explorer Web browser. If you have a PC with Windows 98 installed you should find that you already have a copy on your hard disk. Outlook Express also has the advantage of doubling as a newsreader (see chapter 5).

Eudora Lite Probably the best-known dedicated e-mail software, Eudora Lite is freeware, although its superior big brother Eudora Pro can be purchased cheaply. Eudora Lite can handle every possible e-mail situation, including the creation of separate mailboxes for different users, and mail filtering. You can download it from http://www.eudora.com/eudoralite.

Pegasus Mail Also freeware, Pegasus Mail is comparable with Eudora Lite. You can obtain it from http://www.pegasus.usa.com.

Calypso 32 Download from http://www.mcsdallas.com.

DTS Mail Download from http://dtsoftware.simplenet.com.

Tetrix Reader Plug Download from ftp://sunsite.cnlabswitch.ch/mirror/winsite/win3/winsock/trp110.zip.

CONFIGURING E-MAIL SOFTWARE

Before your e-mail software can send and retrieve mail from your ISP's mail server you will need to type in a few simple settings. Although this isn't difficult, you will need to gather certain pieces of information before you begin. Don't worry, you should only need to do this once, right at the start – once it's out of the way you are almost home and dry.

WHAT DETAILS DO YOU NEED?

There are a few pieces of information you need to know: your e-mail address, the name of your ISP's outgoing mail server (usually the SMTP server), the name of the incoming mail server (usually a POP3 server) and the username and password you need to access the POP3 server. You should already have this information, but if not, a quick telephone call to your ISP should do the trick.

For the rest of this chapter we'll use OUTLOOK EXPRESS. When you run the software for the first time, the program should prompt you to enter the configuration information via the INTERNET CONNECTION WIZARD.

1 Enter your name and click on NEXT.

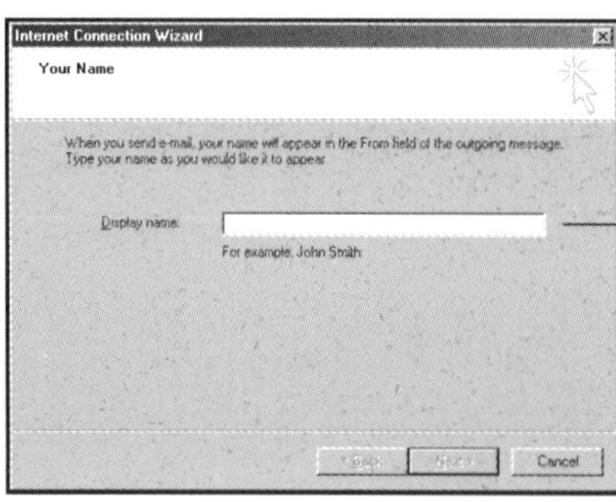

The name you enter here is the "real name" that will be displayed on your e-mails. Some Internet users prefer to enter nicknames.

2 Enter the e-mail address given to you by your ISP. Click on NEXT.

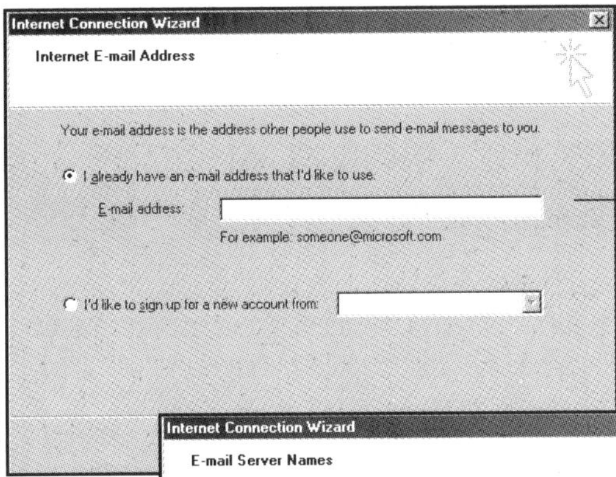

The INTERNET CONNECTION WIZARD allows for the creation of new ISP accounts, but assumes by default that you have already subscribed.

3 Enter the names of the incoming and outgoing mail servers. Click on NEXT.

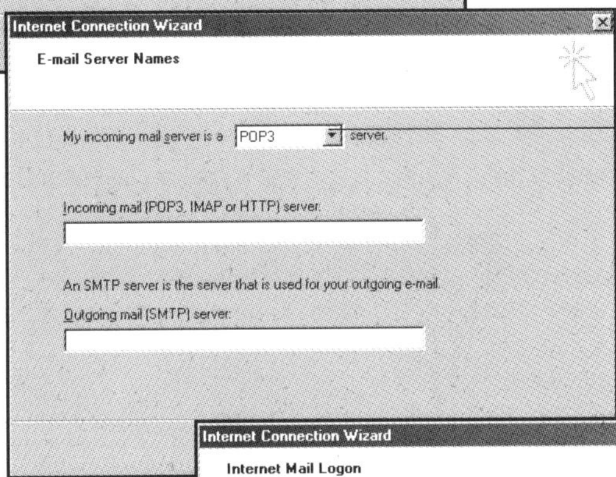

The server type defaults to POP3 (which applies to most incoming mail servers). If necessary, other options can be chosen by clicking on the arrow.

4 Enter your account name and password as provided by your ISP.

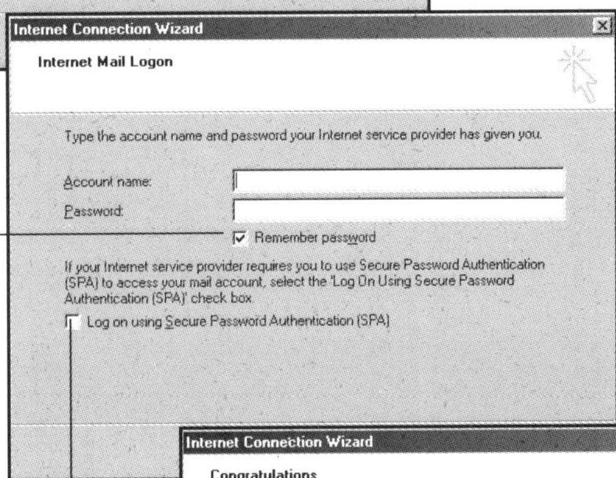

Activate the tick box if you want Outlook Express to remember your password. This makes collecting your mail automatic.

5 Click on FINISH. You are now ready to send and receive e-mails.

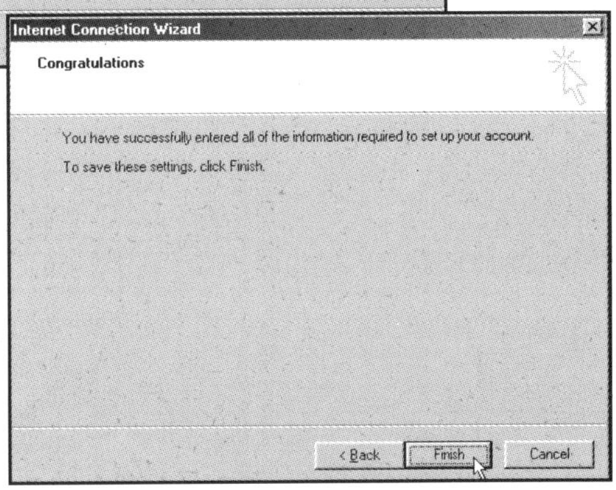

A few ISPs insist that you log in using a "Secure Password". If this applies to your ISP, activate this tick box.

SENDING AND RECEIVING E-MAILS

With your e-mail software now configured you are primed and ready for action. As you are about to discover, sending, reading and replying to e-mails is simplicity itself.

PREPARING TO SEND YOUR FIRST E-MAIL

The next time you run Outlook Express and you are offline (not connected to the Internet), the program will prompt the DIAL-UP CONNECTION dialog box. For the moment you don't need to go online – it's simply a waste of your telephone bill – so click on the WORK OFFLINE button. Now let's write an e-mail.

1 Click on CREATE A NEW MAIL MESSAGE.

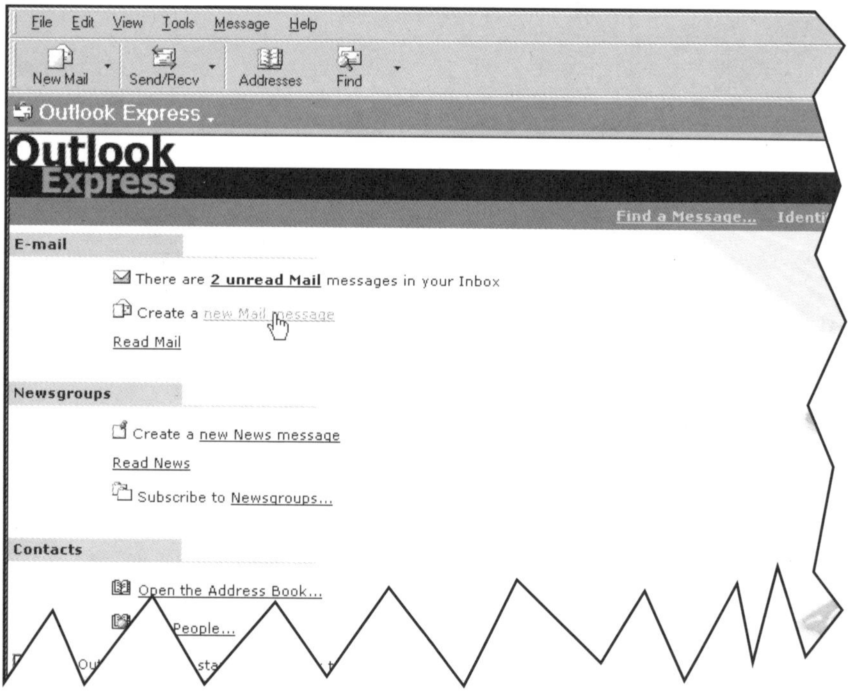

2 Enter the details as required and type your e-mail message.

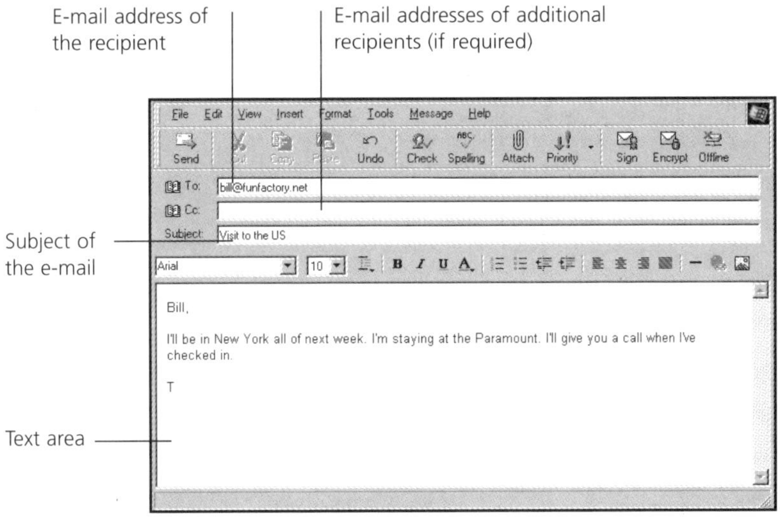

3 Click on SEND.

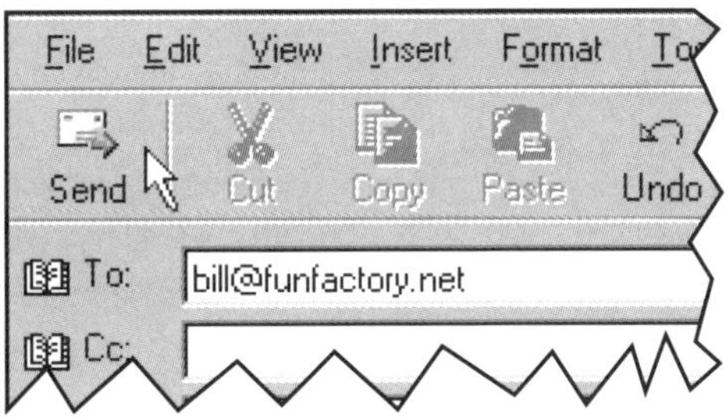

4 Click on OK to post your e-mail in the OUTBOX ready to be transmitted the next time you go online.

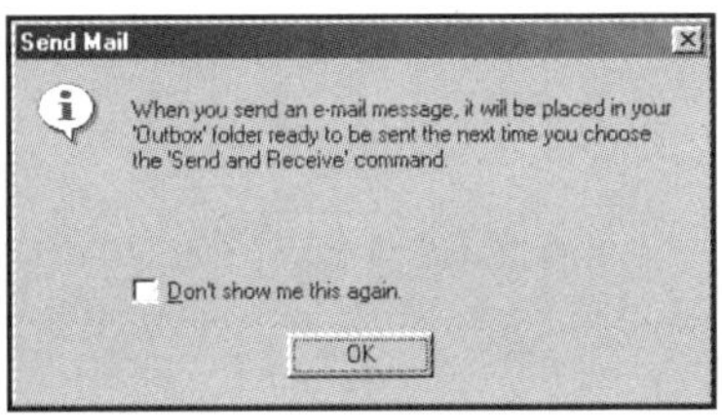

Your e-mail is now waiting in the OUTBOX to be sent. If you want to edit your message all you have to do is click on the OUTBOX folder, which will "collapse" to show its contents. Double-click on the e-mail you want to edit and it will appear on the screen ready for you to alter. If you want to write any more e-mails you should do so while you are still offline.

Over the page you will see how the e-mail is transmitted across the Internet.

SENDING YOUR E-MAIL INTO CYBERSPACE

If you want to transmit your e-mail to its destination you have to go online. This process will send all of the e-mails queued up in the OUTBOX folder.

1 Click on the SEND/RECV button.

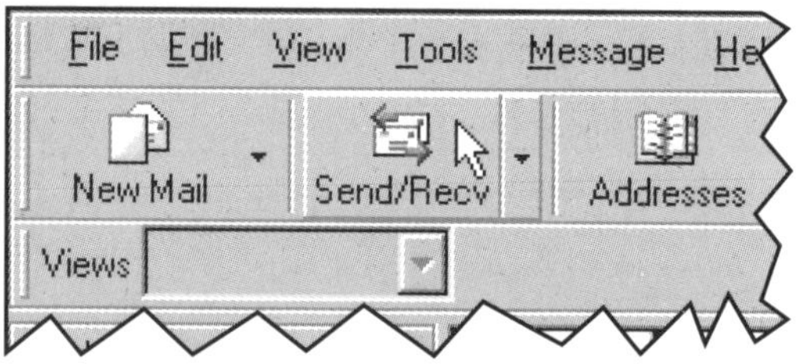

2 Click on YES if you want to go online. This will invoke the DIAL-UP CONNECTION screen.

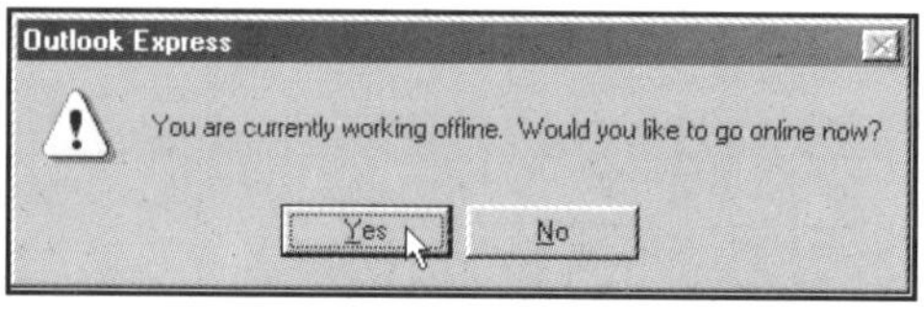

Finally, click on CONNECT in the DIAL-UP CONNECTION dialog box to hook up to your ISP in the normal way. When this has been completed your mails will be sent automatically. Congratulations, you've just sent your first e-mail!

E-MAIL SHORTCUTS

E-mails are extremely informal. When you compose them try to think of them as being more like extracts from a conversation than a traditional letter. Few experienced Netheads begin their e-mails with "Dear Fred..." and end "Yours sincerely...". At best you might get a "Hi, Fred" or just "Fred" at the start of a message – in many cases the text will get right down to business straight away. If you are dealing with large numbers of e-mails each day, then speed is of the essence (if you don't want it to completely take over your life, that is). To this end, a culture of abbreviations for oft-used phrases has emerged. These can be dropped into your e-mails at will. Some of the most commonly used acronyms are shown below and on the right. Beware of using your own abbreviations, though, unless you're really sure that the other person will understand them.

AFAIK	As far as I know	**BCNU**	Be seeing you
BST	But seriously though	**BTW**	By the way
CU	See you	**FWIW (4WIW)**	For what it's worth
FYI	For your information	**IM(NS)HO**	In my (not so) humble opinion
IMO	In my opinion	**IOW**	In other words

E-MAIL SHORTCUTS

KISS	Keep it simple, stupid	**L8R**	Later
LOL	Laughs out loud	**MYOB**	Mind your own business
OAO	Over and out	**OIC**	Oh, I see
OTOH	On the other hand	**PITA**	Pain in the a***
ROFL	Rolls on floor laughing	**TIA**	Thanks in advance
TNX	Thanks	**WTF**	What the f***

Also widely used are emoticons (or "smilies" as they are better known). Created using punctuation keys, when looked at from the side they appear to be faces that convey different feelings.

:-)	Happy	**:-(**	Sad	**:-))**	Very happy	**:-((**	Very sad
;-)	Wink	**>:-)**	Devilish grin	**:-D**	Laughing	**:'-)**	Crying
:-O	Surprised	**:-|**	Unamused	**:-||**	Angry	**:-/**	Mixed feelings
8-)	Wears glasses	**:-w**	Forked tongue	***-)**	Wasted	**:-#**	Man with beard

RECEIVING AN E-MAIL

It's all very well being able to send e-mails, but how do you know when somebody has sent an e-mail to you? To begin with, when you go online the front screen of OUTLOOK EXPRESS will immediately tell you if you have anything waiting.

1 Click on the highlighted text telling you that you have unread mail waiting for you.

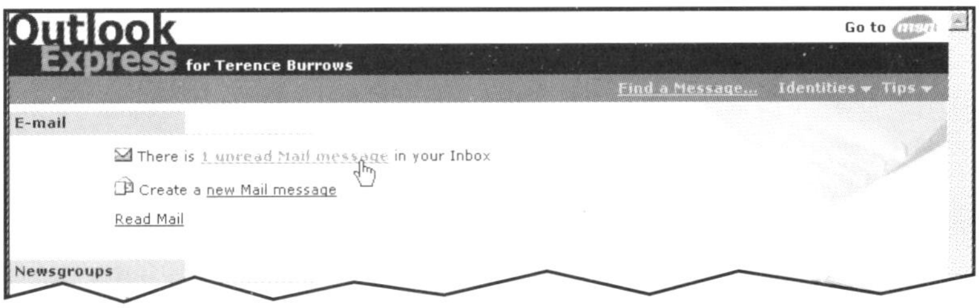

2 This opens the INBOX folder. To read the message, double-click anywhere on the line.

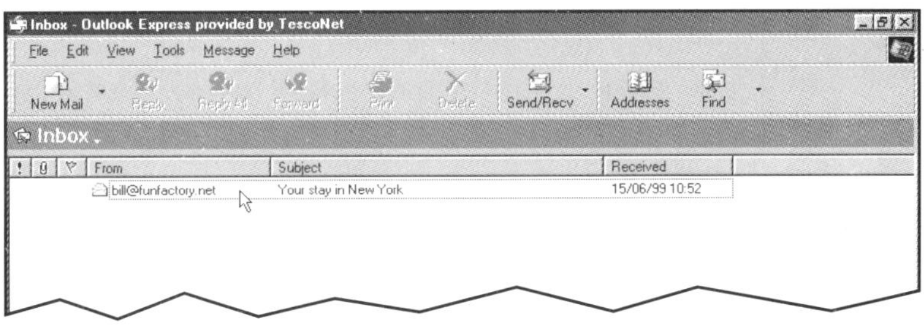

3 The message is displayed in the bottom half of the screen.

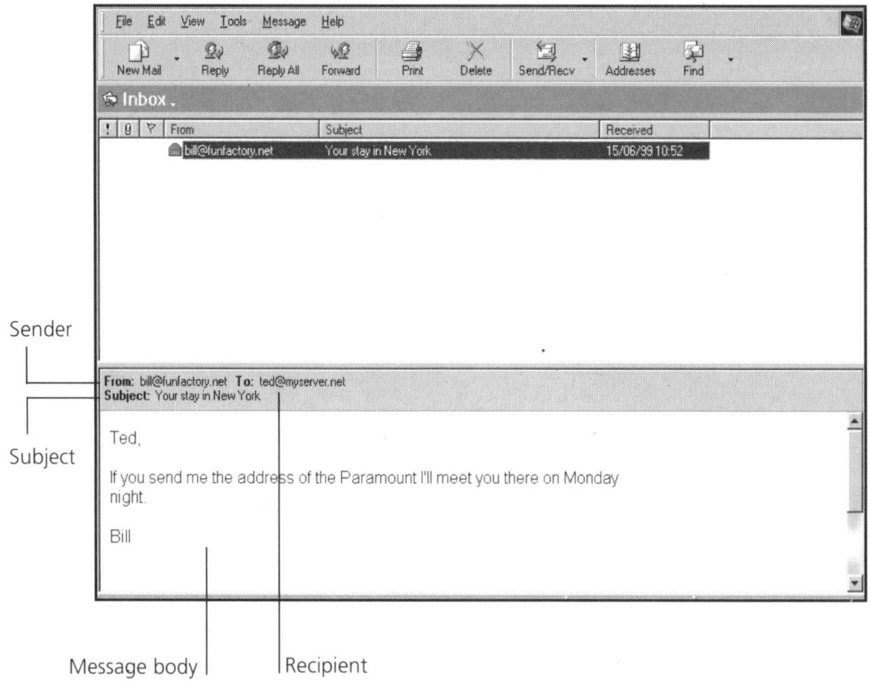

CHANGING APPEARANCES

As you are working through these examples, don't worry if your screen doesn't look exactly the same as it's shown here. Not only is it possible for the various releases of Outlook Express look and work in slightly different ways (or versions for different computers), but the program itself offers the you the flexibility of being able to do the same tasks in a number of alternative ways. Much like a Web browser, you can also configure Outlook Express so that the different tool bars or screens can be displayed in different ways.

REPLYING TO AN E-MAIL

If you want to reply to one of your messages and refer to its contents, you can do it really easily without having to retype the details into a new message. An even greater benefit of doing it this way is that the original text is shown in the body of your message indented by a "greater-than" symbol (">"). This enables you, for eample, to respond directly to questions or issues in the text. When you return the message the recipient will immediately understand those parts of the original mail to which you are referring.

1 Highlight the message in the INBOX to which you want to reply (if the message is currently being read it will automatically be highlighted). Click on REPLY.

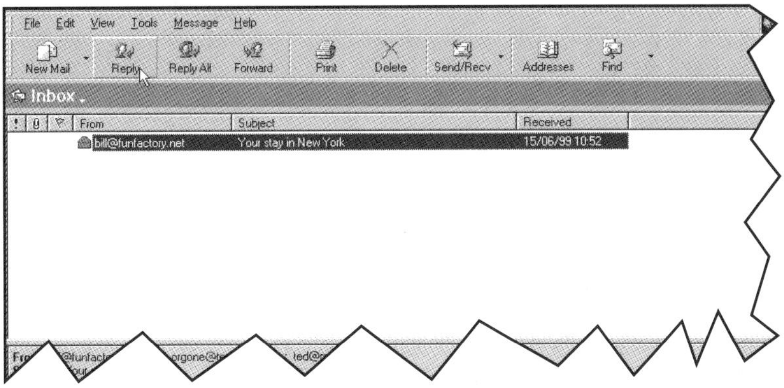

2 The original text appears in the body of the message (note the indentation). This text can be altered or added-to in any way.

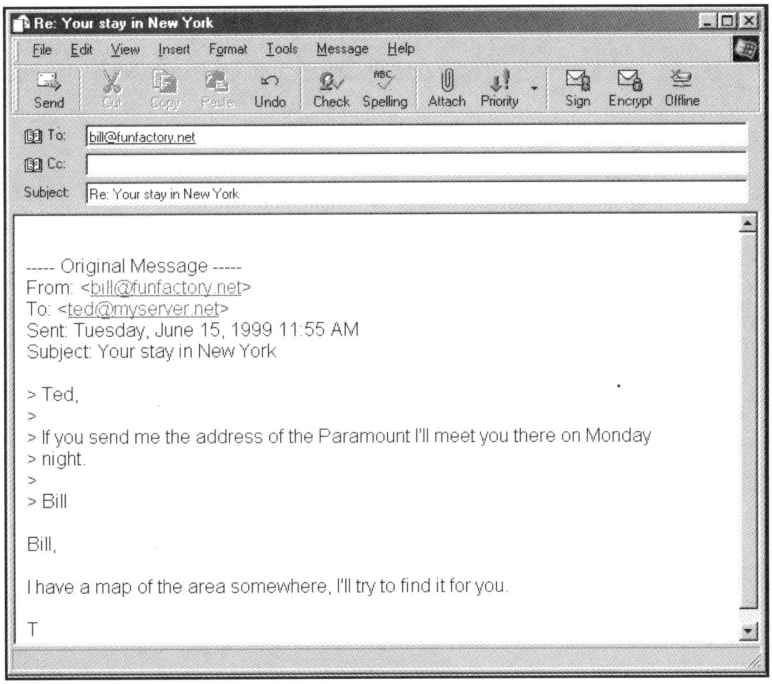

3 Click on SEND.

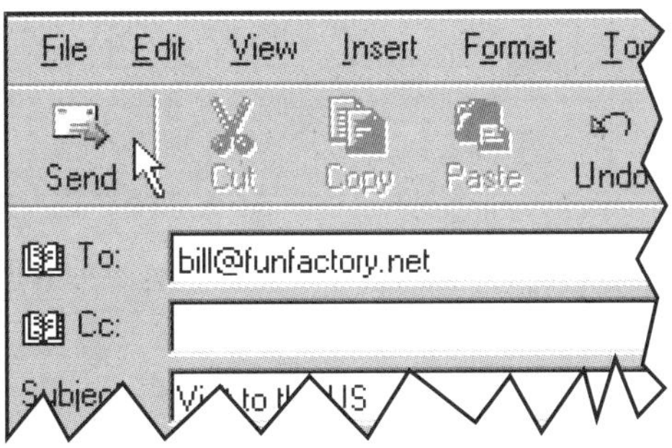

ATTACHING FILES TO YOUR E-MAILS

In addition to simple text-based e-mails, you might occasionally also want to send other files (a sound, image, or text file, for example) as part of your message. formatted for use with specific kinds of software. These extra files are referred to as "attachments".

ATTACHING A FILE IN OUTLOOK EXPRESS

Begin by writing a new e-mail in the way described over the previous few pages. Before you go any further you should locate the folder that contains the file you want to send. This will make things easier when you reach step 3 across the page.

1 Create a new e-mail and write your message.

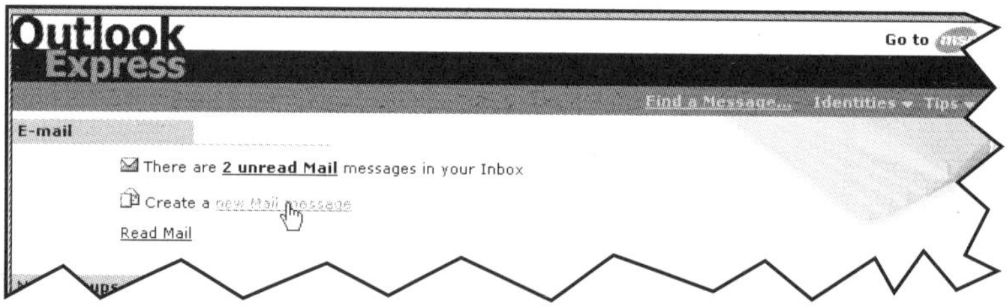

2 Click on the ATTACH button.

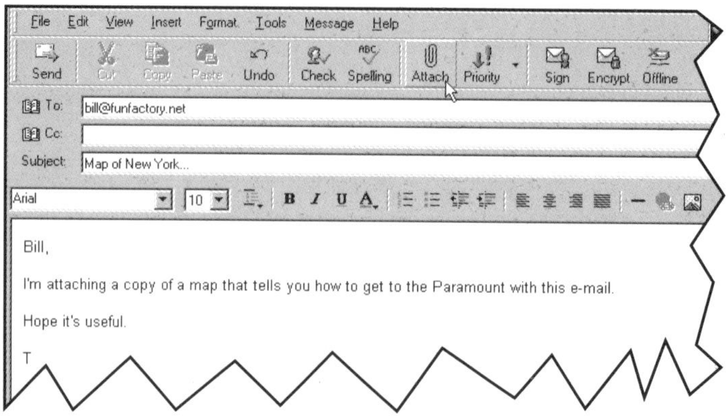

ATTACHMENT ISSUES

Don't overdo your use of attachments, especially large ones which may take an eternity for both you and the recipent to download. As far as the Internet is concerned, there are few things less amusing than waiting for an hour for an unsolicited "humourous" image to complete its arrival in your INBOX. For more information on attachments, read pages 78-79 to see how large files can be reduced in size making them easier to download.

3 The INSERT ATTACHMENT dialog box appears. Select the file you want to send with your e-mail and click on ATTACH.

Select the folder in which the file is stored.

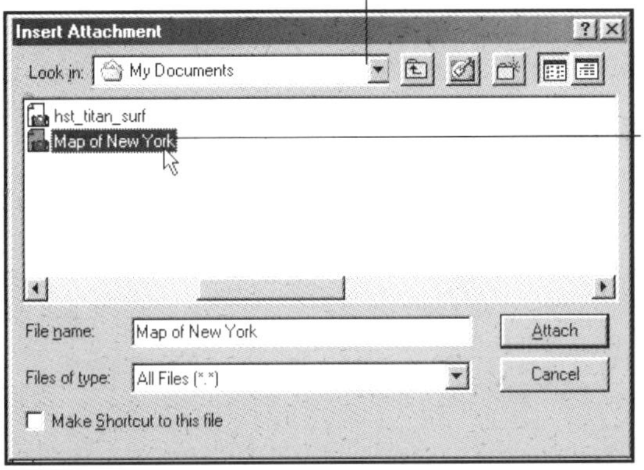

Double-clicking on the file name has the same effect as highlighting and clicking on ATTACH.

4 The attached file name will appear in the ATTACH box. Click on SEND to complete the job.

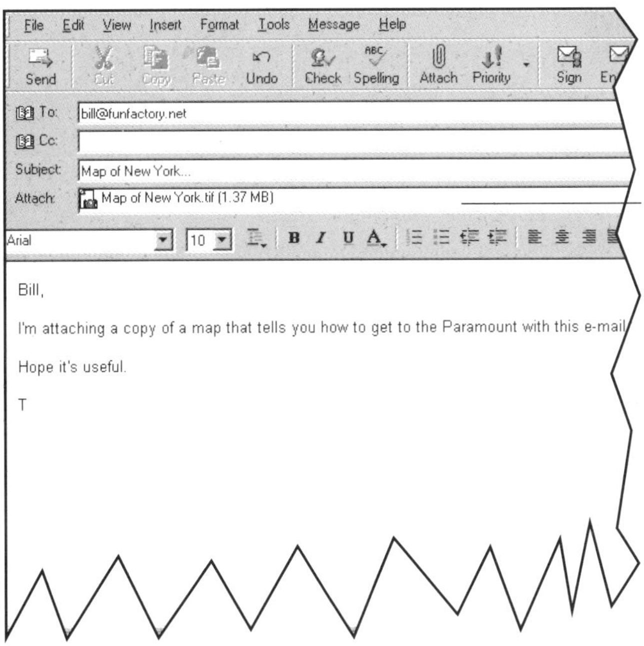

Attached file name appears in the e-mail. The size is shown in brackets.

COMPRESSION

One of the problems of sending files across the Internet is that they can take ages to download (and upload at the other end). A neat solution is to use a data compression program. This scrunches the file to a small proportion – sometimes less than five percent of its original size – making it much faster to send. When the file gets to its destination, a similar program is needed to restore it to its original form.

USING WINZIP

Let's look at an example of file compression using a program called WinZip. Although not conventional shareware, WinZip is widely available on an evaluation basis. In this example we'll see how much smaller we can make the attachment we sent in the previous example – at over one megabyte in size, it would currently be undesirable to send it without compression.

1 Run the WinZip program. To create a new archive click on NEW.

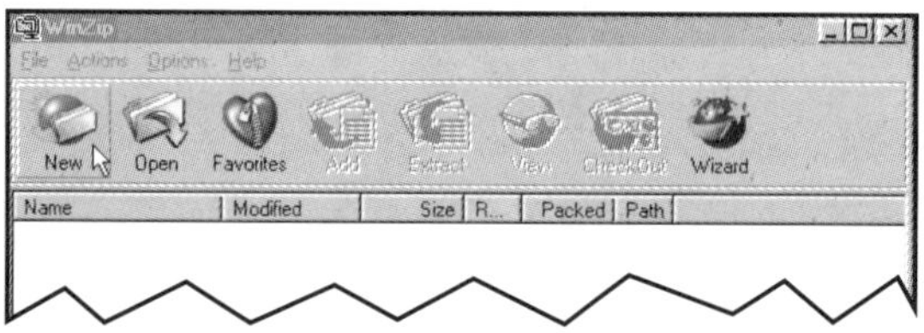

2 Name the new archive and click on OK.

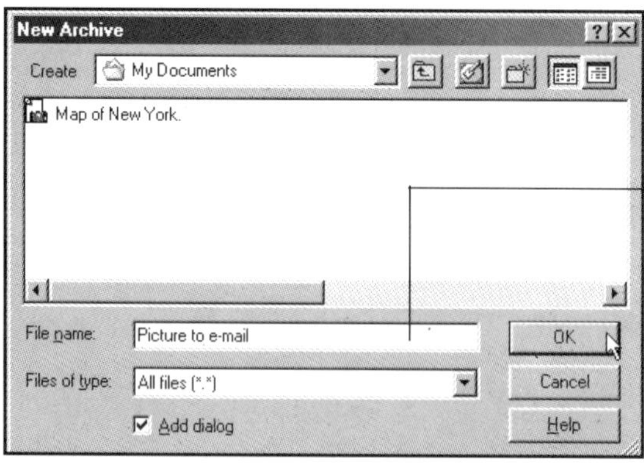

Enter archive name here. A zipped file is called an "archive" as it can contain any number of compressed files.

3 You are returned to the WinZip main menu. To add the file to be compressed click on ADD.

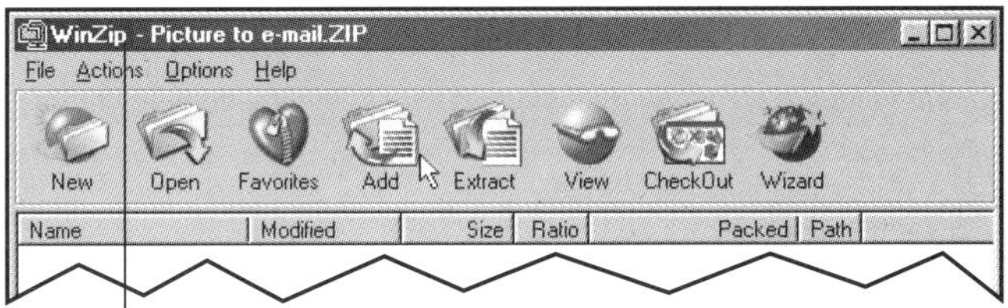

File name is now reflected in the WinZip title bar.

4 In the ADD dialog box, click on the file you want to compress and click on ADD.

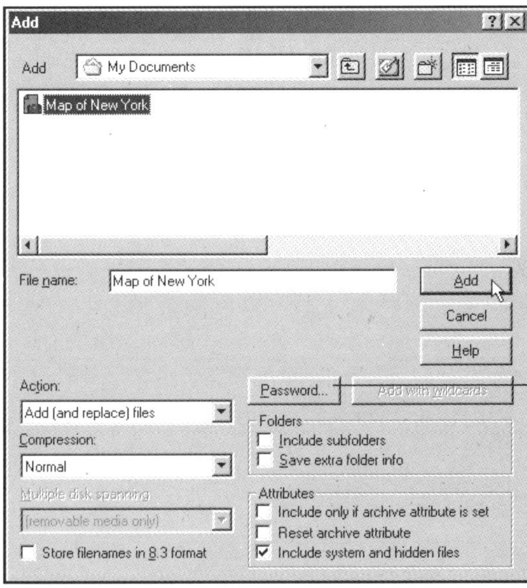

As an additional feature, WinZip allows password protection to prevent "zipped" files being opened by unauthorized persons.

5 The WinZip main menu shows degree of compression achieved for this file.

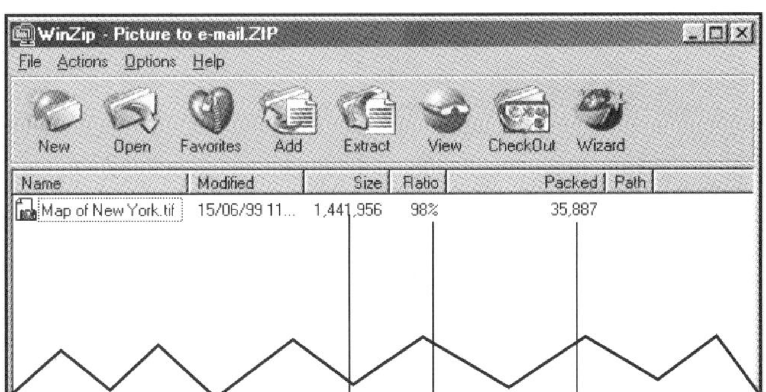

Original file size

New file size

Level of compression

E-MAIL ON THE MOVE

If you are on holiday you can still read your mail wherever you happen to be as long as you have access to a Web browser. Your ISP may offer a secure e-mail service accessible via a Web browser, but if not, all you have to do is open a Web-mail account. The most widely used system is Microsoft's free Hotmail.

USING WEB-MAIL

To use any web-mail system you need to know the name of your ISP's POP3 server as well as your own POP 3 user ID and password. As well as giving an additional free e-mail account, Hotmail allows you to collect mail from up to four other ISP servers. Begin by opening your web browser and logging onto http://www.hotmail.com.

1 If they are already set up, type in your user ID and password and click on ENTER. If you are using Hotmail for the first time, click on SIGN UP HERE and follow the instructions until you have received your ID and password to enter.

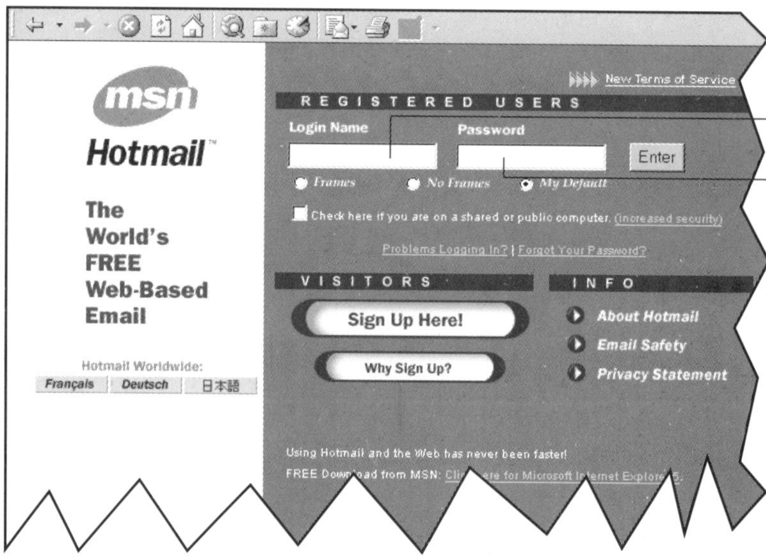

Enter your Hotmail ID here.

Enter your Hotmail password here.

2 In Hotmail's INBOX, enter the POP settings for your ISP(s). These are maintained on the secure Hotmail server.

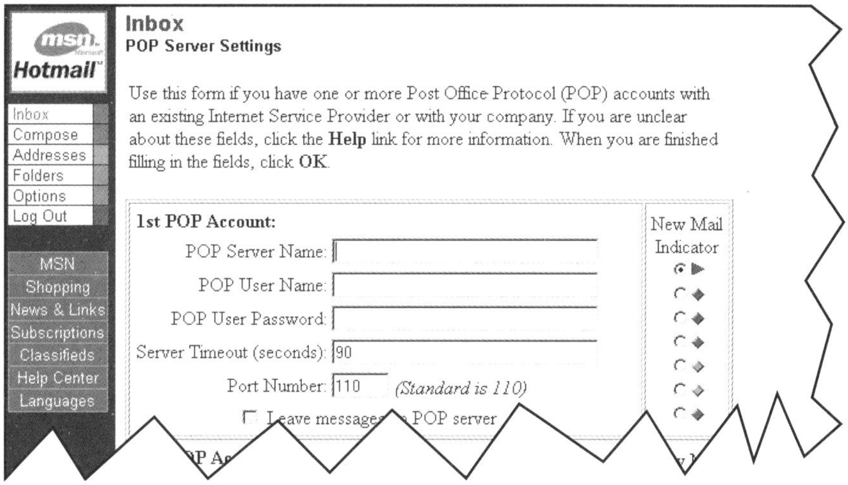

3 In the INBOX, click on POP MAIL.

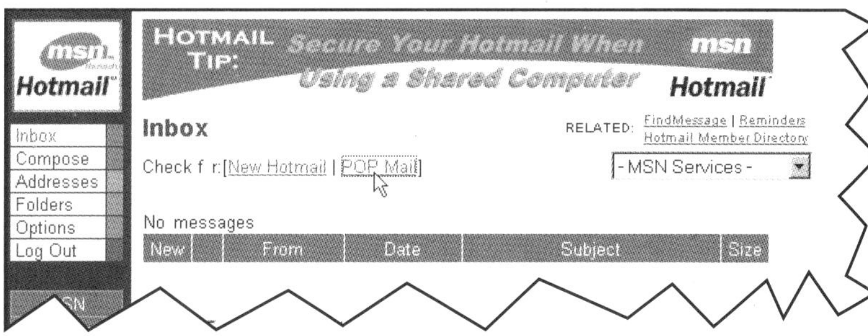

4 Any new e-mail will be displayed in the INBOX. Double-click on the message line to open the e-mail.

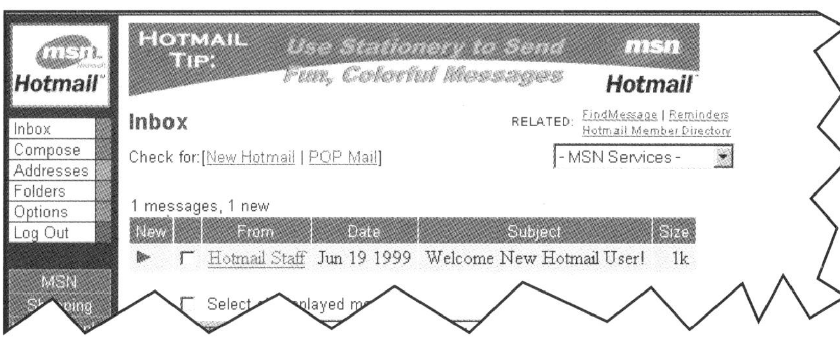

CYBERFAXES

Some ISPs, like Demon (http://www.demon.net), can arrange for you to receive faxes as e-mail attachments, supplying you with a new fax number to give to friends and business contacts. As well as doing away with the need for a fax machine it also means that if you want to receive faxes when you are on the move you can retrieve them at your convenience via a web-mail system like Hotmail.

MAKING E-MAIL EASIER

Like other e-mail programs, Microsoft's Outlook Express has many features that will save you time and effort when sending e-mails and keeping records of your communication.

CREATING AN ADDRESS BOOK

E-mail addresses can be tricky little blighters: one letter out of place or typed in the wrong case and your mails will just get the cyberspace equivalent of "return to sender". Luckily you can set up an address book in your e-mail program. This means that once an individual's details are stored correctly you won't ever have to type them in again. There are many ways you can set up your address book in Outlook Express. This example shows you how you can use incoming e-mails to configure the details.

1 In your INBOX, click on the name that you want to enter into your address book.

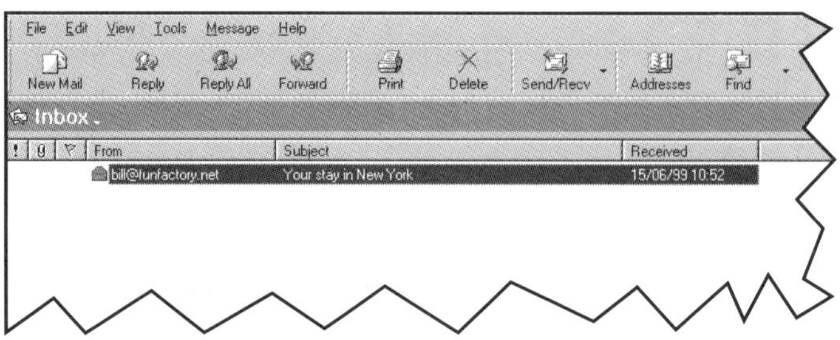

2 With the entry still highlighted, choose the option ADD SENDER TO ADDRESS BOOK from the TOOLS menu.

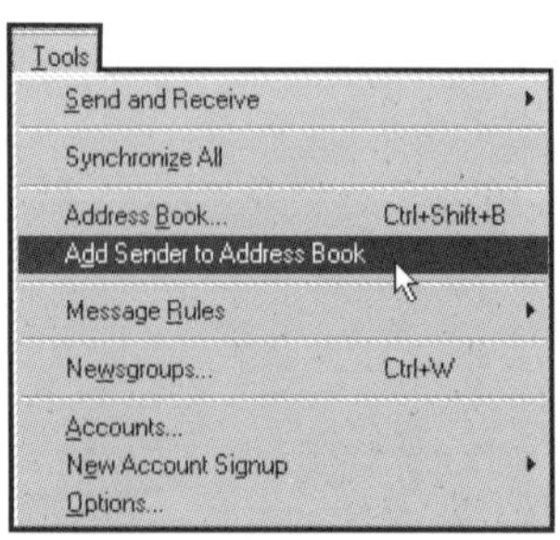

3 Click on ADDRESSES. This opens the ADDRESS BOOK – MAIN IDENTITY.

4 With the new entry highlighted click on PROPERTIES. This opens the PROPERTIES screen.

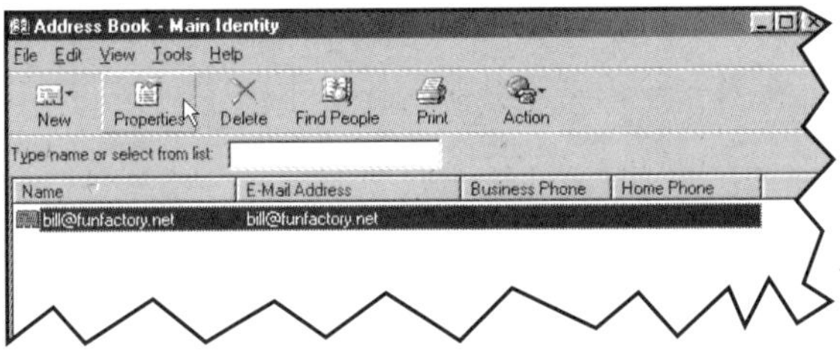

5 Click on the tabs at the top of the screen to add personal information. Click on OK when you have finished.

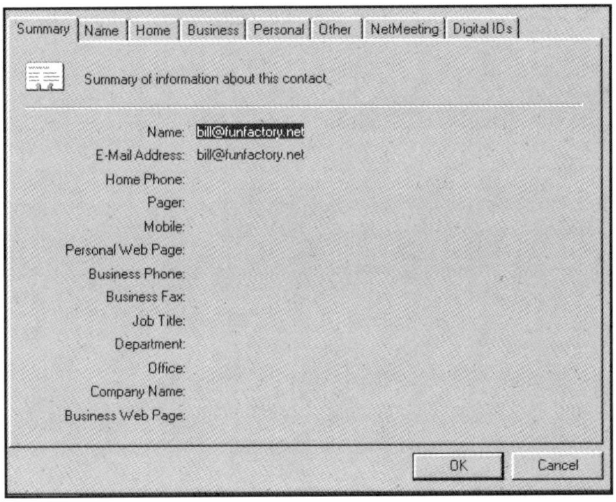

6 New addresses are displayed in the CONTACT box on the bottom left-hand corner of the page. Double-click on an entry to create a new readily addressed blank e-mail.

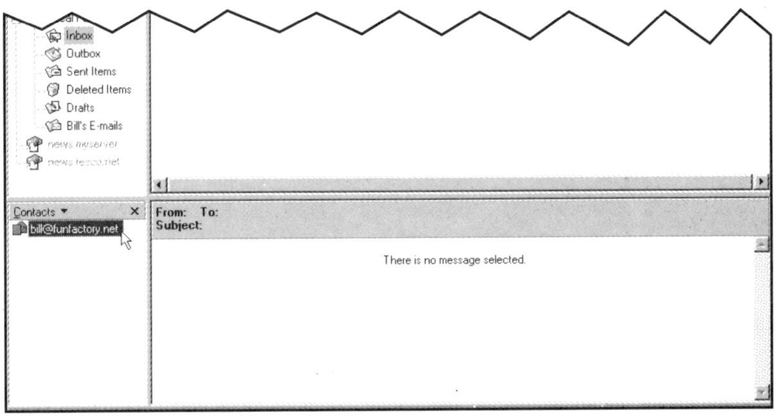

FILTERING

If you get to the stage where you start to receive a lot of e-mails daily, you can easily become disorganized. One way of dealing with this problem is to filter your mail so that it goes into specially allocated mail boxes. You might not even want to see mail from some sources at all, and can just filter it straight into the trash can. Here is a simple example that shows you how to set the rules for filtering your mail.

1 Drag the cursor down to the MESSAGE RULES option in the TOOLS menu. From the sub-menu click on MAIL.

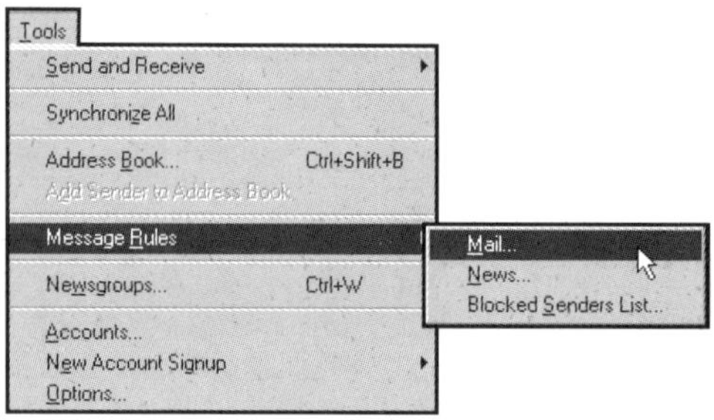

2 Tick the top options in the CONDITIONS and ACTIONS boxes. Click on OK.

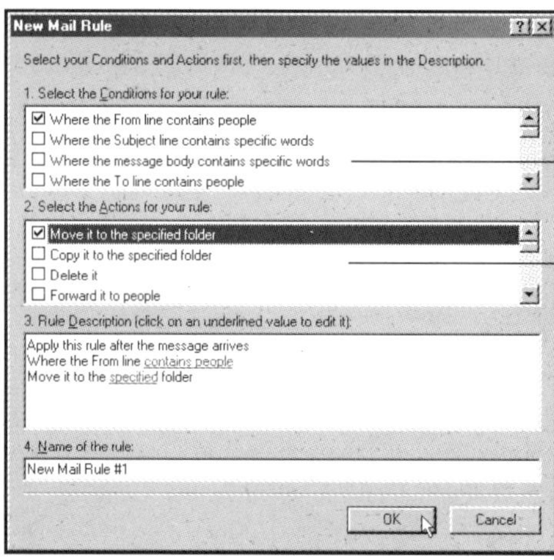

Options in this box are for setting the conditions for the filtering to take place. In this instance, where the "From" line in the e-mail contains the name of a specific person.

Options in this box set the action that must take place when the criteria above have been met. In this case, the e-mail has to be moved from the INBOX to a different folder (as yet unspecified).

3 The SELECT PEOPLE dialog box appears. Type in the name of the person whose messages you wish to filter.

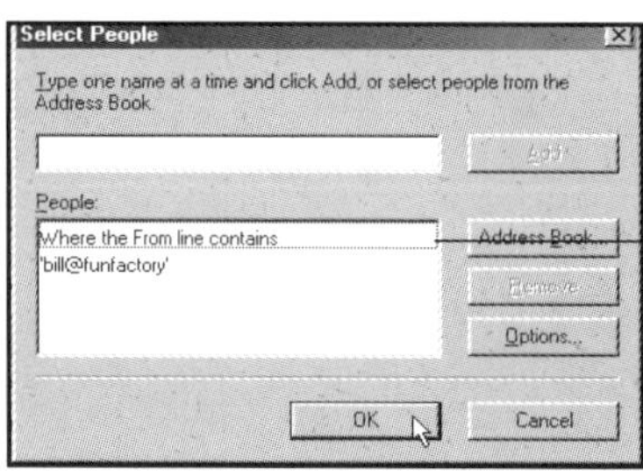

Each time a mail from "bill@funfactory.net" arrives, the action specified in the step that follows will take effect.

3 This returns you to the NEW RULE box. Click on the highlighted text.

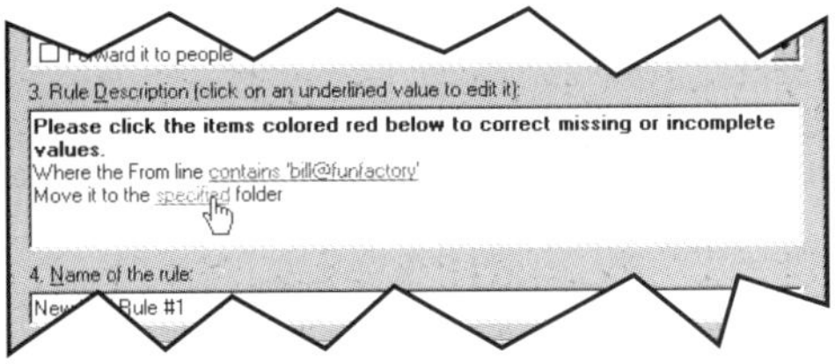

4 The MOVE box gives you the choice of selecting an existing mailbox folder or creating a new one. Click on NEW FOLDER. Enter the name of the new folder in the NEW FOLDER box. Click on OK.

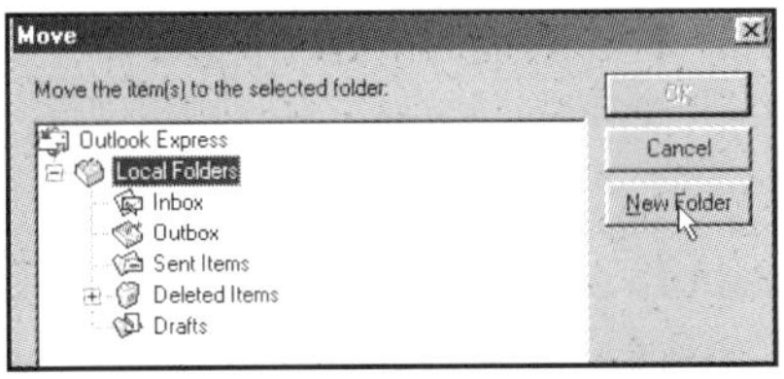

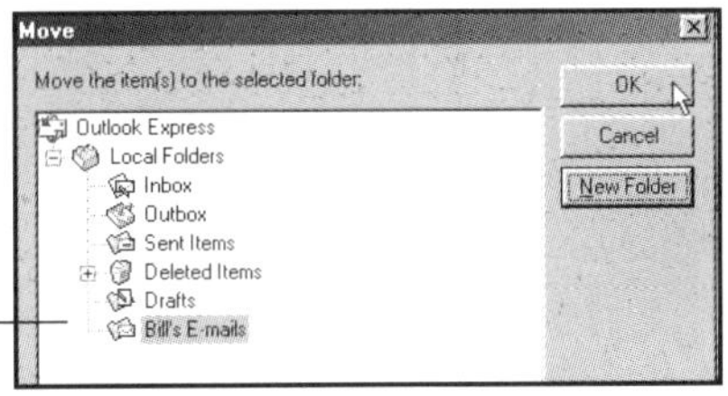

The folder "Bill's E-mails" has now been set up.

5 These conditions and actions are now set up as NEW MAIL RULE #1 and take effect when you click on OK.

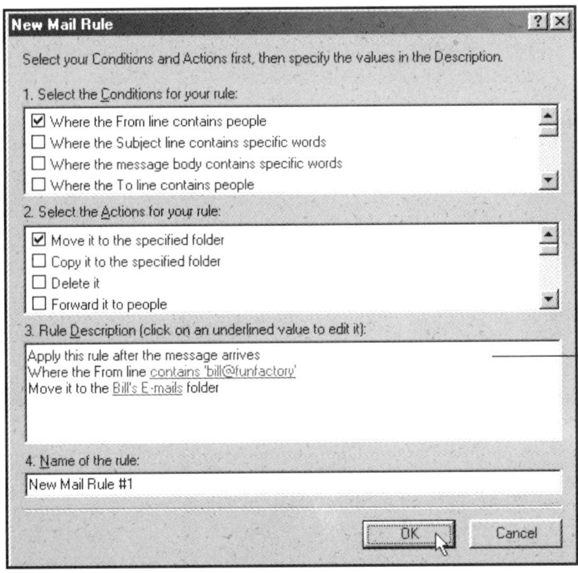

Whenever an e-mail arrives from "bill@funfactory.net it automatically gets sent to the folder "Bill's E-mails".

SIGNING OFF

Appropriately enough, we'll end the chapter on e-mails with a word about signatures. As you'll notice when you start to receive mail, a lot of people end their messages with a standard message of some sort – it may be a full address or perhaps a witty quote. You might wonder why they go to the trouble of typing all that information when their message to you was only one line long. The answer is that they haven't typed it all in on your behalf, they've set up a standard "signature" which is automatically placed at the end of their message. Here is how to do it using Outlook Express.

1 Call the OPTIONS dialog box by clicking on OPTIONS in the TOOLS menu. Click on the SIGNATURES tab and then finally click on NEW.

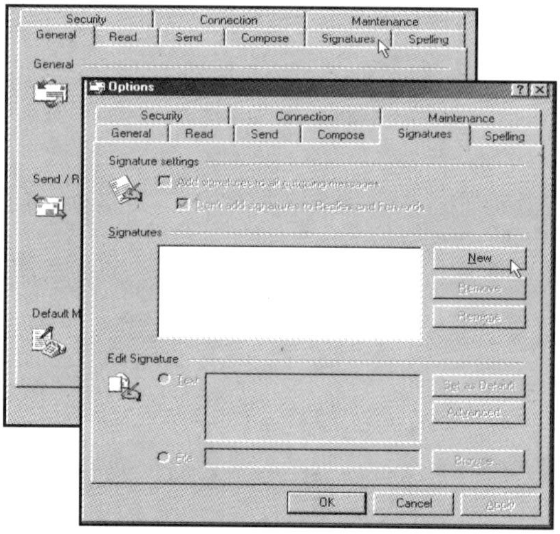

2 In the EDIT SIGNATURE box you can add any text you like. When you are happy with it, click on the ADD SIGNATURES TO ALL OUTGOING MESSAGES box, and then click APPLY.

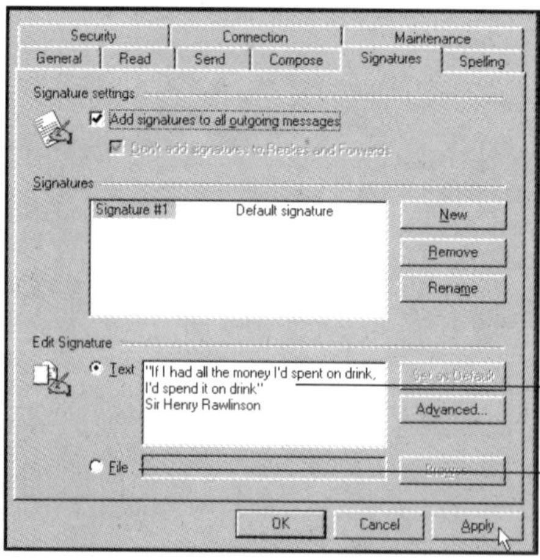

This message will be displayed on the bottom of every e-mail you send.

The option exists to automatically include a file with all of your e-mails.

DOWNLOADING FILES

4

Long before the World Wide Web, the Internet was being used to transfer files between remote locations using a system called FTP – "File Transfer Protocol". Downloading files lets you take advantage of the vast archives of software and documents around the world. File transfer is more commonly performed on the Web these days, and browsers can be used to access the many useful FTP sites that remain.

DOWNLOADING FROM THE WEB

Downloading files from the World Wide Web is very straightforward. You simply click on a few buttons and the whole operation just happens. Here is an example of how to download a piece of software.

DOWNLOADING FROM THE WEB

To download a file from the World Wide Web all you need to know is the URL of the Web site. In this case we're going to download a piece of shareware called "mIRC", which is client software for an Internet Relay Chat server (don't worry about this for now – you'll see it in use in the next chapter). Begin by logging onto the software designer's Web site, which is http://www.mirc.uk.

1 Log onto the site. Amongst the general information you will find an option to download software. From the list of servers that ensues, double-click on the one which is closest to your own location. They will all work, but local servers are more likely to be quicker.

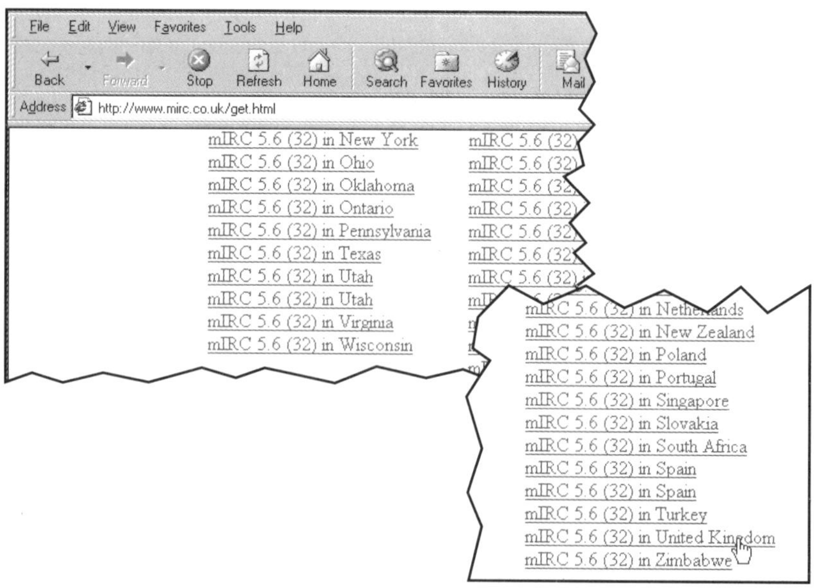

2 You will be presented with the Windows FILE DOWNLOAD box. Select the option to save the file to your hard disk. Click OK.

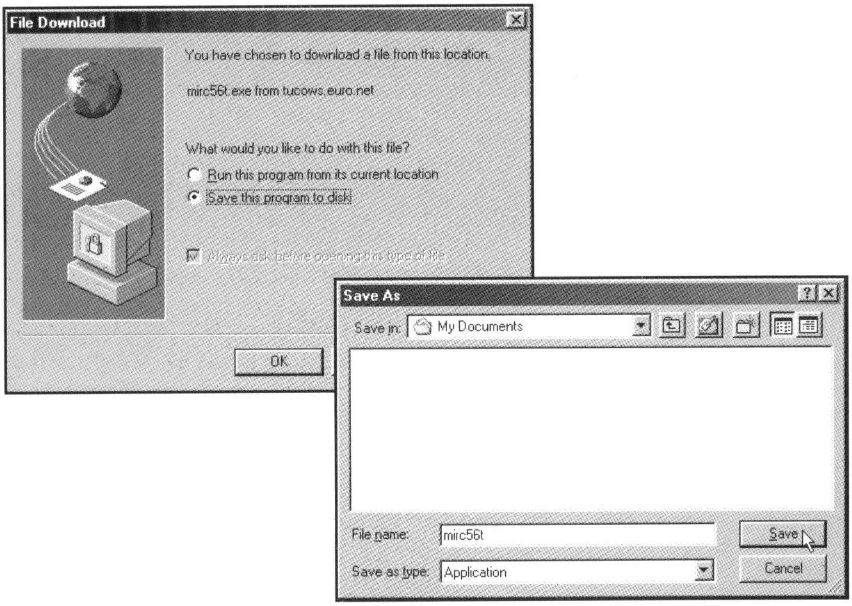

3 The subsequent page asks you which folder you want the file to be saved to. In this case we've specified MY DOCUMENTS.

4 During the download a panel appears telling you its progress and how much longer it is likely to take.

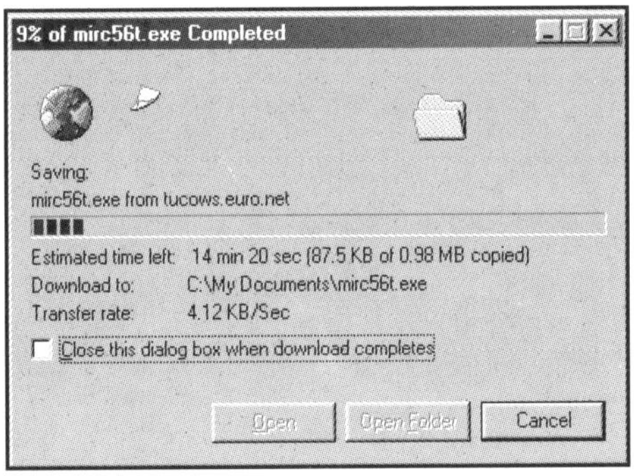

When the completion scale reaches 100% the box will disappear. You will now find the file waiting for your inspection in the folder "My Documents".

MULTI-TASKING

When you are downloading files from the World Wide Web, you can safely leave your browser to carry on downloading "in the background" while you continue to surf the Web for other interesting sites. In fact you can download several files simultaneously, although the speed at which this takes place (and at which you continue to surf) will depend not only on your modem speed, but the speed of your computer processor and the amount of RAM you have installed.

USING FTP

There are two types of FTP. One is private, requiring password permission to make a connection; the other is public (or anonymous), and is free for anyone to use. To see FTP in action you have the can either use your Web browser or software specially designed for the task, which is easier to use.

CUTEFTP

CuteFTP is a popular pieces of FTP software. The examples shown over the next few pages all make use of this program, although you can use the same principles to make other similar programs (or your Web browser) do the same thing. When you first run the program, the FTP SITE MANAGER dialog box pops up. This shows you to see the FTP sites that are already set up (many are supplied with teh software) or allows you to add new sites of your own.

1 In the FTP SITE MANAGER dialog box, click on ADD SITE.

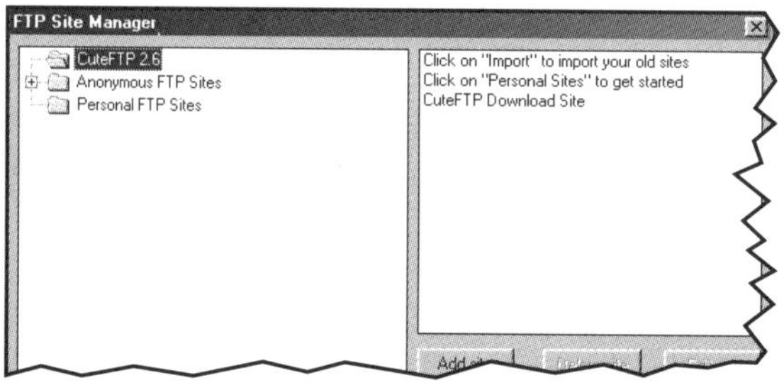

2 In the ADD HOST dialog box, enter the FTP site details and click on OK.

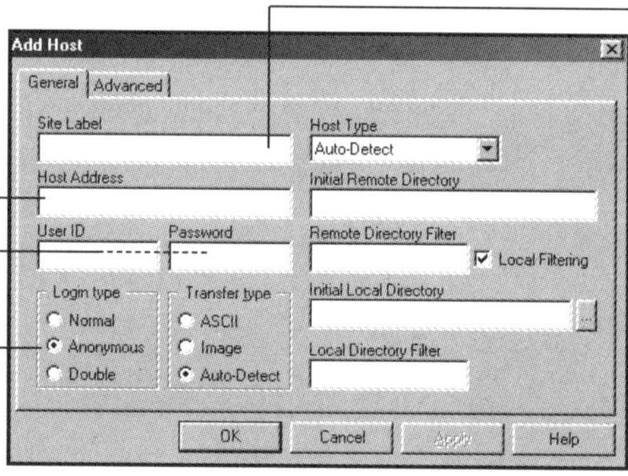

Enter an appropriate name for the site

Enter the address of the FTP site

Enter ID and password if necessary

Select type of connection

CUTEFTP IN ACTION

That example showed you how to set up a connection if you already knew the FTP site details. In fact, CuteFTP comes with a useful selection of sites already in place. If you click on the ANONYMOUS FTP folder in the left-hand side-panel of the FTP SITE MANAGER window, and then from the list of folders that appears, click on PREDEFINED SITES, you will see a further set of folders named according to categories. If you double-click on any of these, you will see a list of FTP sites in the the right -hand box. In this example, we'll download an image from NASA's massive FTP archive.

1 From the "Space Information" FTP sites listed in the box on the right, select NASA IMAGES and click on CONNECT. This opens the main CuteFTP screen.

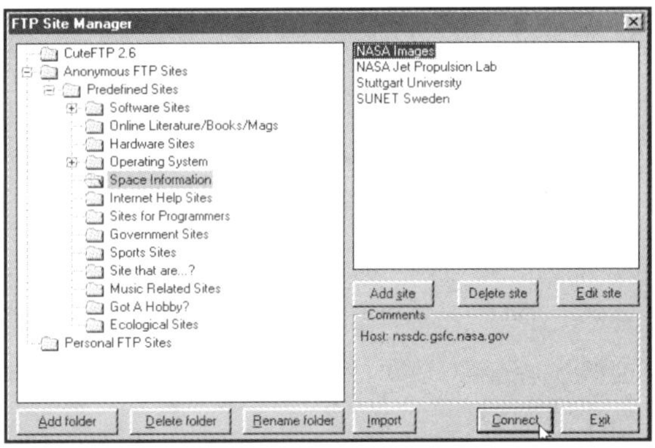

CuteFTP tool bar

Running dialogue of communication between your computer and the remote computer.

Files on your own computer (the folder name is shown at the top of the column).

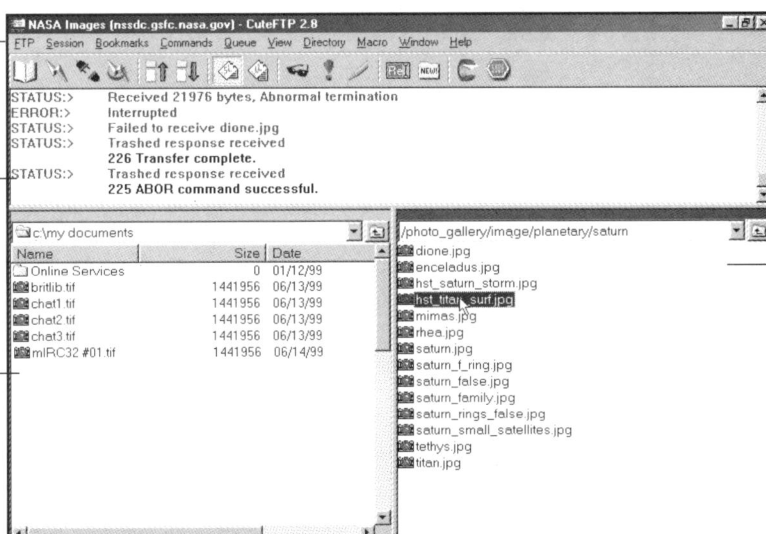

Files on the NASA server that you are allowed to access.

2 Double-click on the graphic file "hst_titan_surf".

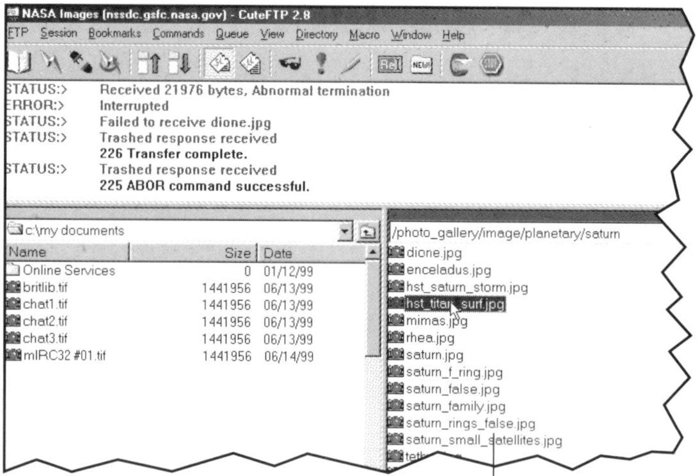

You can also drag the file from the server's list on the right-hand box and drop it into your PC's hard disk on the left-hand box.

3 CuteFTP will ask you whether you really want to download the file. Click on YES.

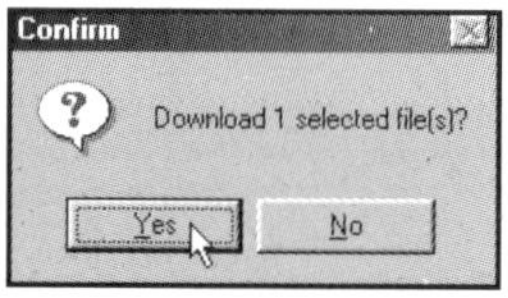

4 The running dialogue will then scroll along until it confirms that the download was successful.

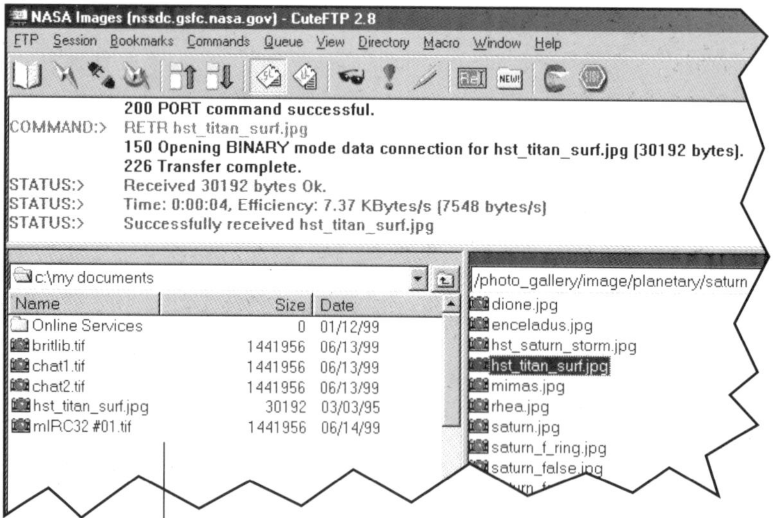

The downloaded file now appears on your computer.

5 Finally you can take a look at the image if you have software that can read "jpeg" files.

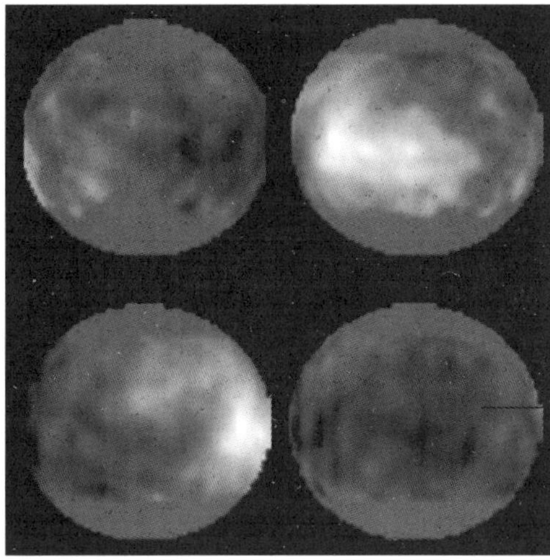

Four views of the surface of Titan, one of Saturn's moons, courtesy of NASA.

WHERE DO YOU GET FTP SOFTWARE?

You can download the most up-to-date shareware version of CuteFTP from http://www.cuteftp.com. There are many other FTP programs that are equally as effective. These include Bulletproof FTP (http://www.bpftp.com), Cupertino (http://www.members.xoon.com/~seanhu), WS-FTP (http://www.ipswitch.com) and Terrapin FTP (http://www.terra-net.com/eu/index.html).

THE TOOLBAR

CuteFTP provides you with numerous options when it comes to downloading files. Many of the most useful functions can be accessed via the toolbar above the dialogue area. If you forget or can't figure out what any of the functions does, all you have to do is hold the mouse cursor over the icon and a descriptive tool-tip will appear.

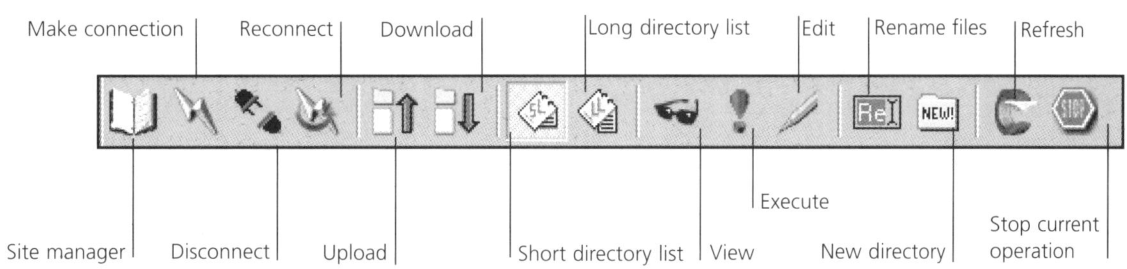

UPLOADING FILES

Seeing how simple downloading files via the Web can be, it might seem that using a dedicated FTP program is a bit of a waste of time. This is not so. There are many excellent free FTP archive resources all over the world that you can only access if you have software suitable for the protocol.

Another important factor is that software such as CuteFTP is also capable of transmitting files in the other direction. This means that you can UPLOAD them from your computer to a remote server. Although Web browsers can be configured to do this, by and large they are nothing like as easy to use. Although you usually would have to get permission to upload to an anonymous FTP site, one area where this has clear practical value is in the uploading of your own personal Web pages to your ISP's web server.

Uploading files follows almost the same the procedure as downloading files. In this case, however, you select the file or files on your PC (shown in the left-hand box using CuteFTP) and drag them across into the remote server (right-hand box).

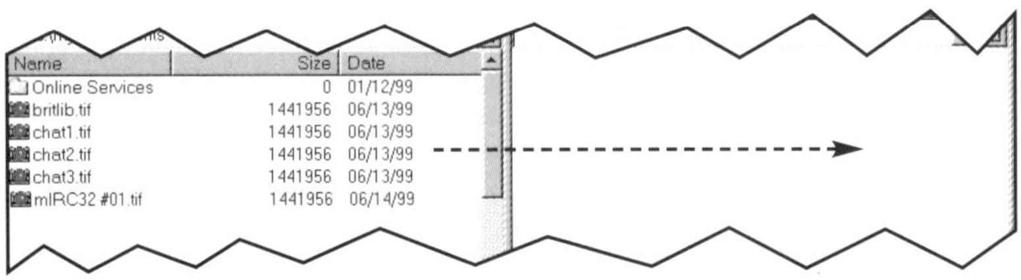

THE PERILS OF DOWNLOADING

One of the potential dangers of downloading files from remote sites across the Internet involves computer viruses. Viruses are almost never passed along by installing legitimate software, which means that the most likely way they spread is on storage media like floppy disks and CD-ROMs passed between machines or downloaded from the Internet, via the World Wide Web, from a newsgroup, or by using FTP. One way you can circumvent this problem is by installing virus detection software which checks all the new documents that hit your hard disk before they are saved. This is STRONGLY recommended. Whilst the majority of viruses are relatively harmless and can be "cured" by running "disinfectant" software, some, like the recent Melissa and Chernobyl viruses can wreck your hard disks. It's estimated that around 400 new viruses are discovered each month, so even the best protection software can date quickly – make sure you get regular updates. There is more about viruses on page 164.

5 GROUP ACTIVITY

You need never be alone on the Internet. Some of the most popular aspects of the Net involve widespread interaction. The most popular type of place to communicate is in a newsgroup, where you can discuss interests with like-minded souls. For a more immediate online exchange, you can pay a visit to an Internet chat room. This chapter will tell you how you can participate in these exciting areas.

NEWSGROUPS

USENET is made up of tens of thousands of newsgroups distributed around the world via computers called news servers. A newsgroup is an Internet forum for public discussion. It is rather like a public notice board on which messages can be posted, read and responded to. To access a newgroup all you need is a program called a "newsreader", the name of your service provider's news server and the name of the group in which you want to participate.

FINDING A NEWSREADER

If you have a PC with Windows 98 installed, you already have a newsgroup reader loaded. This is Outlook Express, which is also an e-mail program. The Netscape Navigator Web browser also has the capability of reading newsgroups. Other popular software includes Free Agent, which you can download from http://www.forteinc.com.

CONFIGURING YOUR NEWSREADER

In this example we'll use Outlook Express. Different versions may look slightly different but can still be configured in much the same way. For now, all you need is the name of your ISP's news server – if you don't know it, a quick telephone call will do the trick.

1 Run OUTLOOK EXPRESS, Select ACCOUNTS in the TOOLS menu.

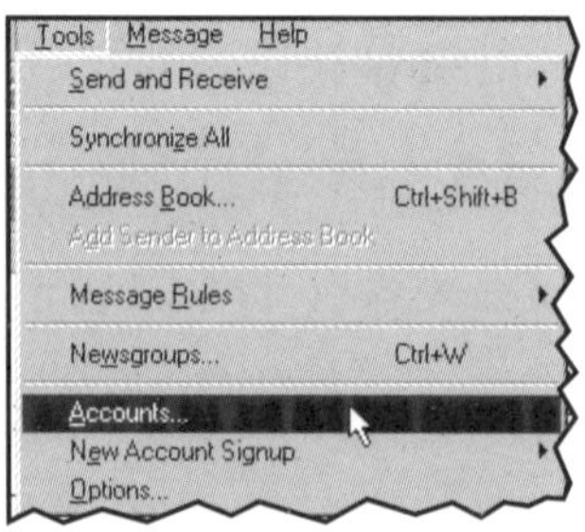

The ACCOUNTS option calls up the INTERNET ACCOUNTS dialog box.

2 In the news areas of the INTERNET ACCOUNTS dialog box, click on the ADD button and then select NEWS from the drop-down menu.

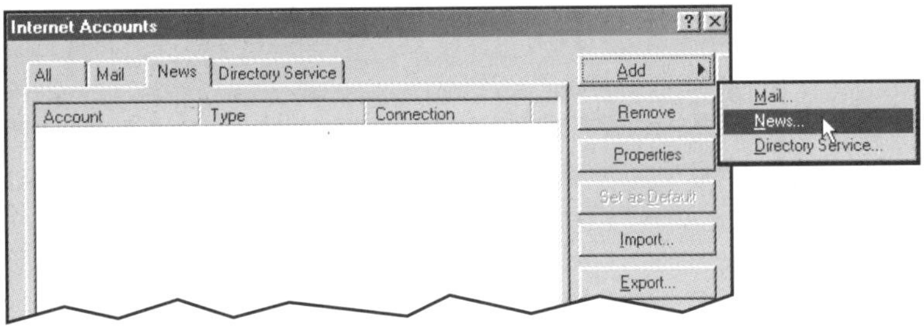

3 Work through the pages of the INTERNET CONNECTION WIZARD. After you've entered the requested details on each page, click on NEXT to move on to the subsequent page.

4 Click on FINISH. You are now set up to read a newsgroup.

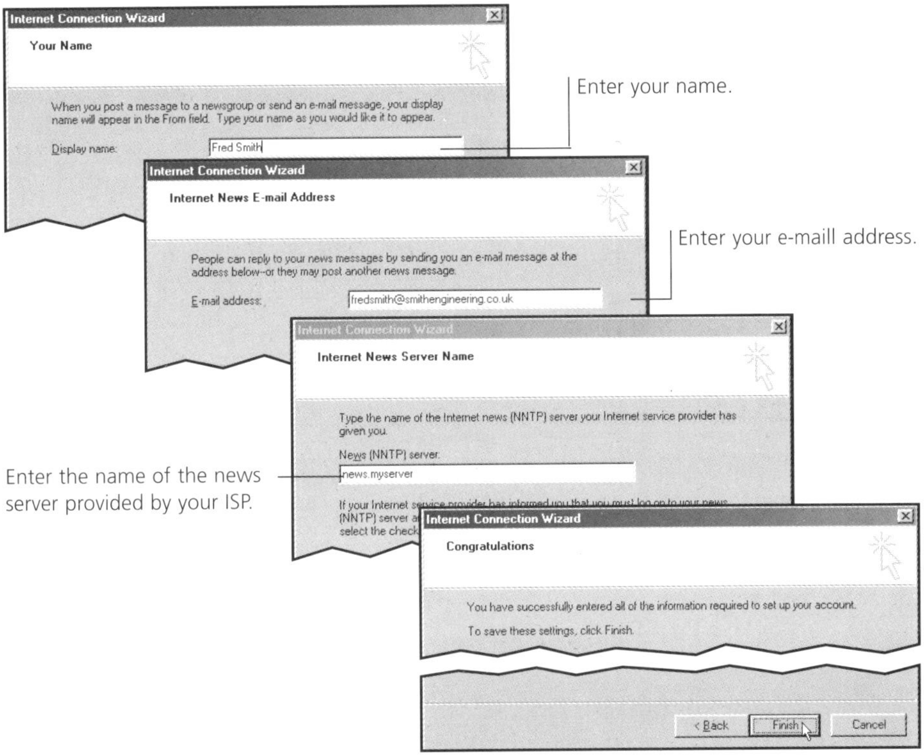

AVOIDING SPAM

A major problem facing newsgroups is the constant threat of "spam". This is the cyber equivalent of junk mail. Spammers use software that trawls through newsgroups looking for e-mail addresses. To avoid unwanted mail, a good tip is to alter the e-mail address you set up in the newsreader so that any software picking it up will not be able to use it. A standard practice is to change from something like fredsmith@smithengineering.co.uk to fredsmith@nospam.smithengineering.co.uk. Legitimate newsgroup users will understand what you have done and will be able to work out your correct address if they wish to contact you.

ACCESSING THE NEWSGROUPS

The next step is find out which newsgroups your ISP supports. This means downloading a list of all available newsgroups. With upwards of 20,000 sites stored by most ISP servers, this process can take a few minutes. Don't forget, that if you have accounts for more than one ISP make sure that the news server name you supplied is for the ISP that you are connected to or obviously it won't work.

1 Click on READ NEWS. You will be asked if you want to see a list of available newsgroups. Click on YES.

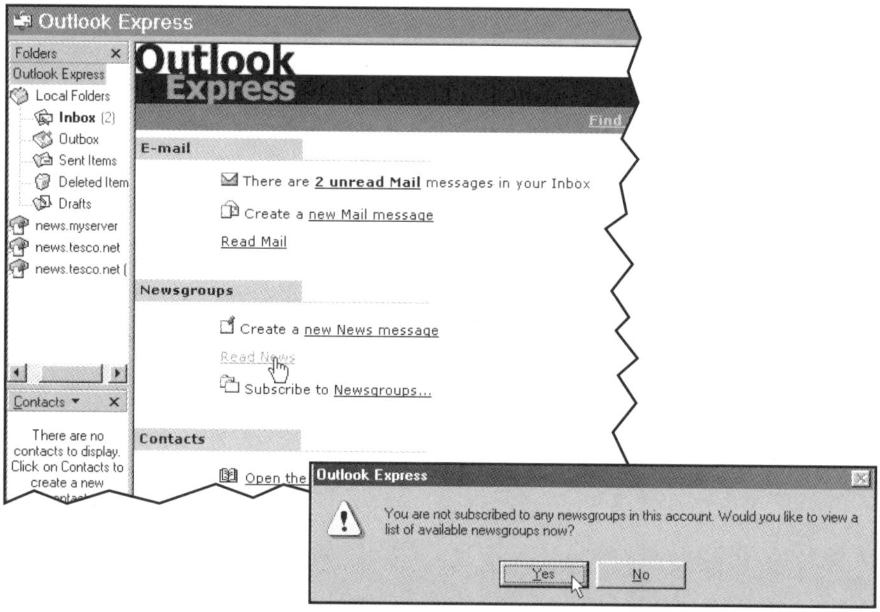

2 A scrolling list of newsgroups currently held by your ISP appears.

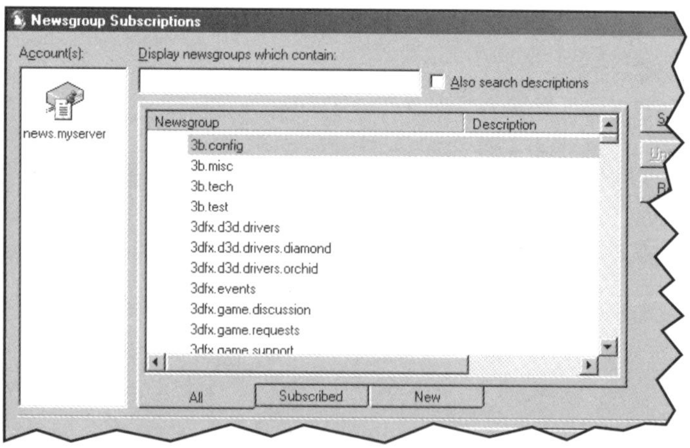

FREQUENTLY ASKED QUESTIONS (FAQs)

When you approach a newsgroup for the first time it's always a good idea to read the FAQ file first. This is usually downloadable from that newsgroup or an associated Web site and will answer some of your most basic questions – the kind that get regular subscribers irritated when they appear.

SUBSCRIBING TO A NEWSGROUP

In Outlook Express, there are two ways you can choose the newsgroups to which you want to subscribe. You can simply scroll down the list – but be warned, there could be getting on for 30,000 names on the list, so it might take a while. The easiest method is to do a keyword search. In this case, we'll see how many newsgroups have the word "Beatles" in their name.

1 Type the word "Beatles" in the DISPLAY box. A list of all newsgroups with the word "Beatles" appears.

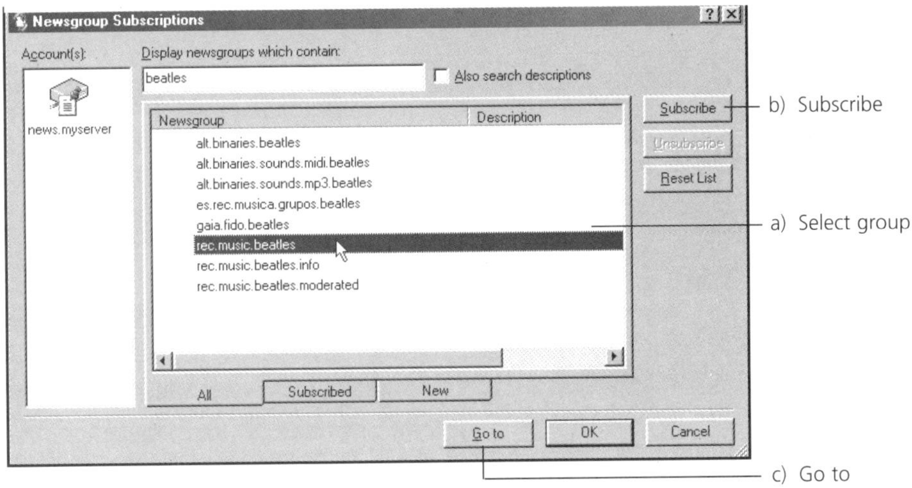

2 Select your newsgroup from the list by highlighting the entry. Click on SUBSCRIBE and then on GOTO. The current postings appear in the top half of the reader.

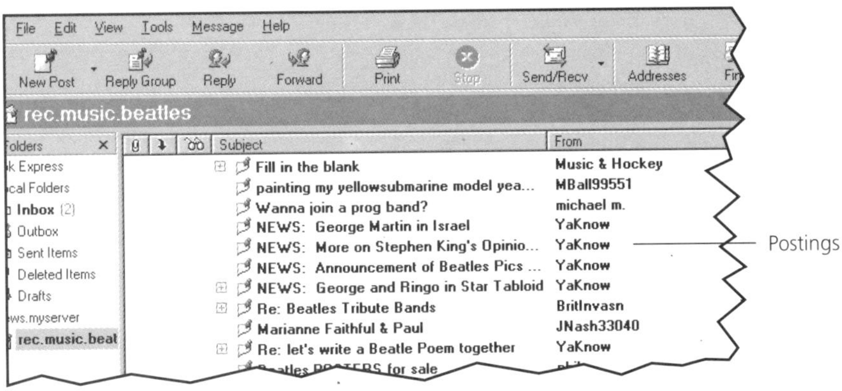

NEWSGROUP NETIQUETTE

LURK Some newsgroups are very narrow in their subject matter and can be intolerent of postings drifting "off-topic". Before you start firing off your postings "lurk" for a few days first - this means that you follow the threads of discussion but don't actually join in.

WASTING TIME Always give your postings a descriptive title. This alerts those who aren't interested in the same subject matter. It's also always a good idea to keep your postings as concise as possible.

MIND YOUR LANGUAGE Although much Internet communication is written in a conversational form, it can be difficult to project certain aspects of speech such as irony or other forms of humour. Don't forget that you are addressing a global audience – what's funny in one country may be dull, weird or downright rude in another. In the early days of the Internet, "smileys" (or "emoticons" to give them their correct name) were developed to convey such subtleties (see page 73).

READING NEWSGROUP POSTINGS

Once the newsgroup messages (known as "postings") have appeared in your reader all you have to do is scan the titles to see if any are look interesting. To open the message you simply double-click on it. Be warned, newsgroup postings can contain pictures that take a while to download. If this inadvertently happens all you have to do is click on STOP to halt the process.

1 To read any posting simply double-click anywhere on the message line.

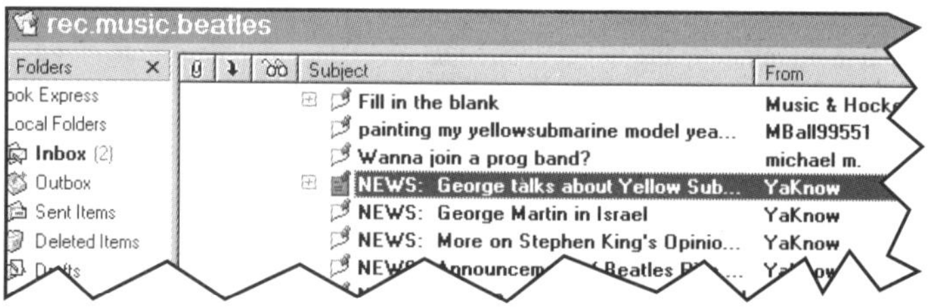

2 The message now appears in full.

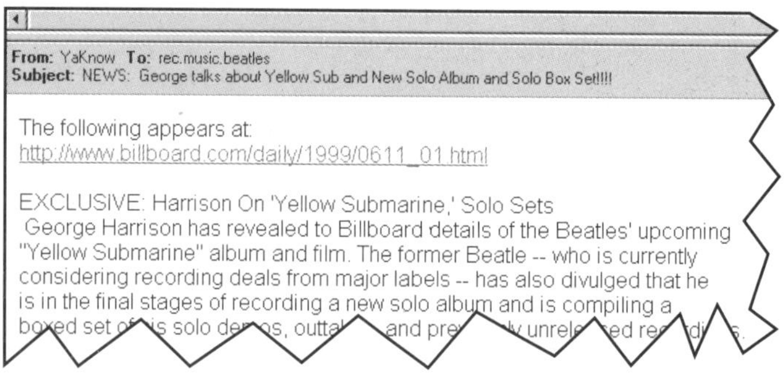

POSTING TO A NEWSGROUP

When you make your own contribution to a newsgroup you are essentially sending an e-mail. There are two different options, you can either respond to an existing posting or send a new one.

1 To make a new posting click on NEW POST. An empty "new message" document appears.

To respond to a posting click on REPLY GROUP. The original posting will appear in the "new message" document each line prefixed by the "greater than" symbol (>).

2 Type in the text and when you are happy with your posting click on SEND. Your posting will update the server and will subsequently appear on the list.

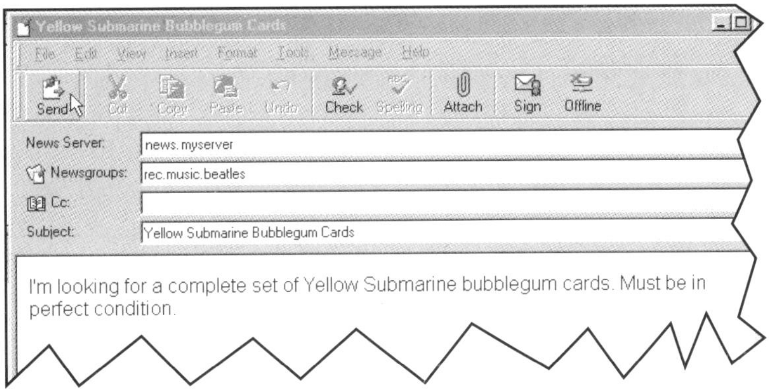

NEWSGROUP NAMES

When you first see a full list of newsgroups you will notice that the same prefixes keep on appearing over and over. This is because there is an informal naming standard at work designed to tell you a bit about the group itself. Here is brief description of the most commonly used suffixes.

alt. ALTERNATIVE. A fairly general prefix that indicates informality and contains everything from the popular (and notorious) alt.sex groups to alt.music.

biz.	BUSINESS	**comp.**	COMPUTERS
misc.	MISCELLANEOUS	**news.**	NEWSGROUP-RELATED
rec.	RECREATION. Includes sport.	**sci.**	SCIENCE

When a general interest newsgroup begins to develop a significant sub-strand of discussion, it's common for those members to break away. For example, rec.skiing started off as a forum for all snowsports, but as snowboarding has become popular, a new group has emerged, discussing only snowboarding issues – rec.skiing.snowboard.

CHAT ROOMS

As fun and useful as newsgroups can be, at best they are just glorified bulletin boards. If you decide to post a message you'll have to check later on to see if you've had any replies. There is, however, one way that you can get an instant response – by visiting an Internet "chat room".

WHAT IS A CHAT ROOM?

A chat room is an interactive zone that creates the illusion that a large group of people are connected to one massive computer terminal. Snippets of conversation scroll on the chat screen. If you type in a text message, it will appear on the screen in a few seconds. Chat rooms can be pretty chaotic places, almost like walking into a party and hearing ALL of the conversations going on at the same time. However, you soon adjust to this way of communicating, and quickly begin to understand which strands of conversation are connected. In other words, it isn't quite the anarchy that it sounds. Like newsgroups, chat rooms are often set up so that participants with common interests can discuss them "live" online. Furthermore, some rooms are controlled by a "moderator" who prevents things getting too much out of hand.

JOINING A CHAT ROOM

There are several different approaches you can take to joining a chat room. The most straightforward is to use a Web-based chat room such as YAHOO! CHAT. These are easy to use but not as fast as some of the alternatives. Online service providers, such as America Online, usually have their own chat rooms open only to their own subscribers. Finally, there is a third type of chat room which actually predates the mass popularity of the World Wide Web – Internet Relay Chat (IRC). This continues to be the most popular way of chatting on the Internet, although you do first have to download special client software to allow you to join in.

CHAT ROOM IN ACTION

To begin with, let's look at a simple example of a Web-based chat room – YAHOO! CHAT. Open your browser and connect to the Internet. Type in the URL http://chat.yahoo.com. The first time, you'll be asked to select a user name and a password for yourself, and to enter a few personal details before you hit the main page.

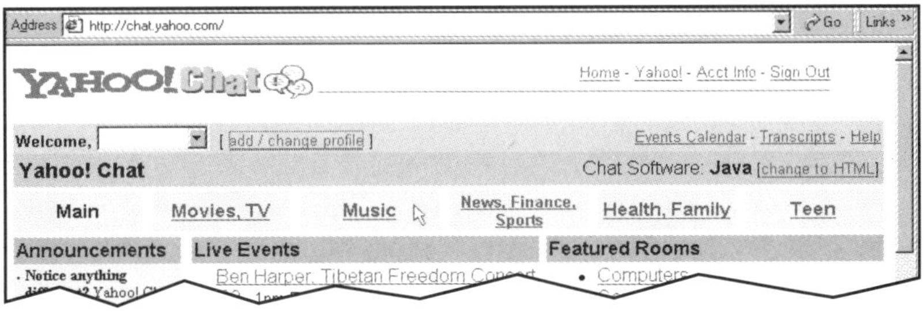

The Chat area. Everything you type in the CHAT message bar appears here alongside your user identification.

Name of the chat room.

List of the people in the chat room. Clicking entries lets you see any information they've logged about themselves. You can also send them a note.

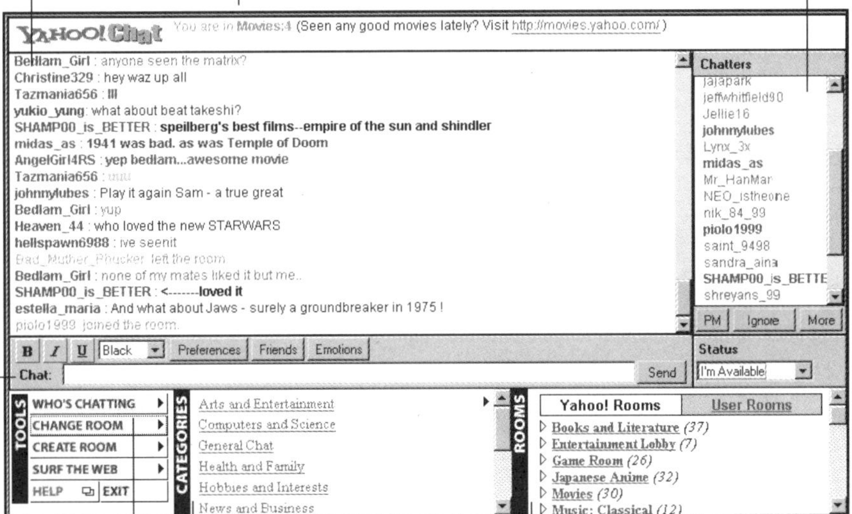

Type anything you want to say in here and press SEND.

Click to move to another room.

List of general categories.

List of rooms under the category *Arts and Entertainment*. The bracketed number shows the number of chatters in the room.

INTERNET RELAY CHAT

Now let's try out Internet Relay Chat (IRC) to see how it differs from the Web example you've just experienced. Net chatters largely seem to prefer the flexibility of IRC, although if you're a newbie it can take a while to figure out.

To use IRC you need to get hold of a piece of "client software" to enable you to get connected to an IRC server. Most of these programs are available either as freeware or shareware. In this example, we'll use a program called mIRC, which, if you've been working through the book in sequence, you should already have downloaded in chapter four (see page 85). If you haven't, now is an ideal time to try it out.

Begin by running mIRC and logging onto the Internet in the usual way.

1 You will first be prompted by the MIRC OPTIONS menu. Fill out the empty boxes and press CONNECT TO IRC SERVER.

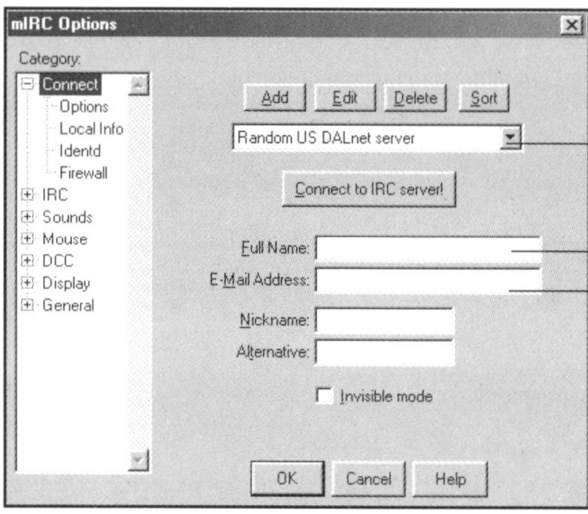

Select server – different servers hold different chat channels.

Enter your name.

Enter your e-mail address.

Enter your nickname – this is how you will be identified in the chat room. Also enter an alternative in the box below in case there is someone already connected with the same name as your first choice.

2 The MIRC CHANNELS list tells you the names of the chat rooms available on the server you logged onto in step 1. Highlight the entry and click on JOIN to enter the room.

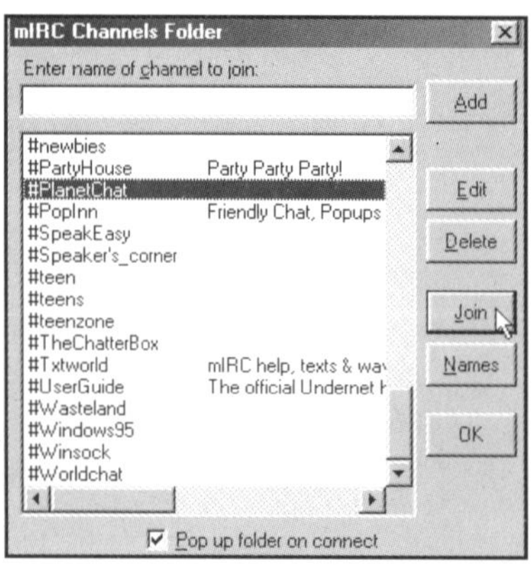

THE MIRC CHAT SCREEN

As you can see, the IRC screen that mIRC creates is quite similar to the web-based chat room we've already seen. The principal features are shown below. As before, you simply type a message in the text box at the foot of the page and press ENTER – it will appear on the screen in seconds.

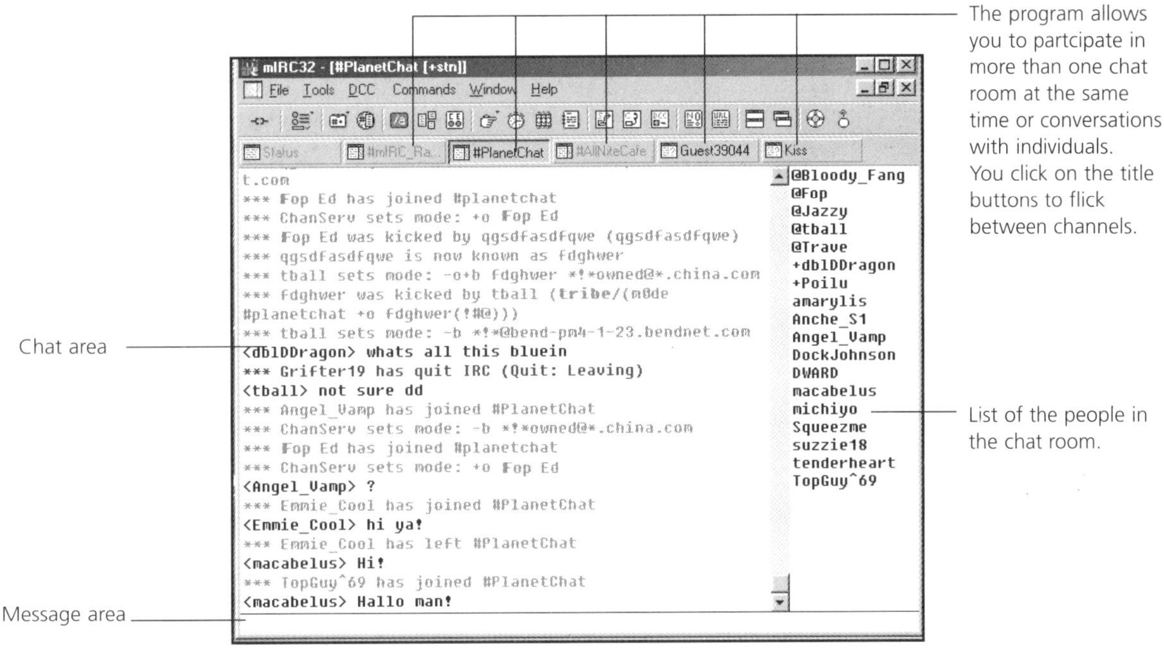

CHAT ROOM SHORTHAND

IRC also has a brief series of commands that you can type into the message box. These will work for all IRC software. Notice that they all begin with a forward slash – if you don't put it in then whatever you type will be viewed by everyone, which might be embarrassing. Here are the main commands.

/HELP	Help for using the other commands.
/JOIN	Use this command to join a new channel (leave off the "#" symbol, though).
/LIST	Tells you all the channels available, their topics and the number of people there.
/MSG	Lets you chat one-to-one with another participant .
/NICK	Change your nickname.
/WHOIS	Enter this command followed by a nickname for information on any other user.

ARE CHAT ROOMS SAFE?

People use chat rooms for all manner of things, from technical advice to dating. But in spite of the numerous scare stories, as long as you take a number of common-sense precautions there are no risks associated with using chat rooms.

- Never give personal details such as home address, home telephone number, credit card information or passwords to anyone in a chat room.

- Take EXTREME care if you allow children to use chat rooms. Online service providers such as AOL have special rooms for kids that make it impossible for them to receive private mail from others in the room.

- If you decide to meet someone you've chatted with, always do it in a public place. It's also a wise precaution to tell a friend where and who you are meeting.

- If you are at the wrong end of behaviour that you think is inappropriate to the room you are in, report it to the service provider or organization running the service. But remember, in some rooms the conversations can legitimately be quite "adult" in nature. If you find such things distasteful then you should leave well alone.

THE FUTURE OF CHAT?

Although text-based chat rooms can be great fun, the future of the online conversation will undoubtedly be with sound and vision. Already "Voice on the Net" (VON) is a reality, albeit a rather crude one. The great appeal in this is that if your computer is geared up with the necessary hardware and software, it becomes possible to hold conversations via a live link over the Internet. And if you think that sounds suspiciously like a telephone system then you would be right! The difference, however, is that you can talk to anyone across the globe for the price of a local connection to your ISP. It's an even better deal for users in the US for whom local calls are generally free. One disadvantage, though is that both parties have to be connected simultaneously, so it's not economically sensible to use it to make local calls (both parties will have to pay for a local call). The natural follow-on from this, of course, is that it makes the "videophone" a reality, although at the moment images have to kept very small and any movements are decidedly jerky.

6 ONLINE SHOPPING

Although still in its infancy, many believe that the future of consumerism lies with e-commerce – online shopping. The advantages of buying certain kinds of product over the Internet are clear – for one thing, you don't need to leave your home to do it. Another benefit is that of choice. Where once you only had local shops or mail order magazines, you can now browse and buy goods from all over the world.

SHOPPING BASICS

Online shopping is really just the next logical step from buying out of a mail order catalogue. You browse the Web, see the product you like, hand over your credit card details and address and eventually the goods will arrive. That's about it. This is a rapidly expanding role for the Internet with radical new ways of parting you from your hard-earned cash coming online all the time.

IS IT SAFE?

This is the first question that any would-be online shopper asks. Frankly, if you take sensible precautions, paying by credit card – which for now is the only practical approach to shopping on the Internet – is among the SAFEST ways to buy goods. The lack of human involvement creates less opportunity for fraud than normal use. That said, as in offline transactions, you should always be wary about handing out your credit-card details to unknown parties. It's always a good idea to look out for "real" contact details – is there an address or telephone number you can call when things go wrong? If you are really concerned, check out the company out over the telephone before you make your order. Dealing with a shopping site that can ONLY be contacted on the Internet is not recommended.

A second precaution is to look out for "secure sites". Reputable online shopping services have a secure payment screen. A message will usually tell you that you are about to enter a secured part of the Web site, but you'll also be able to see a key or a padlock symbol displayed at the bottom of your browser. This tells you that the personal details that you will be transmitting will be scrambled in such a way that they can only be read by the computer at the other end of the line.

You should also bear in mind that paying for anything by credit card immediately gives you some financial protection. If, through no fault of your own, your card is fraudulently used, the credit card company will usually reimburse you. Also, under the terms of the 1974 Consumer Credit Act, the company is jointly liable for goods that fail to arrive or are damaged. Whilst this applies to UK transactions, the rules are a little less clear-cut when you buy from abroad, but credit card companies enjoy a reasonable reputation for looking after their customers so should at least provide you with help if things go wrong.

BUYING ABROAD

As any global traveller knows, the prices of everyday objects can alter drastically from country to country. For example, computer equipment and CDs can be bought in America for at least 30 per cent less than UK prices. This difference will be reflected when you visit US online shopping sites. The good news is that you can take advantage of these low prices. The bad news is that at the end of the day they might turn out to be slightly less of a bargain. The reason for this is that goods bought and delivered from outside of the UK are liable to certain statutary charges. To begin with, VAT has to be paid (currently 17 $^1/_2$ per cent). On top of that there is an import duty of up to 15 percent, depending on the nature of the goods. CDs and videos are charged at 3.8 per cent, so before you make a purchase you need to add on around 20 per cent to the listed price as well as the cost of shipping. They'll still be cheaper, but not quite the bargain they might first have seemed. You'll save more by buying computer supplies since there is no import duty charge, just VAT. Be warned, however; it sometimes takes weeks for the invoices for duty payments to arrive – just because no demand for extra payment appears at the same time as your goods it doesn't necessarily mean you won't be charged later. For a full list of UK import duties take a look at the official Customs and Excise web site (http://www.hmce.gov.uk)

Having bought overseas, you won't necessarily enjoy the same consumer rights as if you'd purchased in the UK. This can turn into major hassle when things go wrong – if you send it back you may incur costly shipping costs. Always carefully weigh up the pros and cons before you decide to purchase.

LET'S DO SOME SHOPPING!

Once you've started looking around the virtual malls of cyberspace, it won't take you long to realise that they all work in pretty much the same way. Here is a typical example of an online shopping site with step by step instructions on how to make a purchase.

WHAT DO YOU NEED?

All you need to go shopping online is the URL of the store you wish to visit and a valid credit card. Here are the main stages of ordering from Amazon, one of the most successful online bookstores (http://www.amazon.co.uk).

1 Enter the URL to enter the online store.

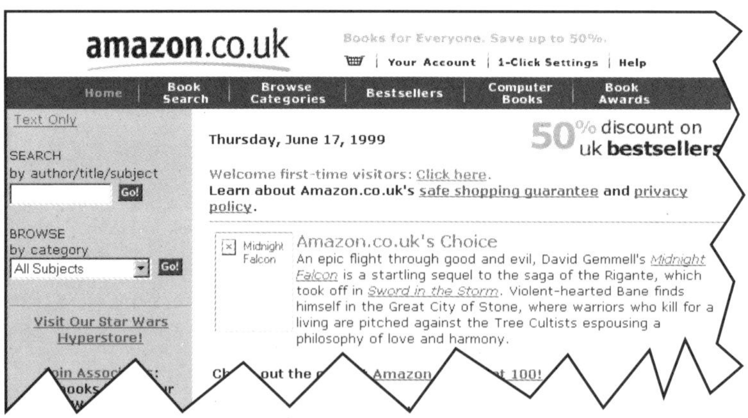

2 Select the product you want to buy. This puts it in your "shopping basket".

3 This screen shows the contents of your basket. Click on PROCEED TO CHECKOUT.

4 To pay for the goods, you work through a series of simple security screens entering your personal details and credit card data when prompted. In this instance, the goods are dispatched within two days of receiving the credit card data.

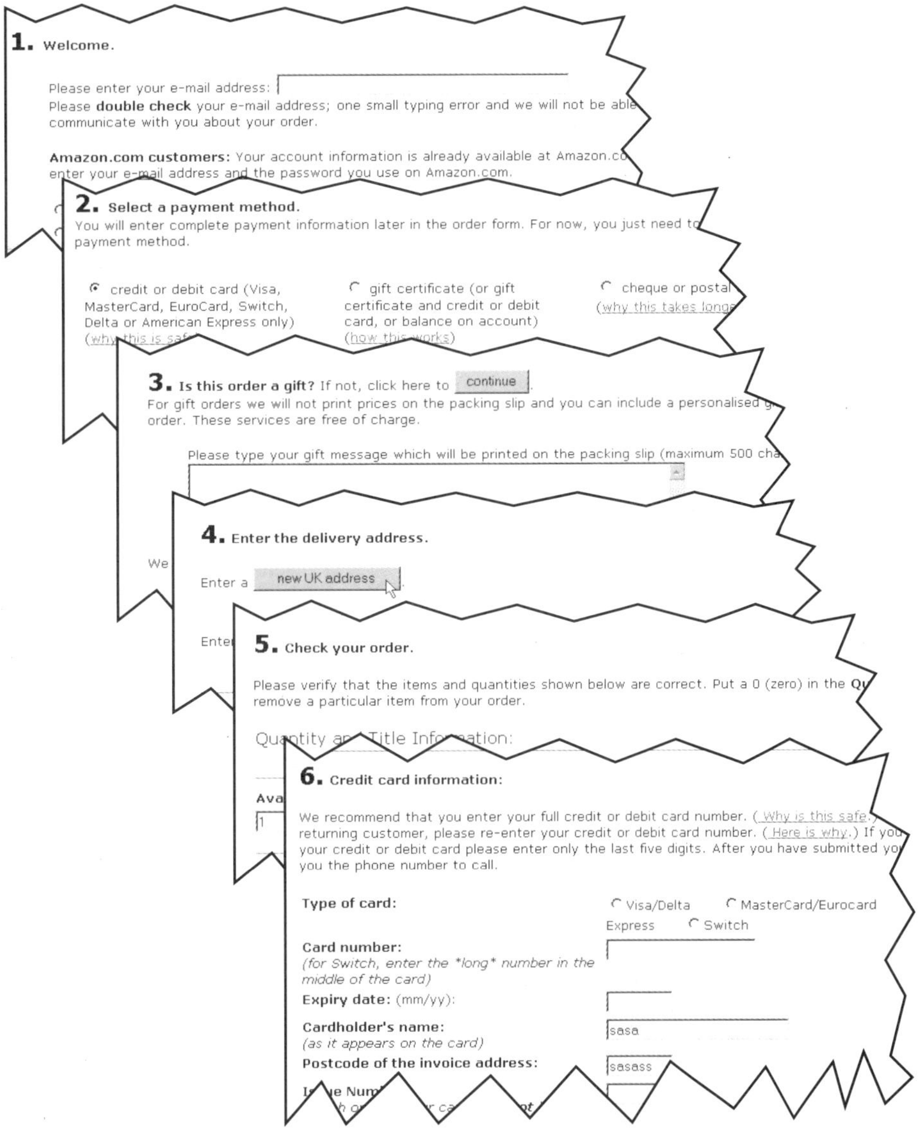

HUNTING OUT THE BARGAINS

Imagine if every time you bought something you knew automatically that you were getting the best deal on offer. In reality this would involve a lot of traipsing around stores and numerous telephone calls. Things are different for online bargain hunters, though. They can call on the services of a virtual shopping assistant.

TOO GOOD TO BE TRUE?

A growing number of shopping web sites are offering what amounts to bargain-hunting search engines. You type in a set of criteria and a search engine comes back with a list of the best deals. This example is from the UK-based cyber-mall *ShopGuide* (http://www.shopguide.co.uk).

1 Click on BARGAIN FINDER on the site's main page.

2 Type in a keyword, select the product category and click on SEARCH.

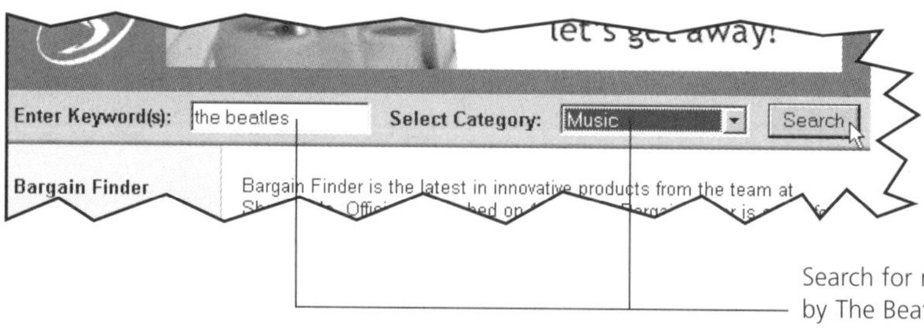

Search for musical products by The Beatles.

ONLINE AUCTIONS

The "online auction" is another burgeoning area of e-commerce that offers the Internet user the chance of a bargain. Online auctions work in much the same way as their "real" equivalents. You can either post a bid in advance – if it doesn't get topped, it's yours – or engage in live bidding online. These auctions are especially good for Internet users who feel intimidated by the stuffy protocol often associated with the real thing. Check out the auction websites listed below if you are interested.

Auction Universe	**http://www.auctionuniverse.co.uk**
Bonhams	**http://www.bonhams.com**
E-Swap	**http://www.eswap.co.uk**
E-Bid	**http://www.ebid.co.uk**
QXL	**http://www.qxl.co.uk**
Sotheby's	**http://www.sothebys.com**

3 This search creates a list of goods available from the retailers searched. Click on BUY NOW for further information.

Retailer list.

4 You can now choose whether or not you wish to buy the product.

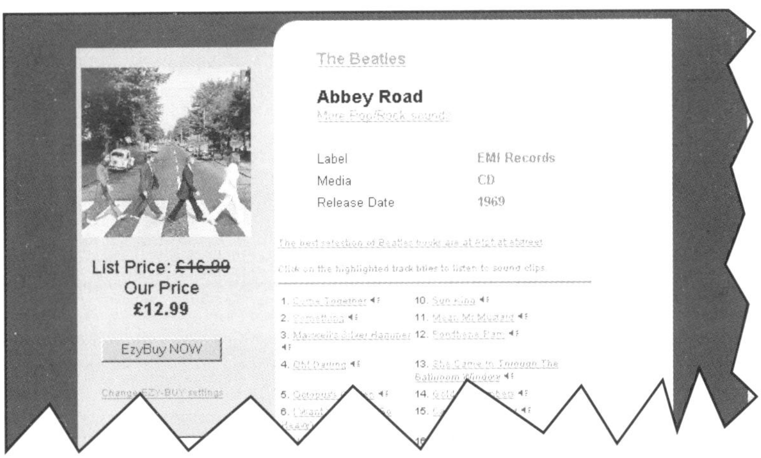

ONLINE BANKING

The idea of dialling-in to a bank to check your account balance is well established. But now, more and more financial institutions are turning to the Internet to provide a greater range of features for online customers.

IS IT WORTH BOTHERING?

It's clear that online banking is in its early stages. Right now there's not much more on offer that you can't achieve just as easily with a simple phone call. This will change, especially if the idea of "Internet cash" – a "virtual currency" with which you can shop online – takes off.

One of the best examples of online banking can be found at the Co-operative Bank (http://www.co-operativebank.co.uk). You can get up-to-the-minute account details, read and print previous statements, pay bills, set up standing orders and direct debits, and transfer funds between accounts. When you log on, a small program is downloaded to run within your Web browser.

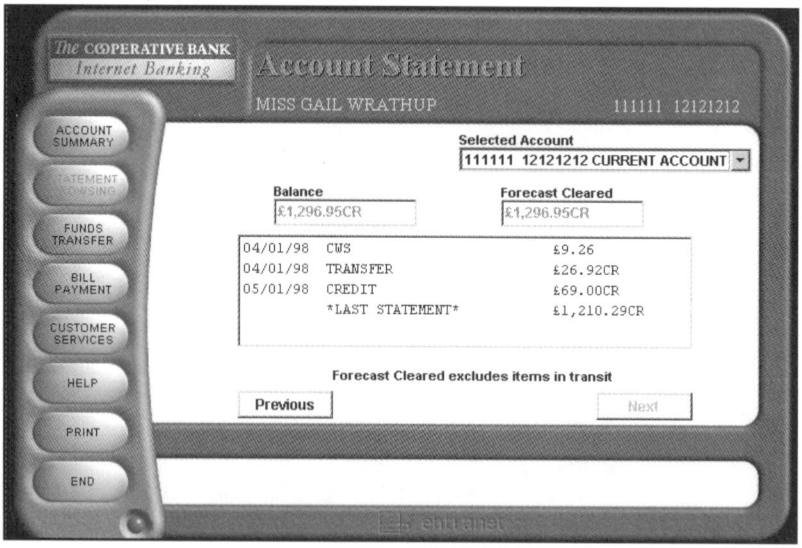

7 GET ON THE WEB

With free Web space now the norm for all ISPs, anyone can create their own Web pages. If you want to tell the world about yourself, your hobbies, or anything else for that matter, there's no easier way to share your thoughts with a global public than by building a your own Web site. Anyone can put together a few simple and effective Web pages using the publishing features provided free with the two main web browsers.

WEB BASICS

If you randomly surf the World Wide Web for more than a few hours, one thing that may strike you is how BAD a significant proportion of the Web sites are. This is usually because they haven't been carefully thought out. Here are some pointers that will help you avoid some of the more obvious errors.

WHY BOTHER?

The vast majority of personal Web sites broadly fall into three categories: autobiographical; fan sites; and business sites; so the chances are that yours will fit into one of the above groups. But before you start worrying about design specifics, you should have a long hard think about what exactly you are trying to do, and maybe even why you want to do it. For example, you may be the world's biggest Rolling Stones fan, but could your own Stones site contribute anything to distinguish it from the several hundred others that exist? In short, ask yourself why anyone would want to visit your little corner of cyberspace. Of course, you might just want to set up your own Web site for a bit of fun, which is an excellent reason for doing it.

PLANNING

Once you've got this far, the next stage is to plan out your site in as much detail as possible. Professional computer systems designers can spend as much as a fifth of the entire duration of a project just planning it out – and your Web page is a piece of system design.

Start by working out exactly how much information you plan to put on your site. A good way of doing this is by coming up with a set of headings that can then be broken down further into sub-headings. For example, if you started with ROLLING STONES as the subject of your Web page, write down separate headings for "THE BAND", "HISTORY" and "RECORDINGS". You might want to further subdivide "THE BAND" so that you

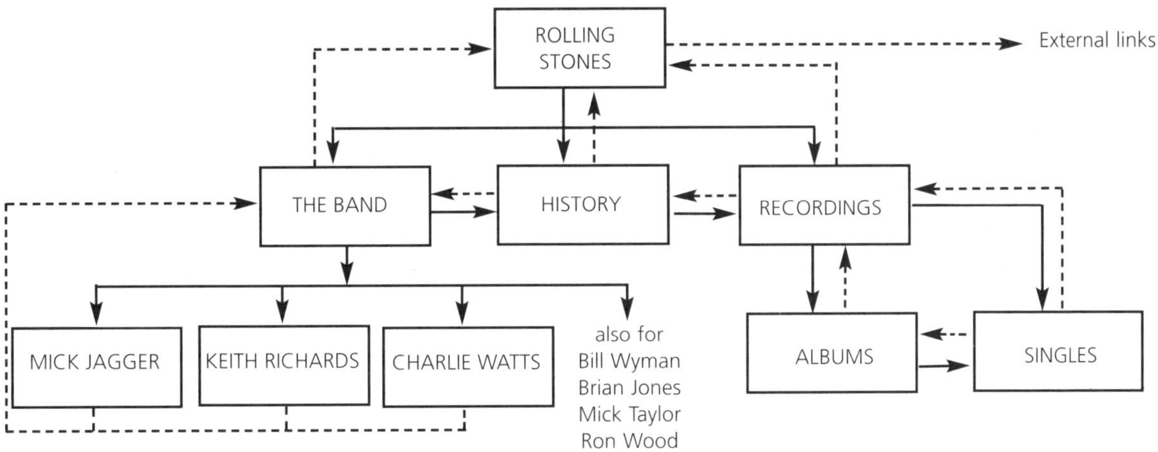

can profile each musician. Similarly, you could sub-divide "RECORDINGS" into "ALBUMS" and "SINGLES".

Each of the headings and sub-headings could be viewed as a separate Web page. If you mark them all out as a series of boxes on a large piece of paper you can see the possible structure of your Web site. You can now start to map out how to navigate through the different levels of information by drawing arrows that join the boxes.

The diagram above tells you that this site requires 13 separate pages. The top-level page will always be named "index.html". If your web address is http://www.fred.myserver, then anytime anyone anywhere in the world enters that URL in their browser, your main ROLLING STONES page will appear. There are three first-level pages which you can get to from the main page. However, assuming you have named one of these pages "band", then typing in http://www.fred.myserver/band will take you straight there. Finally, there are nine second-level pages, seven linked to "THE BAND" and two linked to "RECORDINGS". As before, if you named one of these pages "jagger", then it would be possible to go straight to that page by entering http://www.fred.myserver/band/jagger.

Flow diagrams like the one above also will come in very handy when you come to test out your pages. You can see at a glance how each of the links works.

MAKING A HOME PAGE

Web pages are built using a programming language called HTML. This is very easy to learn if you're that way inclined, and doesn't really require traditional computer programming skills. However, it's possible to bypass HTML by using software that allows you first to type in text and position your images, and then automatically generate the "hidden" HTML code.

USING INTERACTIVE SOFTWARE

One of the most sophisticated interactive Web publishing programs is Macromedia's DreamWeaver, but this is a costly software package aimed mostly at the professional market. The good news, however, is that the full versions of Netscape Communicator and Internet Explorer both now incorporate simple but effective ways for creating and publishing Web pages. Let's look at an example using Netscape Composer (Microsoft's FrontPage works in pretty much the same way).

1 Click on the NETSCAPE COMPOSER icon.

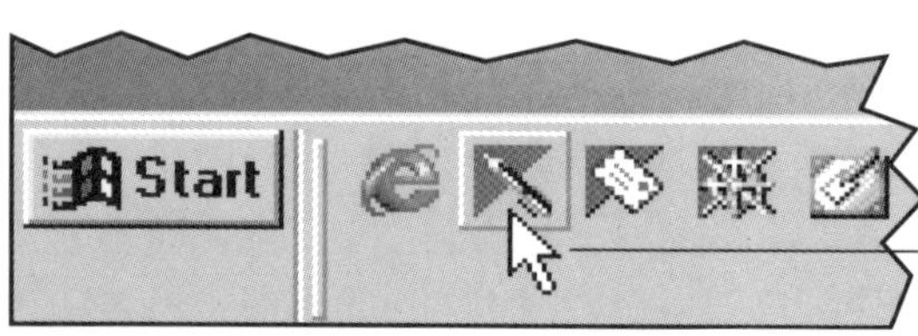

You can also run Netscape Composer from within Netscape Communicator/Navigator.

2 Click on NEW.

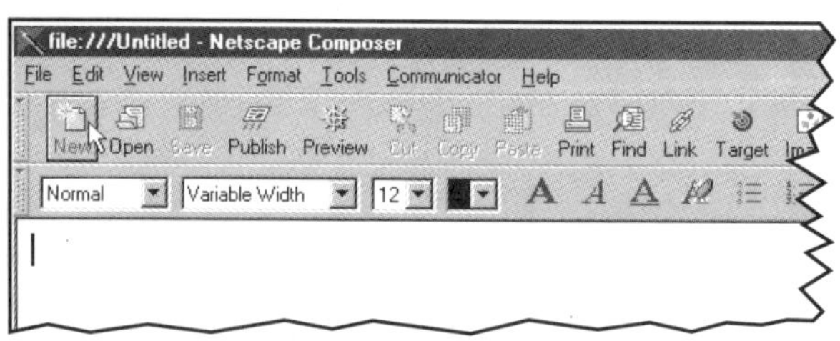

3 In the NEW PAGE dialog box, click on BLANK PAGE.

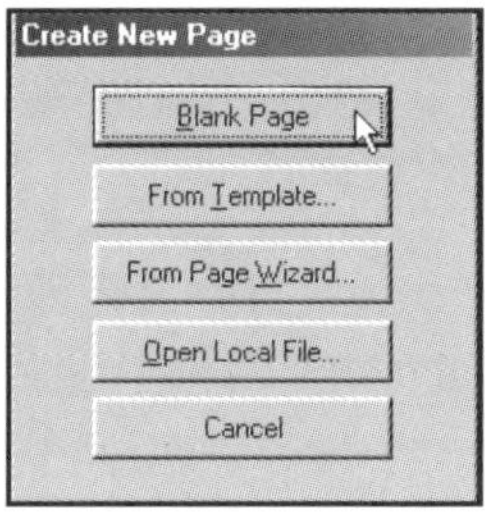

4 Type in the desired text. You can modify it using options in the text toolbar

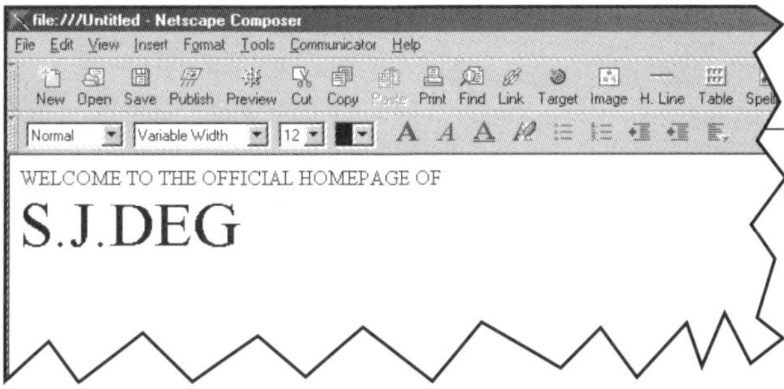

Text toolbar

5 To add an image, set the cursor at the point you want the picture to appear and select IMAGE from the INSERT menu.

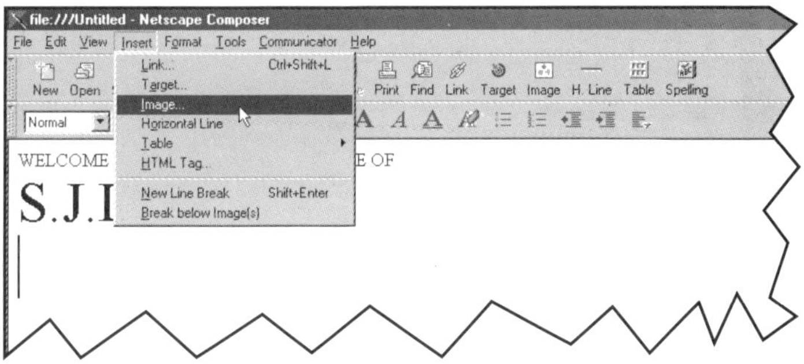

6 In the IMAGE PROPERTIES dialog box, click on the IMAGE tab and enter the file name and path in the IMAGE LOCATION BOX. Click on OK.

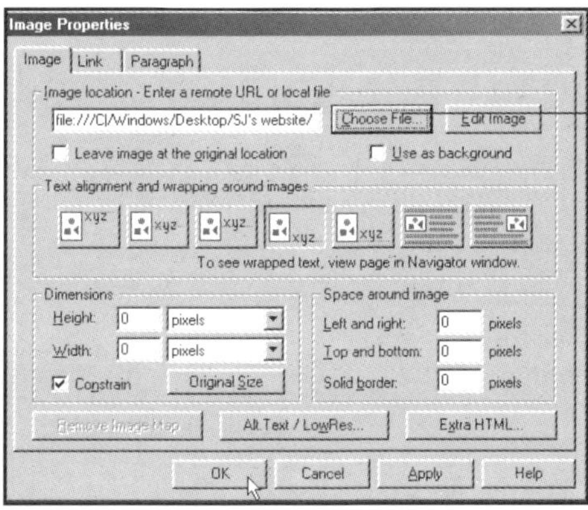

You can also choose the file name and path by clicking CHOOSE FILE and then browsing through the folders on your hard disk.

CREATING HYPERLINKS

You can also set up hyperlinks using Netscape Composer. This means that when your page goes online, Internet users can link to different pages (or different points within the same page) by clicking on the images or words you have specified. Let's continue with the example we started on the previous page.

1 Click on the image so that it is highlighted and then select LINK from the INSERT menu.

2 Enter the full URL of the site to which you want to make a link.

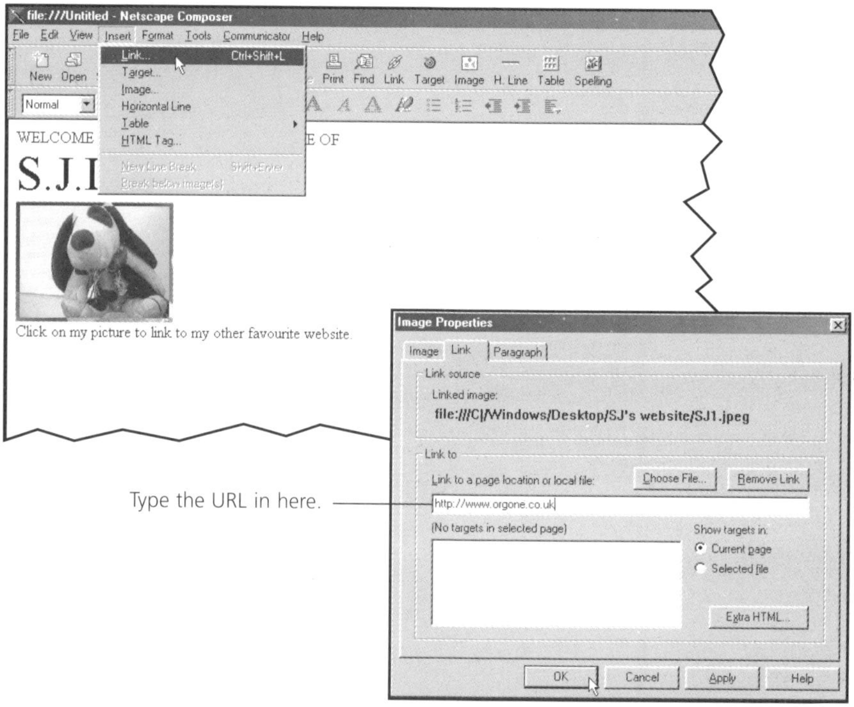

USING PICTURES

Most of the images you see used in Web sites are either "GIF" or "JPEG" files. Although either can be used, it's worthwhile knowing the difference between the two formats. GIF stands for "Graphics Interchange Format". A GIF file (usually suffixed .gif) has between two and 256 colours. JPEG stands for "Joint Photographic Experts Group". A JPEG file (usually suffixed .jpg) can contain up to 16 million colours. A JPEG file will always be bigger than its equivalent GIF file.

The size of a file is clearly important within a Web page – the larger the file, the longer it will take to download. Whilst all types of artwork could be presented in either format, the sensible approach is to save colour photographs and finely detailed artworks in the JPEG format and simpler or less detailed images in GIF format.

3 You can also make a hyperlink using text. Highlight the word or phrase that you want to initiate the link. Select LINK from the INSERT menu and enter the URL in the dialog box as shown.

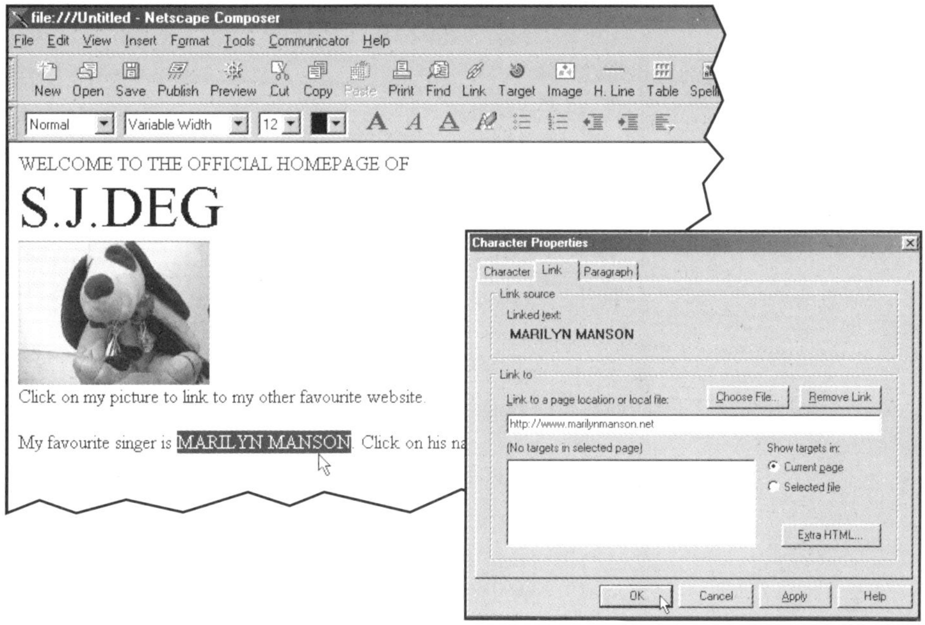

4 To save your Web page click on the SAVE option in toolbar.

5 If this is your main home page – the "top level" of your Web site – it is safest to call it "index.html".

6 Finally, enter the name that will appear in the browser's title bar when it's being read online.

OFFLINE TESTING

Before you make your Web site live it's important that you test it as thoroughly as possible. If your work goes online with images that don't load properly or links that are invalid it reflects poorly on you. It goes without saying that if you run a business from your Web site a shoddy "shop-front" hardly constitutes a great advertisement for your goods or services. Before you publish, make sure you work through this checklist:

- Make a list of the internal links within all of the pages that make up your Web site. Check them one at a time.
- Make sure that you create links that will take users back to previous levels or to the main index page.
- Make sure that images are being displayed correctly.
- There's no way you can actually test the external links without going online. However, when they fail to work this is most commonly because the URLs have been typed in wrongly. One step you can take is to place your cursor over the link – as you do this you should be able to read the name of the linking URL in the status bar at the foot of the browser. This should enable you at least to catch some simple spelling errors.

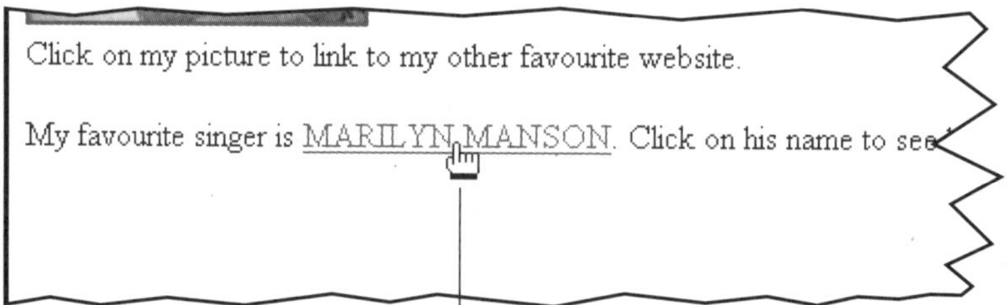

When the cursor covers a hypertext link it changes to a "finger" icon.

The URL appears in the status bar.

READY TO ROLL

Publishing your Web site is the easiest stage. All you need to know from your ISP is where to send it.

1 Click on the PUBLISH icon in the toolbar.

2 Type in the location name to which your web pages will be published. Enter user ID and password if your ISP specifies one. Click on OK.

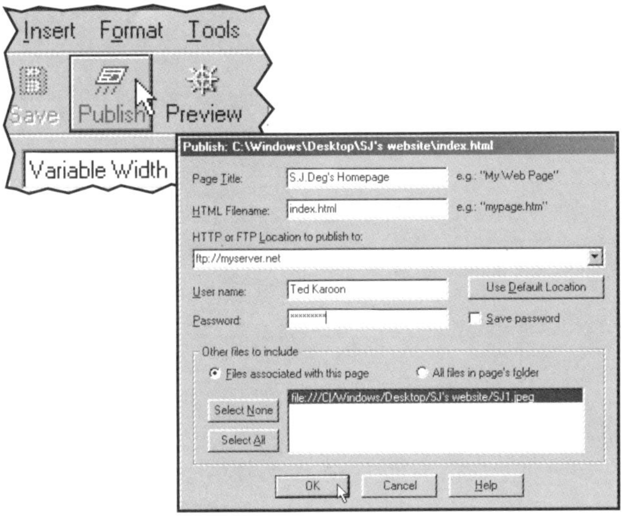

IN CASE YOU'RE INTERESTED

The Web page that we've just created in Nestcape Composer could have been constructed simply by typing HTML code in a text file. If you want to see that in practice, select HTML SOURCE from the VIEW menu. This feature can be useful since it allows you to see how other people's "live" web pages were created. If you want to know more about HTML programming you will find plenty of easy-to-use guides in most book stores.

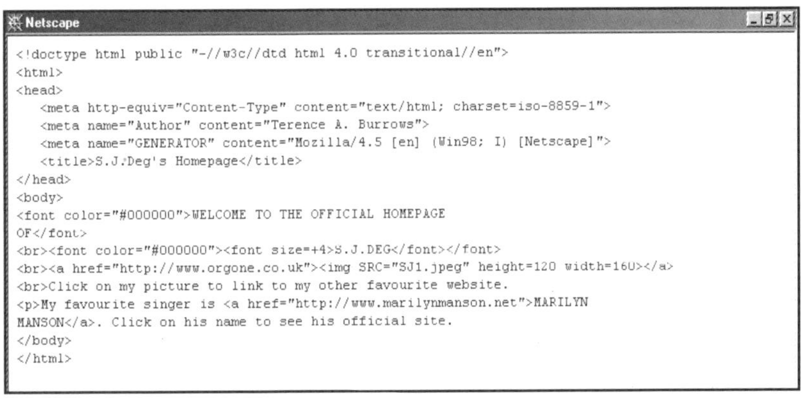
Netscape

```
<!doctype html public "-//w3c//dtd html 4.0 transitional//en">
<html>
<head>
   <meta http-equiv="Content-Type" content="text/html; charset=iso-8859-1">
   <meta name="Author" content="Terence A. Burrows">
   <meta name="GENERATOR" content="Mozilla/4.5 [en] (Win98; I) [Netscape]">
   <title>S.J.Deg's Homepage</title>
</head>
<body>
<font color="#000000">WELCOME TO THE OFFICIAL HOMEPAGE
OF</font>
<br><font color="#000000"><font size=+4>S.J.DEG</font></font>
<br><a href="http://www.orgone.co.uk"><img SRC="SJ1.jpeg" height=120 width=160></a>
<br>Click on my picture to link to my other favourite website.
<p>My favourite singer is <a href="http://www.marilynmanson.net">MARILYN
MANSON</a>. Click on his name to see his official site.
</body>
</html>
```

GETTING KNOWN

There's not a great deal of point in going to the trouble of publishing a Web site if nobody is going to view it. Here are some tips that will show you how to go about publicizing your Web pages.

- The best way to get your site known is to register it with the main search engines. You could do this this on a site-by-site basis, but a more efficient way is to use a site that automatically does this for you. One such site is Register-It (http://www.register-it.com/free). Although they have a large commercial operation, they will do free registration to the best 16 search engines on the Internet – that's not a bad start.
- An alternative registration site is Submit-It! You can find this on http://www.siteowner.linkexchange.com/Free.cfm.
- If yours is a fan site, contact other similar sites or links pages to ask if your URL can be added. Try to get your URL hot-wired into as many other sites as possible.
- If there are newsgroups to which the subject of your Web site is pertinent, send a polite posting to notify their member of your existence. NEVER "spam" newsgroups, though. Just make it a simple posting with a self-explanatory subject header that members can ignore if they are not interested.

GUESSING DOMAINS

If you are running a business from your Web site it's a good idea to register and operate a domain name. This means that if your business is called "Wonder Mowers", you should try to register www.wondermowers.co.uk with one of the domain naming agencies (InterNic for .com names and Nominet for .co.uk names), and set up your Web pages accordingly. Recent research suggests that over a third of all Web site hits are through the user knowing the URL (rather than going through a search engine or link from another site). In short, there's a new breed of Internet-literate shopper out there who moves around cyberspace by "guessing" URLs – most commonly suffixing known business names with either .com or .co.uk to see if a Web site exists.

8 SURFING THE COOL SITES

The World Wide Web really is a wonder of the modern world. Here is a selection of cool Web sites. They're themed under the general headings of news, music, cinema, sports, food and drink, art, health, politics, education, finance, comedy, careers, science, weird stuff, travel, and kids' stuff. The plushest sites are financed by Big Business, but many interesting ones are put there just for fun by regular Netheads.

NEWS AND CURRENT AFFAIRS

In the age of the Internet, you don't necessarily have to wander along to your local newsagent to read a daily newspaper since many of the most popular tabloids, broadsheets and magazines provide their own online versions on the Internet. Experiencing the news in this way also gives you access to the most important news media all over the world.

BBC NEWS
http://news.bbc.co.uk

It comes as no great surprise that with its vast news resources, the good old BBC provides what is probably the best on-line news service available anywhere. News is updated throughout the day (as it should be – not all online services manage this) and it also provides selected live audio and video links. Like many of the online newspapers you can also dip into their archives and pull out old news stories. With its famed World Service links, the BBC site is also especially strong on international news.

ITN NEWS
http://www.itn.co.uk

An alternative take on the news events unfurling throughout the world from ITN, the BBC's longstanding rivals.

THE INDEPENDENT ONLINE
http://www.independent.co.uk

Quality broadsheet news but, like its paper equivalent, is only updated on a daily basis. *The Independent Online* is extremely easy to navigate with an index along the left-hand side of the screen organized in much the same way as the different sections of the newspaper, covering such areas as international news, sport, travel and education. An online version of *The Independent On Sunday* is also produced.

TELEGRAPH ONLINE
http://www.telegraph.co.uk

Online version of the *Daily Telegraph* newspaper. Like some other news services, when you first go online, you are allocated a password and user name that you have to enter on future visits, but this is a fairly painless process. *Telegraph Online* is especially strong for its easy-to-use archive system that allows you to search for news stories dating back to 1996.

THE WASHINGTON POST
http://washingtonpost.com

One of the world's most famous newspapers, *The Washington Post* is best-known outside of the US as the paper whose ground-breaking investigative reporters came up with the "Watergate" story that brought down President Nixon in the 1970s. A full version of the newspaper appears daily on the Web site.

THE DRUDGE REPORT
http://drudgereport.com

The *Drudge Report* is a fine example of Internet obsession that got out of hand. Starting life as a one-man project, Matt Drudge has turned his Web site into one of the most influential in the world. Indeed, this was the site where the Monica Lewinsky affair first alerted other newspapers to strange goings-on at the White House. The colourless text-based layout is dull beyond belief, but the lack of images also makes it just about the fastest news site to download. Not only is the *Drudge Report* a fine source of sometimes obscure information and views, but if you scroll to the bottom of the headline page you will find hyperlinks to just about every other significant news site in the world. This is definitely one to bookmark if you're serious about your news.

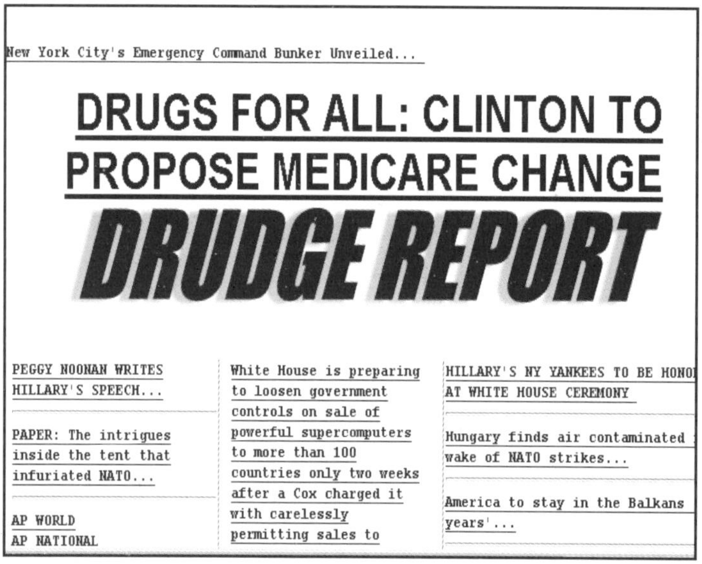

PA NEWS CENTRE
http://www.pa.press.net

The Press Association is one of those organizations that feeds news stories to the media. The *PA News Centre* is a cut-down version of the same service that journalists can access (although it only takes payment of a subscription fee to earn you exactly the same status). You'll also find this site especially useful if you're a sports fan since many major international sporting events are given up-to-the-minute coverage.

THE NATIONAL ENQUIRER
http://www.nationalenquirer.com

For news of a rather different kind, why not tap into America's smut-rag supreme, The *National Enquirer*. A safe haven from the real world, the *Enquirer* tells us the celebrity marriages that are in jeopardy and where Elvis has been seen lately.

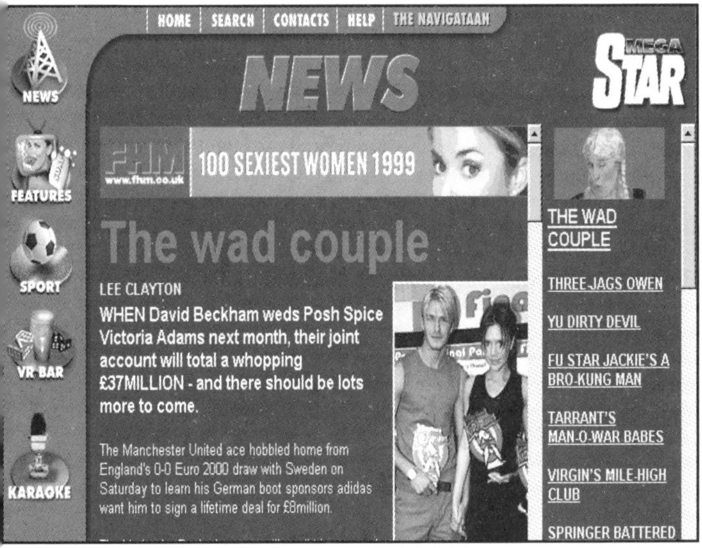

MEGA STAR
http://www.megastar.co.uk

If you like the *National Enquirer* you might also enjoy *MegaStar*, the online equivalent of Britain's *Daily Star* newspaper. *MegaStar* is widely concerned with dishing the dirt on the rich and famous, but also has a certain fondness for pictures of women's breasts.

WORTH A VISIT...

Here are some other news sites that you might find of interest:

ABC News	TV news network	**http://www.abcnews.com**
CNN Interactive	In-depth news world news	**http://www.cnn.com**
Daily Mirror	UK tabloid news	**http://www.mirror.co.uk**
The Express	UK tabloid news	**http://lineone.net/express**
The Guardian	UK broadsheet	**http://guardian.co.uk**
LA Times	Hollywood lowdown	**http://www.latimes.com**
MSN	Microsoft's condensed world news	**http://www.msn.co.uk**
News Resource	Global news	**http://www.newo.com/news**
New York Times	Top US broadsheet	**http://www.nytimes.com**
One World News	Human Rights and Ecology	**http://www.oneworld.org**
Sky TV	News and sport as it happens	**http://www.sky.co.uk**
Slate	US news with attitude	**http://www.slate.com**
The Smoking Gun	The stories you won't see elsewhere	**http://www.thesmokinggun.com**
The Times	Historic British broadsheet	**http://www.the-times.co.uk**
Wall Street Journal	US news with a financial slant	**http://www.wsj.com**

MUSIC

Another area in which the Internet often excels is in bringing music fans into contact with their idols. Music sites fall into two categories, "official" sites which are often little more than plush adverts, and fan sites, which are usually online fanzines.

Q ONLINE
http://www.qonline.co.uk

One of Britain's most popular grown-up music magazines, Q is a cut-down version of its paper equivalent. Whatever it would like to think about itself, Q's content is decidedly mainstream, although the amount of space it dedicates to album reviews makes it worthwhile in itself. As such, the most useful aspect of Q Online is that you can view every album review ever printed in the magazine using a handy search tool.

NME MUSICAL EXPRESS ONLINE
http://nme.com

Although aimed at a younger audience than *Q*, the once mighty *New Musical Express* charts equally safe territory. Updated daily, the online site provides a reasonable cross-section of the magazine's indie-based content, but scores especially well as the UK's best gig guide.

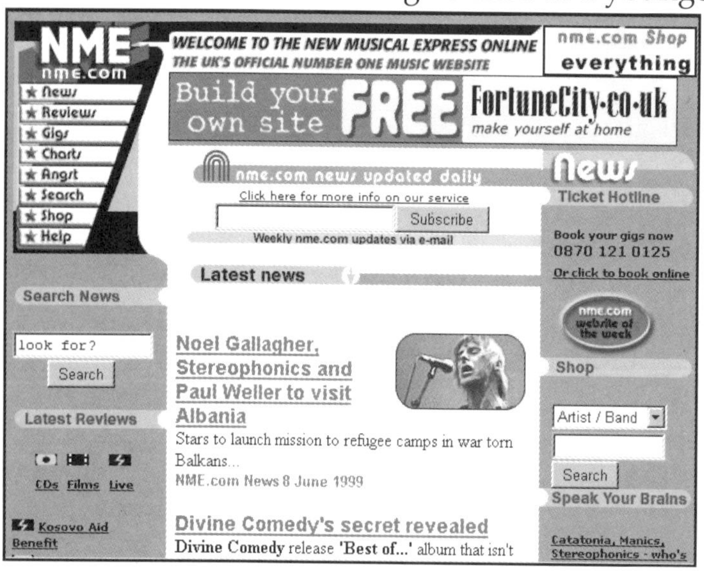

ROLLING STONE NETWORK
http://www.rollingstone.com

Not the band, but the vintage American rock magazine. A haven for po-faced middle-aged fans who like to take their music far too seriously.

BOWIENET
http://www.davidbowie.com

Even if you can't stand his music, it's worth checking out David Bowie's Internet service (the term "Web site" doesn't really do it justice) to see an all-encompassing multimedia system in action. Besides the usual biographies, discographies and online sounds, *BowieNet* features online facilities allowing fans to chat, as well as other interesting concepts, like a recent competition in which fans were asked to provide lyrics to an unfinished Bowie song which the Man himself would then record. It's also an Internet provider, so you could find yourself with an e-mail address that goes fred-smith@davidbowie.com. Cool.

JAZZ ONLINE
http://www.jazzonln.com

The ultimate jazz buff's site featuring a splendid overview of the history of every major jazz genre. Also features new releases as well as audio and video performances.

WORTH A VISIT...

Band Link	Information and links	**http://www.ubl.com**
Classical Net	Classical music releases	**http://www.classical.net**
IUMA	Underground music archive	**http://www.iuma.com**
Kaleidoscope	Independent music links	**http://www.kspace.com**
MP3.com	Site devoted to MP3 sound format	**http://www.mp3.com**
Mumz Global links	Independent music links	**http://www.orgone.co.uk**
Real Networks	Site devoted to RealPlayer format	**http://www.real.com**
Synth Museum	Online museum of synthesisers	**http://www.synthmuseum.com**
The Theremin	The original synthesiser	**http://www.nashville.net/~theremin**
Top 100 Guitar Sites	Guitar-related signpost	**http://topguitars.hypermart.net**
World Charts	Music charts throughout the world	**http://www.lanet.lv/misc/charts/**

CINEMA

Whilst the current limitations of technology make watching movies on the Internet a little impractical, this is certain to be an exciting online option at some point in the near future. For now, there is plenty of entertaining and informative material in cyberspace to keep most movie fans reasonably happy.

POPCORN
http://www.popcorn.couk
Popcorn is an online movie magazine aimed at mainstream movie fans. It provides news, views, gossip and features on the latest Hollywood releases. It also sometimes features video trailers for forthcoming movies.

INTERNET MOVIE DATABASE
http://uk.imdb.com
There are very few Web sites that truly deserve to be called the "ultimate" in their field, but the *Internet Movie Database* is one of them. With extensive detail on almost 200,000 films, this is the site to visit when you just have to know who the make-up artist on *The Great Escape* was (Emile LaVigne, if you were interested). Also listed are reviews submitted by the movie-going public as well as the availability of videos, DVDs and audio soundtracks. A field day for every movie anorak.

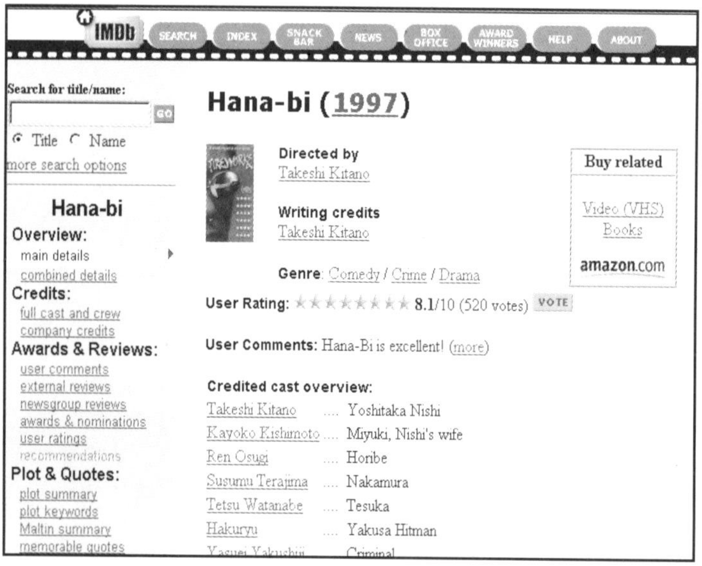

STAR WARS
http://www.starwars.com
With the spate of "prequels" now underway, interest in *Star Wars* is at an all-time high. This official

WORTH A VISIT...

Ain't It Cool News	Movie gossip	**http://www.aint-it-cool-news.com**
American Zoetrope	Site for would-be scriptwriters	**http://www.zoetrope.com**
Cowboy Pal	Site for Western fans	**http://www.cowboypal.com**
Disney	Details of Disney releases	**http://disney.co.uk**
Film.Com	Video clips in RealPlayer format	**http://www.film.com**
Hollywood Online	New Hollywood releases	**http://www.hollywood.com**
James Bond	Spy site	**http://www.mgmua.com/bond**
Movie Cliches	Clips of the worst ever dialogue	**http://www.like.it/vertigo/cliches.html**
Mr Showbiz	Movie reviews and links	**http://www.mrshowbiz.com/reviews**
The Palace	Tribute to pre-1950 Hollywood	**http://www.palace.com**
VirginNet Film Finder	Locates films at Virgin cinemas	**http://www.virgin.net/cinema**

site is one of the plushest ever to hit the web. Not only is every last detail about any of the films at your fingertips, you can also download QuickTime video clips.

MOVIE REVIEW QUERY ENGINE
http://www.cinema.pgh.pa.us/movie/reviews

An signpost site that points you to reviews of any current or recent film. Type in the title and click on Find Reviews to get a hypertext list of reviews that have been published in magazines and newspapers all over the world. Clicking on the review you want to see links you to the relevant Web page.

VARIETY
http://www.variety.com

Hollywood's most famous cinema newspaper, which is required reading for all those in the "biz".

IFILM
http://www.ifilm.net

Movie search engine that works like the IMDB but concentrates on independent movies. Fill out your personal details and you can receive regular e-mail updates of new releases.

SPORTS

On the World Wide Web you'll find sites devoted to every sport you could possibly imagine, and quite a few that you couldn't. As is common in other areas, many of the best and most reliable sites are set up by official bodies – although if you look hard enough you'll also find plenty of excellent fan sites.

CARLINGNET
http://www.fa-premier.com

One of the most important Web sites for many British football fans, *CarlingNet* is the official site of the Premiership. Team names appearing in the league table double as hyperlinks. Click on any one to find club details: from results and fixtures to how to get to the stadium from the local railway station.

SYDNEY 2000 OLYMPIC GAMES
http://www.sydney.olympic.org

This is the official Web site of the Sydney Olympics, which takes place during the Summer of 2000. The site gives in-depth details about every sport for which a gold medal can be awarded. Among other things, it also describes the somewhat comical process by which spectator tickets are allocated. During the Games, the site will provide live reports for competitions in progress.

CNN SPORTS ILLUSTRATED
http://www.cnnsi.com

Sports reporting from all over the world, although headlines tend to focus on US national sports such as baseball and football (of the American sort, that is).

SPORTSWEB
http://www.sportsweb.com

With information provided by Reuters, *SportWeb* focuses its attention specifically on what's going on in the UK and the rest of Europe. The navigation buttons on the main screen can take you to any of 14 different sports. Details of minor sports require further navigation.

WHEN SATURDAY COMES
http://www.dircon.co.uk/wsc

A fan's-eye view of the football scene from *When Saturday Comes* – the "Half-Decent Football Magazine". Unlike most people involved in the sport, *WSC* is both intelligent and funny.

LORD'S: THE HOME OF CRICKET
http://www.lords.org

Apart from the scorecards for all of the county and tests series, the main feature of this site is a Web-camera positioned on top of the famous Lord's Pavilion, providing live pictures of matches being played throughout the season.

WORTH A VISIT...

PA Sports Headlines	Sports action as it happens	**http://www.pa.press.net/sports**
RFU Online	Rugby union site	**http://www.rfu.com**
FIFA	World football federation	**http://www.fifa.com**
Sporting Life	General sports	**http://www.sporting-life.com**
Boxing Monthly	Online version of magazine	**http://www.boxing-monthly.co.uk**
SkiCentral	Skiing and snowboarding	**http://www.skicentral.com**
UK MotorSport	Any sports with wheels	**http://www.ukmotorsport.com/uk.html**
GolfWeb	Professional and amateur golf	**http://www.golfweb.com**
Nationwide League	UK football's lower divisions	**http://www.football.nationwide.co.uk**
ESPN	Major US sports	**http://espn.co.com**
Racenews	Horse racing in the UK	**http://www.racenews.co.uk**

FOOD AND DRINK

Culinary Web sites are often no more than online adverts for products, companies, magazines or TV shows. Whilst some of them do have excellent content, the most interesting sites are often the ones that have been put there by ordinary Internet users.

THE SPICE GUIDE
http://www.spiceguide.com

Jointly sponsored by the spice industry, *The Spice Guide* tells you everything you could every want to know about every different kind of spice. Features include spice recipes, tips on how to use different spices and even a "kid's corner". Also includes the detailed "encyclopedia of spice". Very tasty.

THE INTERNET CHEF – ICHEF
http://www.ichef.com

For cooks everywhere, *ICHEF* is an online cookbook and much more besides. Not only is there a searchable database of recipes, but *ICHEF* also includes the intriguing *Cook's Thesaurus*, a page which, as its name suggests, offers substitutions when you can't obtain crucial ingredients. The tips and hints section also describes how you can "repair" your food in the event of one of those tragic cooking disasters that we all have from time to time.

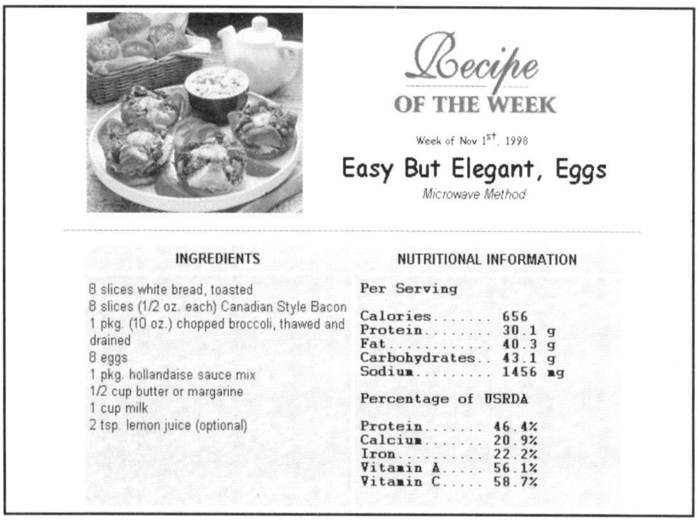

FODOR'S RESTAURANT GUIDE
http://www.fodors.com/ri.cgi

Where to eat out in hundreds of cities throughout the world. The restaurants listed in Fodor's are generally upmarket and above average in price.

WORTH A VISIT...

All India...	Indian recipes and restaurants	**http://www.gadnet.com/foodx.htm**
Beer Info Source	Beer from around the globe	**http://www.beerinfo.com**
Chopstix	Chinese recipes and restaurants	**http://chopstix.co.uk**
Epicurious Food	Serious food and drink site	**http://www.epicurious.com**
Food Channel	All things culinary	**http://foodchannel.com**
Planet K	More recipes	**http://www.kelloggs.com**
Ready Steady Cook	Tips from TV's culinary contest	**http://www.bbc.co.uk/readysteadycook**
TeaTime	Everything about tea	**http://www.teatime.com**
Usenet Cookbook	Searchable recipe database	**http://astro.cf.ac.uk/misc.recipe**
The Virtual Bar	Hangover cures and bar tricks	**http://www.TheVirtualBar.com**
Where To Eat	Dining in the UK	**http://www.where-to-eat.co.uk**

FOOD AND DRINK
http://www.bbc.co.uk/foodanddrink

Over 150 online recipes shown on the top culinary television programme. Grouped into convenient categories, many created by leading chef Antony Worral Thompson. Authoritative advice on the subject of wines and beers is also dispensed by experts Oz Clarke and Jilly Goolden.

THE CHILE-HEADS HOME PAGE
http://www.neptune.netimages.com/~chile.

If you're a fan of the really hot stuff - and who isn't? – look no further than this site devoted to the joys of the chilli pepper. Among other things, you can find out just how hot the hottest habañero pepper really is. The site also holds an exhaustive list of hyperlinks to other chilli sites.

CADBURY'S
http://www.cadbury.co.uk

One of the world's biggest names in confectionery has created this informative history of chocolate: from the Mayan cocoa growers who started the whole thing off to the present day.

THE ART WORLD

Most of the art world's great galleries and institutions have already introduced their own Web sites, making the Internet a gateway to some of the world's greatest art. Most of these sites aim to tempt future vistors to the galleries they represent, but they can also be both entertaining and a valuable reference source.

NATIONAL GALLERY
http://www.nationalgallery.org.uk
The traditional face of the art world, London's National Gallery boasts paintings from the 13th century onwards. The paintings are beautifully presented but the accompanying text, though very detailed, is written in a turgid academic style which may deter some Net surfers.

CENTRE GEORGES POMPIDOU
http://www.cnac-gp.fr
In its brief life, the "Pompidou Centre" in Paris has established itself as one of Europe's most important modern art institutions. The Web site offers a neat guided tour around the museum's permanent exhibitions with the paintings sympathetically displayed on a plain white background – just like the real gallery. There is also a series of interesting online exhibitions.

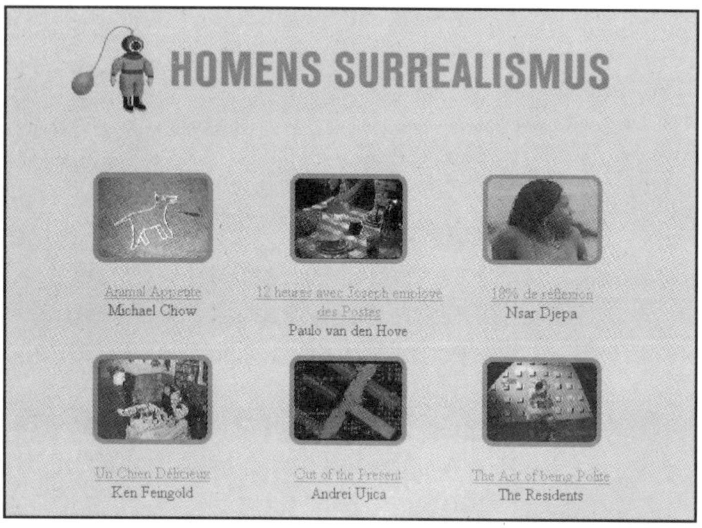

THE GUGGENHEIM MUSEUMS
http://www.guggenheim.org
The Solomon R. Guggenheim Foundation owns some of the most important works of 20th century art, which it houses in its esteemed galleries in New York,

Berlin, Bilbao and Venice. A colour-coded virtual trek through these galleries will provide you with an excellent overview of all the major artistic movements of the century from Cubism to Abstract Expressionism (both well represented).

MUSEUM OF LONDON
http://www.museum-london.org.uk

Devoted not only to art but also the history and culture of the capital, the Museum of London's Web site is a good balance of clever graphics and lengthy texts. Subjects range from the haunts of Charles Dickens to debates on whether the post-war concrete tower blocks should be protected or demolished.

VICTORIA AND ALBERT
http://www.vam.ac.uk

One of the best cultural Web sites on display, the interactive nature of the online version of London's Victoria and Albert Museum makes it especially appealing to children. Unsurprisingly, textiles and fashion are well to the fore, the numerous images usually accompanied by text which manages to be easy-to-read without being patronizing.

WORTH A VISIT...

Art Guide	Art in Britain and Ireland	**http://www.artguide.org**
Art History Network	Art, archeology and architeture	**http://www.arthistory.netThe**
Getty Centre	Treasures of the Getty Empire	**http://www.getty.edu**
History of Art Virtual Library	Art history and technology	**http://www.hart.66k.ac.uk/ VirtualLibrary.html**
Metropolitan Museum of Art	New York gallery	**http://www.mdq.org**
Musée de Québec	Canada's best-known gallery	**http://www.mdq.org**
Museum of Web Art	Virtual gallery	**http://www.mowa.com**

GOOD HEALTH

The Internet is full of ideas about ways in which you can improve your health. As always, you need to exercise some caution when seeking advice on medical matters – a Web site is not a good replacement for a doctor! That said, there are many reputable sites that offer high-quality information as well as useful support for sufferers of serious illnesses.

BRITISH HEART FOUNDATION
http://www.bhf.org.uk
Heart disease is the number one killer in the West. In a high proportion of cases such illness can be avoided. The official BHF site offers a neat depiction of how the heart works and all the nasty things that we do to harm it, as well as lifestyle tips on how to keep our organs in a healthy state.

PATIENT (UK)
http://www.patient.co.uk
If you only delve into one medical site make it Patient (UK). Essentially a signpost site, good, simple design makes it easy to find good information from the hundreds of well-organized links within. Also strong on newgroups for sufferers of specific diseases.

PHARMWEB
http://www.pharmweb.net
Aimed more at the professional medic, Pharmweb can provide technical information on every drug currently on the market. The general public would be best advised to stick with the "Patient Information" section of the site

WORTH A VISIT...

Active	Healthy living	**http://awww.health.co.uk**
Aidsmap	Aids information	**http://www.aids.map.com**
BDHF	British Dental Health Foundation	**http://www.dentalhealth.org.uk**
RNIB	Royal National Institute for the Blind	**http://www.rnib.org.uk**
Trashed	Drug education	**http://www.trashed.co.uk**
Wrecked	Alcohol education	**http://www.wrecked.co.uk**

since reading a list of potential side-effects of even the most commonly used drugs can make scary reading.

LIFESAVER
http://www.lifesaver.co.uk

Trying to kick the habit? Lifesaver offers sound practical advice for would-be ex-smokers.

THE NATURAL HEALTH GUIDE
http://marches.county.net/health

Excellent overview of alternative and complementary treatments currently available, along with their various practioners.

THE NHS
http://www.nhs50.nhs.uk

Developed as a part of the 50th anniversary celebrations for Britain's beleaguered National Health Service in 1998, this site gives a good potted history of health issues in post-war Britain.

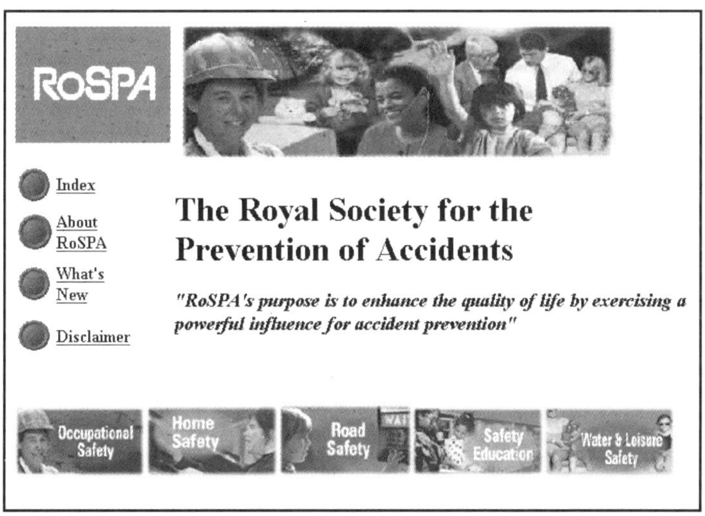

ROSPA
http://www.rospa.co.uk

The Royal Society for the Prevention of Accidents runs a comprehensive Web site. Big on statistics and legislation, this site will strongly appeal to those who like to pepper their conversations with "did you know...?"

POLITICS

If politics is your bag you'll find plenty to keep you occupied on the Web. Not only do the major political parties all have their own Web sites for you to study, but you also have access to similar sites for most countries in the West and beyond.

POLITICAL RESOURCES ON THE NET
http://www.stm.it/politic

This Italian site is possibly the best starting point for politics on the Web. With a map of the world on its home page, you can click on any continent for a hypertext list of sites relating to your choice.

THE WHITE HOUSE
http://www.whitehouse.gov

One of the most famous Web sites in the world, this is the US government's official cyberspace presence. It's also pretty impressive. The epitome of "infotainment", The White House combines a guided tour in which we meet the President and his family, with a potted history of democracy in America, and details of the day's governmental business. If you really want to, you can also "Write the President" – you never know, you might just get a personal reply.

GREENPEACE
http://www.greenpeace.org

Proponents of direct action when it comes to the protection of the environment, the Greenpeace site acts as a news service for their ongoing activities and focuses on current ecological issues.

PRIVATE EYE

http://www.compulink.co.uk/~private-eye

The online version of Britain's best-loved satirical magazine mixes some of its fortnightly content with additional material exclusive to the Web. Includes an extended "Colemanballs", "Pseud's Corner" and, of course, the covers for which the magazine is famed.

AMNESTY INTERNATIONAL

http://www.amnesty.org

A sobering website that highlights appalling political injustice and human rights violations. As they put it: "If you think virtual reality is interesting, try reality".

UK CITIZENS ONLINE DEMOCRACY

http://www.democracy.org.uk

A Web site that works more like a newsgroup; postings are sent by e-mail and appear in the sequence in which they arrive. A place for serious political debate, this site has gained a reputation from the fact that well-known politicians have sometimes been prepared to participate in discussions.

WORTH A VISIT...

Conservative Party	Political party	**http://www.conservative-party.org**
Green Party	Political party	**http://www.greenparty.org**
Houses of Parliament	Home of British government	**http://www.parliament.ukLabour**
Labour Party	Political party	**http://www.labour.org.uk**
Liberal Democratic Party	Political party	**http://www.libdems.org.uk**
Monster Raving Loony Party	Political party	**http://www.ravingloony.pv.org**
Plaid Cymru	Political party	**http://www.wales.com/political-party.plaid-cymru/emglishindex.html**
Scottish National Party	Political party	**http://www.snp.org.uk**
Spunk Press	Anarchist magazine	**http://www.spunk.org**
UN Development Program	UN humanitarian work	**http://www.undp.or**

REFERENCE AND EDUCATION

The Word Wide Web is the ultimate reference tool. It's almost like having a row of specialist libraries at your fingertips. Indeed it's hard to imagine how writers and researchers ever got along without it.

GUIDE TO WRITING RESEARCH PAPERS
http://www.webster.comment.edu/mia.htm
Invaluable advice how to put together and present your ideas on paper. In spite of its name, the information presented is as useful to school projects as those preparing doctoral theses.

THE DISCOVERY CHANNEL
http://www.discovery.com
The Discovery network creates science and history programs for television. Their Web site complements these broadcasts with features such as an interactive tour of Cleopatra's Palace.

ENCYLOPEDIA BRITANNICA
http://www.eb.com
The most famous name in its field, *Encylopedia Britannica Online* is by far the most comprehensive Internet reference system. The downside is that you have to pay a small subscription – less than £5 a month – for the privilege. Easy to use, you can perform keyword searches in a matter of seconds that would take hours working with the paper editions.

WORTH A VISIT...

Bartlett's Quotations	Dictionary of quotations	http://www.columbia.edu/acis/bartleby/bartlett
Berkeley Digital Library	Outstanding search facilities	http://www.sunsite.berkeley.com
Dynamo	BBC for primary schools	http://www.bbc.co.uk/education/parents/dynamo
EduWeb	Links for teachers	http://www.eduweb.co.uk
Lingua Franca	Life in academia	http://www.sevenbridgespress.com/lf
MIT Media Lab	Premier scientific university	http://www.media.mit.com
MuseumNet	Listing of UK museums	http://www.museum.net
Roget's Thesaurus	Site for synonyms	http://www.thesaurus.com
THES	Times Higher Education	http://www.thesis.co.uk

ALT.CULTURE
http://www.altculture.com

A hip, attitude-filled online encylopedia highlighting significant aspects of modern-day culture. Keyword searches are possible but a more entertaining approach is to hit the "random" button.

DICTIONARY
http://www.dictionary.com

An online version of *Webster's Revised Unabridged Dictionary*, this Web site is easy to use, especially with the annotated hyperlinks. It is American, though, so watch out for those weird spellings.

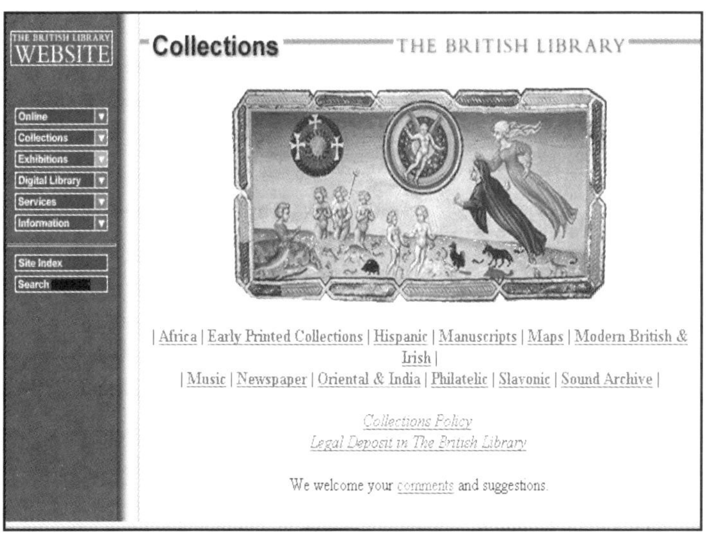

THE BRITISH LIBRARY
http://www.bl.uk

Comprehensive but hard work, the British Library allows you to search its main catalogue and lists its special collections.

LIBRARY OF CONGRESS
http://lcwed.loc.gov/homepage

More visual than its British counterpart, the Library of Congress also allows detailed searches of Congressional records and changes in legislation.

FINANCE

Although some users are a little supicious about bringing money and the Internet together, there is a whole lot of valuable information online that can advise you how best to spend or save your money. The World Wide Web is expecially strong on its global stock market data.

INLAND REVENUE
http://www.inlandrevenue.gov.uk

In spite of what you might have imagined from filling out your tax return, the official Web site of the British Inland Revenue is a well-designed and comprehensive affair. Especially useful to the many last minute tax-payers is the facility for downloading blank self-assessment forms.

MONEYWORLDUK
http://www.co.uk

If, like most people, your brain switches off the second your financial adviser opens his mouth, you may need *Moneyworld UK*. Aimed at the general reader, this site provides a surprisingly easy-to-follow guide to every aspect of personal finance: from pension plans to mortgages. *Moneyworld UK* also offers a news service and links to most of the significant financial institutions you can name.

FINANCIAL TIMES
http://www.ft.com

The online version of one of the most famous finance newspapers in the world.

EMUNET
http://www.euro-emu.co.uk

The issue of the single European currency is still a matter that confuses many people. *EMUNET*, the offical Web site of the Euro, aims to promote the currency and show the doubters of Europe how they will be positively affected by its eventual arrival.

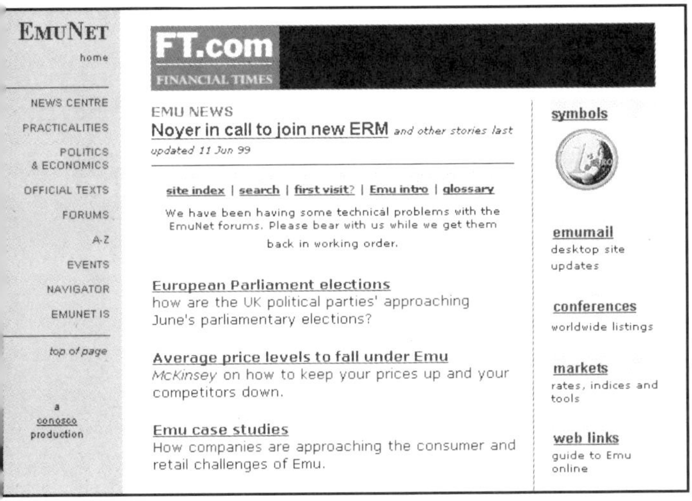

QUICKEN.COM
http://www.quicken.com/retirement

This site helps earners of all ages work out how much money they need to save, and how safe their pension investments need to be to guarantee them early retirement. Frightening stuff.

CHARTING UK SHARES
http://www.metronet.co.uk/bigwood/shares/index.htm

A useful summary of all the action on the London stock market, supplemented with charts and graphs that show the fastest moving prices in either direction. *Charting UK Shares* is a good introductory site for the novice or small-time investor, or for anyone who wants an overview of the market.

WORTH A VISIT...

AAA Investment Guide	Tips for investors	**http://www.wisebuys.co.uk**
Bankfacts	British Bankers Association	**http://www.bankfacts.org.uk**
Business Link	Guide for small businesses	**http://www.businesslink.co.uk**
Fidelity	Fund management	**http://www.fidelity.co.uk**
First Direct	PC banking	**http://firstdirect.co.uk**
Interactive Investor	Online Investments	**http://www.iii.co.uk**
Legal and General	Online insurance	**http://www.landg.co.uk**
MoneyeXtra	Cheap loans database	**http://www.moneyextra.co.uk**
National Savings	Premium bonds online	**http://www.nationalsavings.co.uk**
Charles Schwab	Online Investments	**http://www.schwab-worldwide.com**
Screentrade	Online insurance	**http://www.screentrade.co.uk**

COMEDY

We can all use a good laugh from time to time, and the Internet can be an excellent source of comic relief. You will find humour to suit all tastes – if you're looking for jokes about banjos, you'll find them. Lots of them. Be warned, however, quite a lot of the material you find on the Internet is not quite what you would expect to see broadcast on the television.

BORED.COM
http://www.bored.com
Aimed at the slacker/surfer, *BORED.COM* claims to link to the most interesting sites on the Internet, such as the "Densa" quiz in which you can measure your own stupidity.

UK LAUGHTER LINKS
http://www.link-it.com/comedy/link.html
First stop for fans of British television comedy. Click on any of the stations on this nifty tube-map design and you will get a list of hyperlinks to websites – official or otherwise – devoted to that show. Covers the extremes of British comedy from "Are You Being Served" to "Father Ted".

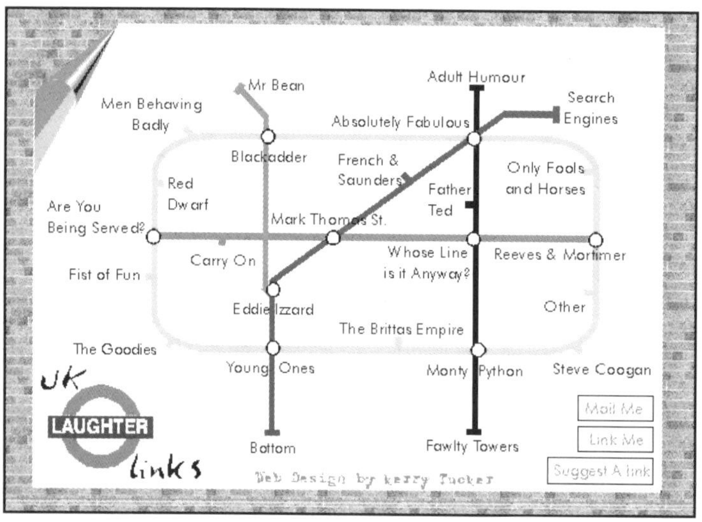

EDDIE IZZARD ONLINE
http://www.izzard.com
The excellent official Web site of the funniest comedian ever to have lived. Not only can you find out what the maestro is up to at the moment but you can also download classic examples of his stunning "stream-of-consciousness" comic rants.

MICHAEL MOORE
http://www.michaelmoore.com

Not exactly comedy, the mild-mannered yet often hard-hitting Michael Moore rails againsts social injustice in the US. His perennial direct action on behalf of the downtrodden worker against bureaucracy and the machinations of Big Business is both funny and provocative.

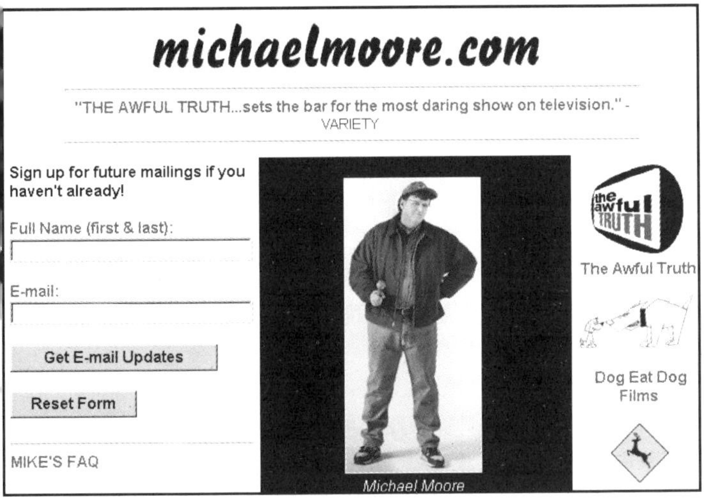

PYTHONLINE
http://www.pythonline.com

US site devoted to Monty Python's Flying Circus, the semi-official *PythOnline* contains news updates and games as well as a chance to join the "Spam Club".

HARRY HILL
http://www.harryhill.com

Plenty of downloadable quotable quotes from the man who asked the question: "A dolphin will jump out of the water for a piece of fish – imagine what he'd do for some chips".

E-MAIL JOKES ARCHIVE
http://www.emailjoke.com

A never-ending list of gags on every topic imaginable. Sign up and receive a joke via e-mail every day.

WORTH A VISIT...

The Black Piano	Strange strip cartoon	**http://www.blackpiano/freeserve.co.uk**
Caricature Zone	Cartoons of the stars	**http://www.magixl.com**
The Comedy Zone	BBC comedy site	**http://www.comedyzone.beeb.com**
Lee and Herring	Childish (and very funny)	**http://mudhole.spotnet.uk.com/fist**
The Stand	Scottish comedy site	**http://www.thestand.co.uk**
Mark Thomas	Comedy agit-prop	**http://fnord.demon.co.uk/markt.html**
Viz	Un-PC magazine	**http://www.viz.co.uk**

CAREERS AND JOBS

When Big Business latched onto the Net, employers quickly realised that they could advertise vacancies for a fraction of the cost of using newspapers. Since then, job agencies have sprung up on the Net, advertising jobs and displaying CVs for potential employers. Take a look at these Web sites – they could guide you to a new and fulfilling career.

JOBSITE
http://www.jobsite.co.uk

One of the biggest and best online agencies, *Jobsite* contains live vacancies from all over Europe. To use the site you enter a job title into the keyword search box. This will produce a number of job title categories which you can then click on to see the jobs listed. *Jobsite* also offers its "Jobs by Email" feature, so if nothing suitable is currently on offer you simply enter your details. If and when a new vacancy arises you will be contacted automatically via e-mail .

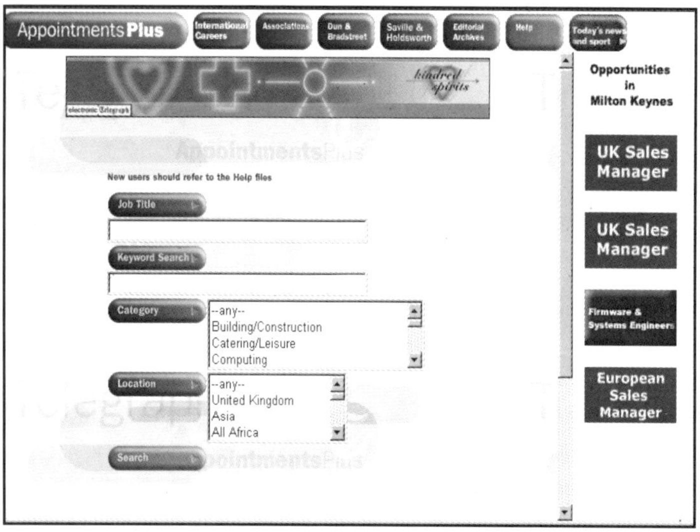

APPOINTMENTS PLUS
http://www.appointments-plus.co.uk

For the more upmarket career move, *Appointments Plus* shows all of the positions advertised in the *Daily Telegraph.*

CAREERZINE
http://www.careerzine.co.uk

UK and European database listing over 3,000 current positions in a variety of industries. *Careerzine* also features an e-mail option.

THE MONSTER BOARD
http://www.monster.co.uk

A particularly good job site. In addition to the usual option to search by job title, one of the most useful features of the *The Monster Board* is the "Career Centre". Here you can build yourself an online CV which potential employers can view. Beware, though. This can take a while and will give your telephone bill an unwanted push, so it's best to take the offline option.

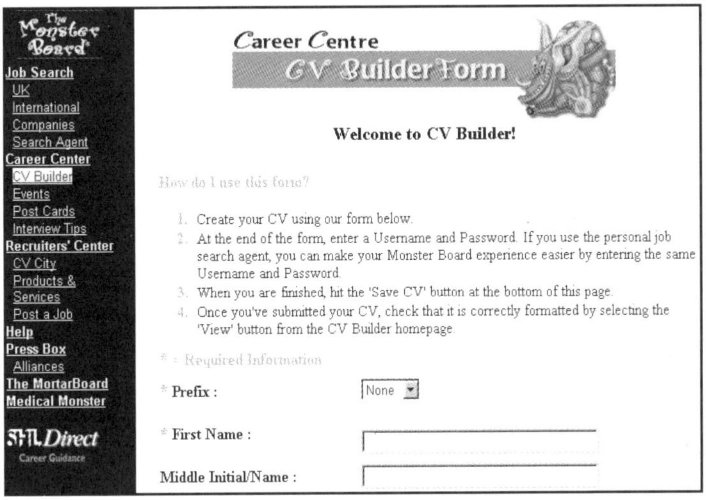

JOB HUNTER
http://www.jobhunter.co.uk

A collection of job advertisements from regional newspapers all over Great Britain.

HEADHUNTER
http://www.HeadHunter.Net

One of the biggest employment databases in the world, *Headhunter* boasts almost 300,000 jobs in nearly every possible industry and at levels from first-timer to CEO. Almost 200,000 CVs are maintained online.

WORTH A VISIT...

Top Jobs	Searchable database	**http://www.topjobs.co.uk**
JobNet	Vacancies in Australia	**http://www.jobnet.com.au**
PeopleBank	Worldwide vacancies	**http://www.peoplebank.co.ik**
Media Centre	Media jobs	**http://www.mediamasters.ndirect.co.uk/mediacentre/jobs/**

As well as using Web sites, a number of newsgroups may help with a job search.

alt.job	**alt.jobs.offerred**	**alt.jos.overseas**	**aus.ads.jobs**
comp.jobs.computer	**eunet.jobs**	**euro.jobs**	**jobs.offered**
uk.jobs	**uk.jobs.contract**	**uk.jobs.offered**	**uk.jobs.wanted**

TECHNOLOGY AND SCIENCE

Given its early geek-dominance, it's hardly surprising that the Internet is particularly strong on science and technology resources. Many of the best sites are official education or government bodies, but there are also some good online supplements to well-established magazines and television programs.

THE HISTORY OF THE INTERNET
http://www.internetvalley.com

Comprehensive history of this sprawling mass we call the Internet, from its beginnings as the US military's ARPANET to the latest developments on the World Wide Web.

MICROSOFT VRML
http://www.microsoft.com/vrml

Virtual Reality Modeling Language (VRML) enables Internet users to click and drag on a Web site picture or photograph and thereby manoeuvre around and see three-dimensional views of that same image. Among the impressive sample sites is a tour of the Great Wall of China.

HOTWIRED
http://www.hotwired.com

The online version of the hardcore techie magazine *Wired*. Ideal for Netheads who like to speak to each other in code.

WORTH A VISIT...

British UFO Research	"Official" UFO site	**http://www.bufora.org.uk**
EPA Global Warming	Ecological science	**http://www.epa.gov**
Greenwich Observatory	Excellent science links	**http://www.ast.cam.ac.uk**
Horizon	High-brow BBC science show	**http://www.bbc.co.uk/horizon**
Periodic Table	Click on any element for details	**http://www.shef.ac.uk/chemistry/web-elements/index.html**
The Quest	For UFO nuts	**http://www.netfeed.com**
Science Museum	Exhibitions and experiments	**http://www.nmsl.ac.uk/welcome.html**
Slashdot	Anti-establishment techie e-zine	**http://www.slashdot.org**
Tomorrow's World	Low-brow BBC science show	**http://www/bbc.co.uk/tw**
The Why Files	Science for kids	**http://www.whyfiles.news.wisc.edu/**

SCIENCE A GO GO
http://www.scienceagogo.com

Online magazine that discusses new scientific developments in terms that a reasonably intelligent layman could comprehend.

RITA THE ROBOT
http://www.cs.bham.ac.uk/~axg/Rita.html

Control a robot using commands sent across the Web.

NASA
http://www.nasa.gov

The final word on anything out of this world, the official NASA website is vast. Sounds, images and movies accompany the latest developments in Mankind's knowledge of the solar system.

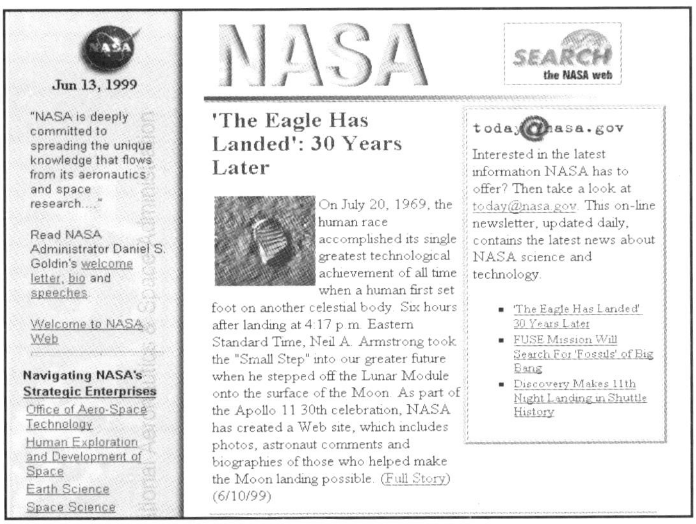

NEW SCIENTIST
http://www.newscientist.com

Leading science magazine that's just about comprehensible to the lay reader. *New Scientist* not only contains features from the current printed edition but gives access to an archive containing every story to have made the online site.

WEIRD STUFF

Now let's take a look at some Internet oddities – the places where you can find anything from duct tape fetishists to those with proof that Elvis shot JFK. There seems to be no logical reason for many these sites to exist, but they do. And some are very entertaining – even if they leave you scratching your head.

THE SURREALIST COMPLIMENT GENERATOR
http://pharmdec.wustl.edu/cgi-bin/jardin_scripts/SCG
Forge a new reputation in your social set with such greetings as: "A suburban distance lying across your chest, a purpled frock befitting the asphyxiated, cans of lima beans upon your knees, you are truly a goddess of disturbed tranquility!" Keep clicking for more randomly generated nonsense.

JESUS DANCE
http://www.jesusdance.com
A variety of religious icons jiggle away on the screen to a merry "ho-down" (for which the lyrics are thoughtfully provided, so you can join in). Possibly profane; definitely amusing.

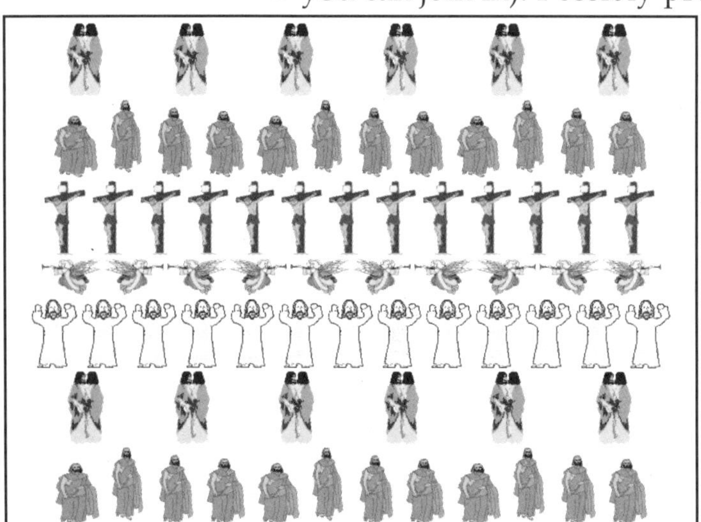

THE CIRCLEMAKERS
http://www.head-space/com/circlemakers.html
A long-standing and mysterious brotherhood that claims to be behind most of the crop circle mysteries that continue to baffle scientists and UFO experts.

KPU
http://www.moebius.psy.ed.ac.uk
The Koestler Parapsychology Unit conducts research into all matters

psychic. This site allows you to join in with their experiments and perform a series of ESP tests of your own. The scores will tell you if you have any psychic potential.

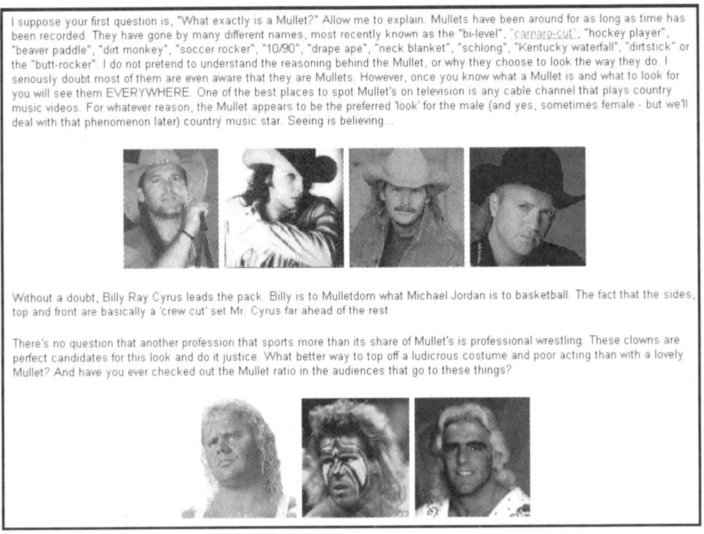

I suppose your first question is, "What exactly is a Mullet?" Allow me to explain. Mullets have been around for as long as time has been recorded. They have gone by many different names, most recently known as the "bi-level", "camaro-cut", "hockey player", "beaver paddle", "dirt monkey", "soccer rocker", "10/90", "drape ape", "neck blanket", "schlong", "Kentucky waterfall", "dirtstick" or the "butt-rocker". I do not pretend to understand the reasoning behind the Mullet, or why they choose to look the way they do. I seriously doubt most of them are even aware that they are Mullets. However, once you know what a Mullet is and what to look for you will see them EVERYWHERE. One of the best places to spot Mullet's on television is any cable channel that plays country music videos. For whatever reason, the Mullet appears to be the preferred 'look' for the male (and yes, sometimes female - but we'll deal with that phenomenon later) country music star. Seeing is believing...

Without a doubt, Billy Ray Cyrus leads the pack. Billy is to Mulletdom what Michael Jordan is to basketball. The fact that the sides, top and front are basically a 'crew cut' set Mr. Cyrus far ahead of the rest.

There's no question that another profession that sports more than its share of Mullet's is professional wrestling. These clowns are perfect candidates for this look and do it justice. What better way to top off a ludicrous costume and poor acting than with a lovely Mullet? And have you ever checked out the Mullet ratio in the audiences that go to these things?

THE NORTH AMERICAN MULLET PAGE
http://www.geocities.com/Hollywood/Hills/6906/

An online celebration of that most maligned (though perhaps not without reason) of hair styles, the mullet. Seemingly still popular with professional wrestlers and country singers, if you like your hair long at the back and short on the top you might well already find yourself featured in this peculiar Web site.

DIGITAL LANDFILL
http://www.potatoland.org/landfill

Cyperspace has its very own dumping ground where Net users can go to download unwanted documents and code. Press the button and watch it decompose and (hopefully/doubtfully) turn into something new and usable.

WORTH A VISIT...

Atlas of Cyberspace	Internet viewed from space	**http://www.cybergeography.org/atlas/**
Bonehead of the Day	Random stupidity	**http://www.bonehead.oddballs.com**
Duct Tape on the Web	For fans of duct tape	**http://www.octane.com/ducttape**
Ghost Sites	Digital junkyard	**http://www.disobey.com/ghostsitesThe**
Live Deformed Frog Cam	Pollution control	**http://www.freddo.pca.state.mn.us/frogcam2.html**
Museum of Dirt	Everything related to dirt	**http://www.planet.com/dirtweb/dirt.html**
Technosphere III	DIY evolution	**http://www.technosphere.org.uk**
Virtual Pet Cemetary	In loving memory...	**http://www.lavamind.com/pet.html**
Web Stalker	An "anti-browser"	**http://www.backspace.org/iod**
World Dogbite Service	Send dogbites via e-mail	**http://www.sassydog.com**

HOLIDAYS AND TRAVEL

Travel is one area in which the Web excels. It's a great way to research a holiday – a few hours of surfing can easily turn up some unexpected ideas. Once you've settled on a destination, you can find information on the locale, as well as researching (and even booking online) some of the best travel and accomodation deals.

MAPQUEST
http://www.mapquest.com

Very detailed online maps of most of the world's major cities – especially strong for travelling in the US.

ROUGH GUIDE TO TRAVEL
http://www.roughguides.com

A well-thought-out Web site from the makers of the popular youth-oriented *Rough Guide* books. More than 4,000 destinations are listed, many of which have full-length features. If you register your e-mail address with the site you can receive periodic updates.

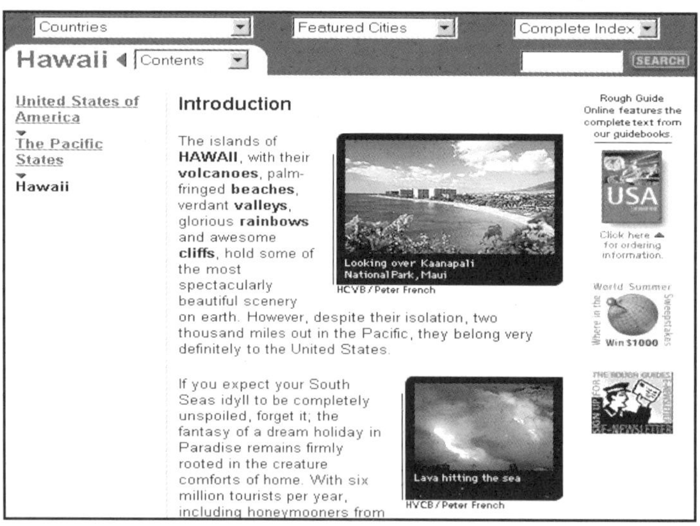

FODOR'S TRAVEL ONLINE
http://www.fodors.com

A good place to begin if you are in the throes of preparing for an overseas holiday. By entering your details as you navigate the site you are able to create your own personalised "mini-guide" itinerary.

WORTH A VISIT...

Bargain Holidays	last-minute cheap holidays	**http://www.bargainholidays.com**
Greatest Places Online	Exotic locations	**http://greatestplaces.org**
Lonely Planet Online	Exotic locations	**http://www.lonelyplanet.com**
Online Weather	Weather in 6,000 cities	**http://www.onlineweather.com**
RAC	Royal Automobile Club	**http://www.rac.co.uk**
Railtrack Travel	Rail travel in the UK	**http://www.railtrack.co.uk/travel**
Time Out	City guide to Europe and US	**http://www.timeout.com**
Travel Resources	Travel links	**http://www.travel-resources.com**
Tourist Offices	Official tourist information	**http://www.towd.com**
Wish You Were Here	BBC travel show	**http://www.wishyouwerehere.com**

VIRTUAL LONDON
http://www.a-london-guide.co.uk

The official London Tourist Board guide to the city. Besides giving you limited theatre listings, *Virtual London* will let you visit Buckingham Palace, 10 Downing Street and Tower Bridge all at the click of a mouse.

HEALTH ADVICE FOR TRAVELLERS
http://www.doh.gov.uk/hat/emerg.htm

Official Department of Health guidelines that tell you how to protect yourself from disease when travelling abroad.

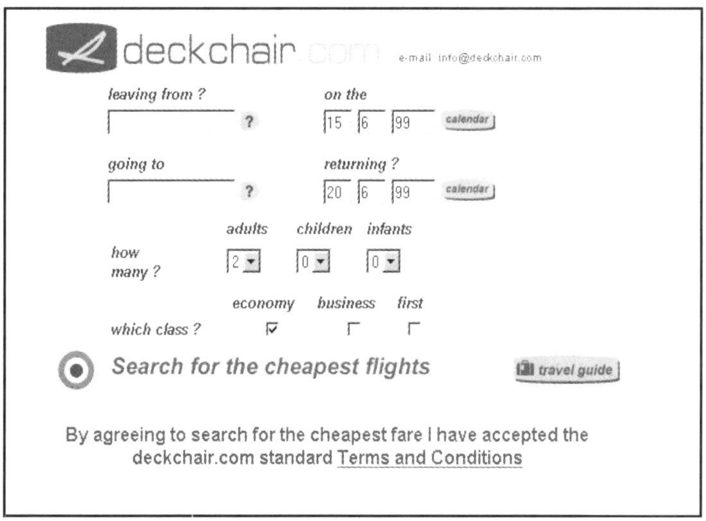

DECKCHAIR.COM
http://www.deckchair.com

The brainchild of former pop star Bob Geldoff, *Deckchair.com* is a devilishly straightforward idea for booking cheap air flights. By entering your travel dates, the site (which is linked directly to most of the major airlines) can tell you the cheapest fare available for those dates and let you book it directly. Alternatives sites do exist, but none of them are quicker or simpler than this.

FUN, GAMES AND KIDS' STUFF

Wasn't it Walt Disney who said that we were all kids at heart? The World Wide Web has masses of sites devoted to keeping children of all ages amused.

GAMES DOMAIN
http://www.gamesdomain.co.uk
This is one for all games fans to bookmark. Not only do you get the lastest buzz from the gaming industry, you also get a huge database of freeware and shareware games (designed for every type of computer) that you can download. *Games Domain* also has an area devoted to games for young children.

TIDDLEYWINKS
http://www.tiddlywinks.org
This classic children's game now has a world-wide following among adults. The entertaining *Tiddleywinks* Web site tells you everything you could want to know about the sport, from its history, to clubs across the globe.

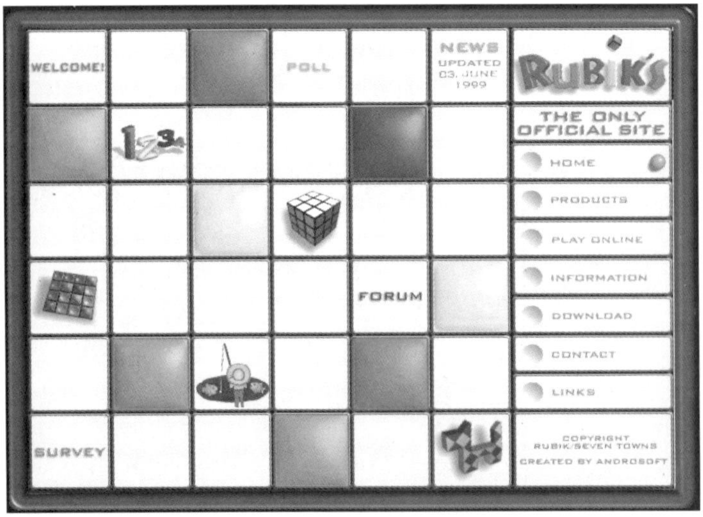

RUBIK'S ONLINE
http://www.rubiks.com
The Rubik's Cube took over the world at the end of the 1970s, and then fell from fashion before its recent relaunch. The Rubik puzzles have now become classics of their kind. The official Rubik site has online versions of all the puzzles as well as a rather cool screensaver that you can download onto your PC.

JASPER
http://www.spectrum.lovely.net/

As perverse as it might seem, there are some very clever techies out there who have seen fit to create an online emulation of the Sinclair ZX SPECTRUM, a home computer from the early 1980s. This had a whacking great 48K of RAM and no hard disk. *Jasper* lets you play all those classic games like "Jet Set Willy" and "Chuckie Egg". An amusing history lesson for anyone under 25; nostalgia for everyone else.

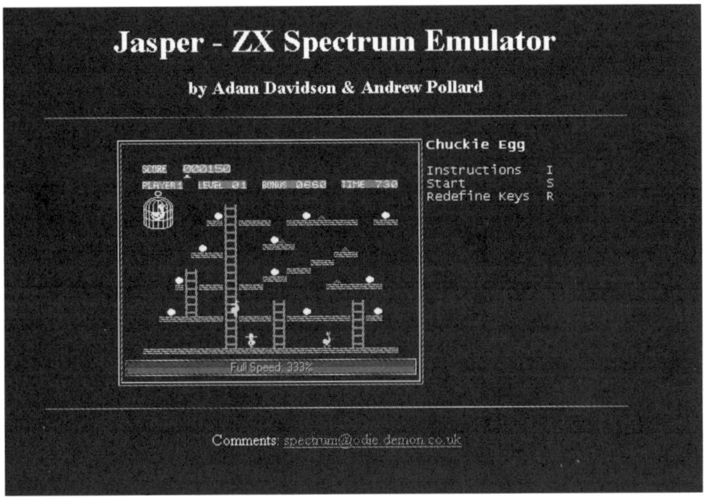

ACCESS DENIED
http://www.accessdenied.com

An extremely powerful source of information on all manner of gaming the world over. No matter how obscure your interests may be, this site will point you at someone, somewhere around the globe who shares your passion.

PLAYSTATION EUROPE
http://www.playstation-europe.com

As you might expect from the maker of the world's premier game platform, the official Playstation site is one of the slickest on the Web. In addition to advertising features, the site also has a section on playing tips for many of the most popular games.

WORTH A VISIT...

21	Online gambling site	**http://www.casinos-gambling.com**
Backgammon Galore!	Everything about the game	**http://www.bkgm.com**
Cheat Elite	Tips on unfair play	**http://www.alienmoon.com**
Games and Puzzles	Games and links	**http://www.gamesandpuzzles.com**
Play Better Chess	Hints and tips	**http://www.infochess.com**
Web Dice	Roll dice on the Web	**http://www.irony.com/webdice.html**
WebRPG	Role playing games	**http://www.webrpg.com**
World Pinball	Gobal directory	**http://www.daveland.com/pinball**

DISNEY.CO.UK
http://www.disney.co.uk
Although *Disney.co.uk* is merciless in the way its features are linked to product marketing, it's one the finest children's sites on the Web. Superbly designed and easy to navigate including several very speedy online games.

CRAYOLA
http://www.crayola.com
Excellent site aimed at parents surfing the Web with their young kids. The site features pictures you can download to colour-in (with your Crayola crayons, obviously), and also a special area that displays children's drawings.

MERPY
http://www.merpy.com
The cute animated adventures of a cartoon character called Merpy and her friend Jeremy Dragonfly.

RAINFOREST ACTION NETWORK
http://www.ran.org/kids_action/index1.html
Easy-to-follow educational site that aims to foster an interest in ecological matters among children.

WORTH A VISIT...

These sites are especially recommended for pre-teenage children:

Argo Sphere	Activity site for under 10s	**http://www.argosphere.net**
Infant Explorer	Nature for kids	**http://www.naturegrid.org.uk/infant**
Kids Domain	Fun and games	**http://www.kidsdomain.com/kids**
KinderArt	Art activities for youngsters	**http://www.kinderart.com/lessons**
Robots in Space	Educational site	**http://www.brookes.ac.uk/rms/robots**
Yahooligans!	Yahoo! search engine for kids	**http://www.yahooligans.com**

REFERENCE SECTION

9

We'll finish with a mixed bag containing some of the issues that may not affect you directly, but of which you ought to be aware. We've already discussed computer viruses briefly. Here you'll see how to combat them in practice. You'll also find some common-sense tips on avoiding the wrath of the law. Finally, although the Internet is great for kids, there are some ideas on how you can check that your child is using the Internet safely.

LEGAL STUFF

The existence and growth of the Internet has posed numerous challenges to the world's greatest legal minds, but its global nature has turned up a number of issues which can make the law difficult to enforce.

THE LAW OF THE LAND

Most of the crimes that we hear about in relation to the Internet have their direct equivalents in the "real" world. One of the most common misdemeanours is copyright infringement in relation to personal Web pages. Even if you have set up the best fan Web site for your favourite band and have taken millions of "hits" from other Internet users, if you quote lines of lyrics, include snippets of sound recordings, or even in some cases images, you are breaking copyright laws. In some cases this will bring you to the attention of music business lawyers, who may legitimately be able to slap a "cease and desist" order on your site (although the more enlightened companies often tolerate fan sites). Refusal to comply often ends with prosecution.

It's important to remember that when you set up a Web site, in the eyes of the law you are responsible for its content. If you include defamatory material on your site, it would be rather like publishing the same content in a newspaper.

The same holds true for other areas of Internet activity, such as newsgroups and e-mail. If you have access to e-mail in your place of work, you should certainly think twice before spreading malicious gossip about your boss – your employer "owns" all of the mail that's sent from within the company's intranet. Even if you delete the offending mail from your machine, there will probably remain a record of it somewhere on the network.

INTERNATIONAL ISSUES

Whether in cyberspace or not, if you break the laws of your own country you face prosecution. However in the international arena this can be far more complex. What happens when an act is committed on foreign soil that contravenes no laws, but is a crime in another state? For example, what if British "official secrets" mysteriously turn up on an ISP's server in Turkey, where the British legal system has no jurisdiction? There is often little that can easily be done. Many similar cases have taken place, where Internet users have sought to bypass their own national laws by issuing "public interest" material on a foreign site. But these can still lead to prosecution, even though it may be long and protracted. In recent times, prosecutors have turned to the ISPs themselves in the hope that they can be made responsible for web content and newsgroups found on their servers. This is a story that will run and run.

PIRATE SOFTWARE

On a more mundane level, far and away the most common form of computer-related crime involves illegal software. Whilst there are many excellent and perfectly legal sites from which freeware and shareware can be distributed, there are also numerous sites where illegal software can be had for free. Whilst all of us like the idea of getting something for nothing, the simple fact of the matter is that downloading and using pirated software is theft and is illegal. No matter how you might like to think about it, if you use a bootleg program you're not too far away from having walked into a computer store and shoplifted the software.

There's little doubt that software piracy is widely viewed as a minor petty crime – akin to stealing pencils from an employer's stationery cupboard. But it does cost the likes of Microsoft millions (maybe billions) of dollars in lost revenue every year. There are wider issues here, though. For as long as software piracy remains "acceptable" it actually works in favour of the major established players in the industry. Let's be honest, Bill Gates and his chums can afford to lose a small fortune in this way, but the next generation of young innovators coming up with the software that might well change our lives a few years down the line may not be so fortunate. So we should also face the fact that software piracy helps to suppress progress and competition, which will prove to be of harm to our own interests in the long run.

THE VIRUS THREAT

One of the great mysteries of the PC age has been the periodic unleashing of computer "viruses". These are tiny programs, usually passed across the Internet, which are specifically designed to do harm. At worst this can mean corrupting crucial data on your hard disk, even rendering it unusable.

WHY DO THEY BOTHER?

During 1999, a virus was unleashed on the Internet to become effective on the anniversary of the Chernobyl nuclear disaster. When the day came, tens of thousands of PCs around the world – mostly in Southeast Asia – were infected. Many had the data on their hard disks damaged beyond repair. This all begs the question as to why an individual with such impressive software engineering skills would want to use them in this way – surely his or her undoubted talents could earn serious money creating something worthwhile?

Yes, it's baffling but it seems to be happening more and more. Indeed, thousands of new viruses are discovered each year, even if the vast majority of them are relatively benign. The growth of this threat now means that it is becoming increasingly important for every computer to be kitted out with an "anti-virus" program of some kind.

The principle is simple – each time you download data from the Internet (or from any other external source, such as floppy disks, CD-ROMs or Zip cartridges) it will be vetted by the program for known viruses.

VIRUS SCANNING SOFTWARE IN ACTION

One the most widely used anti-virus packages is McAfee's VirusScan. You can find out more about it from their home Web site (http://www.mcafee.com). Like other anti-virus software, VirusScan can be updated each month to take account of new developments in the world of computer viruses.

You can set up the software so that it automatically scans new files that come onto your hard disk or you can perform manual scans. If you have the software loaded, click on MCAFEE VIRUSSCAN CENTRAL.

1 Click on SCAN.

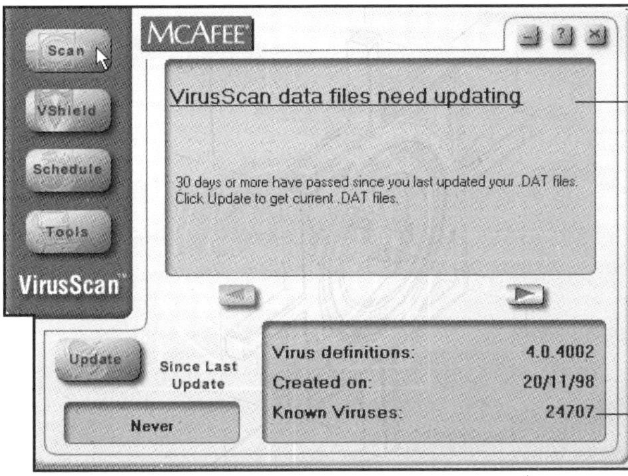

The program warns you that you need to download the most recent anti-virus data.

The number of known viruses your copy of the program can detect.

2 In the dialog box, click on the WHERE & WHAT tab to select the drive you wish to scan. Click on ALL FILES. Click on SCAN NOW.

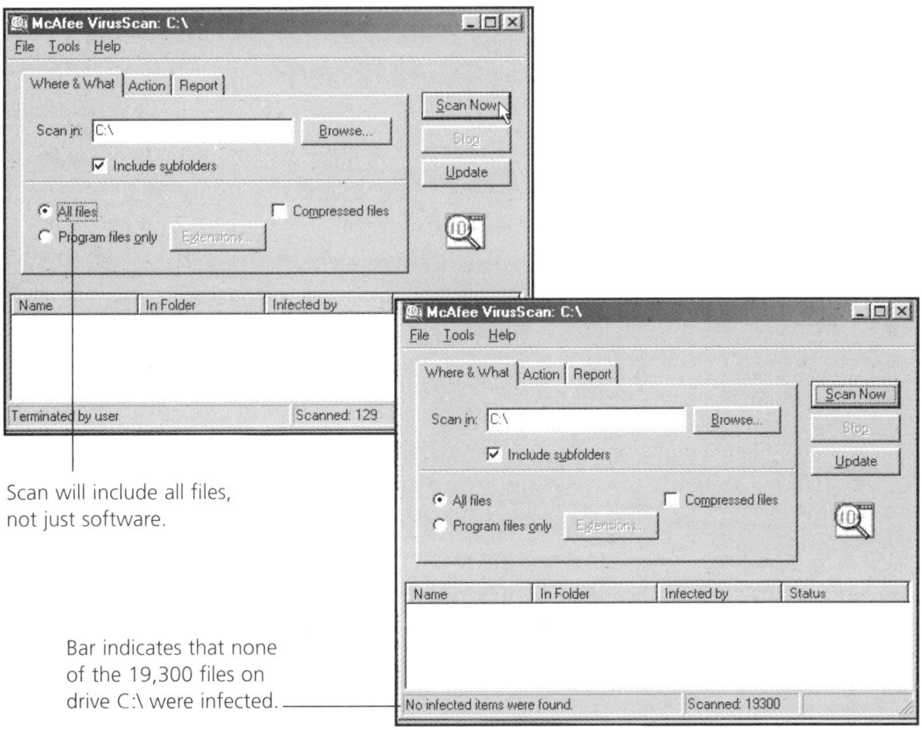

Scan will include all files, not just software.

Bar indicates that none of the 19,300 files on drive C:\ were infected.

THE DARK SIDE

The Internet is rather like a huge "virtual" metropolis. But just like a real city, danger may lurk in some areas. In spite of what scaremongers may claim, you won't be greeted by an endless stream of hard-core porn or the rantings of insane political bigots the second you go online. These things are certainly out there, but you have to search them out – they rarely come looking for you. This still has serious implications for parents who are rightly concerned that their kids are not exposed to some of the less wholesome aspects of life on the Net.

POLICING THE NET

One of the things that makes the Internet so truly unique is that, unlike any remotely comparable product, nobody actually owns it. The first wave of Netheads took great pride in this very fact and have fought hard through its rapid commercialization to keep it that way. When the subject of censorship rears its head for any reason it gets treated as an attack on personal liberty. Indeed, when the US government attempted to push through the Communications Decency Act in 1997, aimed at limiting porn on the Web, it fell foul of America's famed constitutional right to free speech. But the problem of controlling what ought to be allowed on the Internet is much more complex. The main problem is that the Internet is a GLOBAL phenomenon. The soft porn found in British tabloid newspapers would barely raise an eyebrow in Europe and yet may well constitute gross indecency in America's Bible Belt. But if laws were passed, how would governments stop their own citizens from browsing "illegal" content in a different country? The simple answer is that it just can't be done.

IS IT SAFE FOR KIDS, THEN?

As adults, most of us feel capable of making our own decisions as to whether or not we want to log onto "adult" sites, but the issue becomes more difficult where children are concerned. Frankly, how many of us could truthfully say that if the Internet had existed in its current form when we were kids we, too, wouldn't have been at least a little intrigued by its forbidden zones? This is not an insurmountable problem, though. As far as pornography on the Web is concerned, almost all of these sites are commercial ventures, so without a credit card you can't get in. That's a pretty effective deterrent.

However, there *are* two areas of the Internet to which you should think seriously about blocking access – newsgroups and chat rooms. Newsgroups, particularly those beginning with alt.sex... and alt.binaries... are where the vast majority of the Internet's hard-core material is to be found. But sex is not the only issue. Other newsgroups may expose your children to extreme political or racist views, or unacceptable language. As many of the chat channels are "adult" in content, reasons for concern hardly need spelling out.

If some of this sounds rather bleak, don't panic! The benefits your child will gain by access to the Internet – especially in surfing the Web – INFINITELY outweigh the potential dangers. The good news for parents is that there are practical steps that can be taken to limit access. A wise starting point is to try to set some ground rules of acceptability with your children, in the same way as we tell them that they shouldn't talk to strangers. You can also discuss with your ISP which newsgroups are available to their subscribers. You will find that some do not support the prefixes mentioned above. A third alternative is to seek out software solutions. We'll take a look at some of these over the page.

NEED SOME ADVICE?

Further reading about children on the Internet can be found in a number of useful Web sites. The Internet Watch Foundation reports dubious Web sites and attempts to have them removed.

http://www.yahooligans.com/docs/safety
http://www.netparents.org
http://www.nchafc.org.uk/internet
http://www.internetwatch.org.uk/

BABYSITTERS

One approach to pacifying those parents concerned about their children using the Internet has been the development of "software babysitters", programs that run in the background and use parameters set by the parents to decide whether content is suitable. If any of the predefined key words or phrases are discovered the program denies access.

NET NANNY

Here is one of the most popular "babysitter" programs in action. Not only can Net Nanny block access to specified Web sites and newsgroups but it can also be used to prevent certain words being used by other specified computer programs. NetNanny runs in the background and can only be turned off with the use of a password. These programs are seen as a positive new development which not only protects children but also maintains freedom of speech on the Internet.

SOFTWARE SOLUTIONS

Here is a list of some of the best babysitter programs and Web sites where you can find out how to acquire them. Image Censor works on a different principle to the others in that it specifically looks for flesh-coloured tones in pictures – if it finds too much it covers it up.

NET NANNY	**http://www.netnanny.com/home/html**
SURFWATCH	**http://www.surfwatch.com**
CYBERSITTER	**http://www.pow-dist.co.uk**
CYBERPATROL	**http://www.microsys.com**
IMAGE CENSOR	**http:www.microtrope.com/icensor.html**

BARRING NEWSGROUPS

To specify the newsgroups that are to be inaccessible, click on OPEN in the toolbar. The OPEN LIST screen appears.

1 Select INTERNET NEWS GROUPS#1 and click on OK.

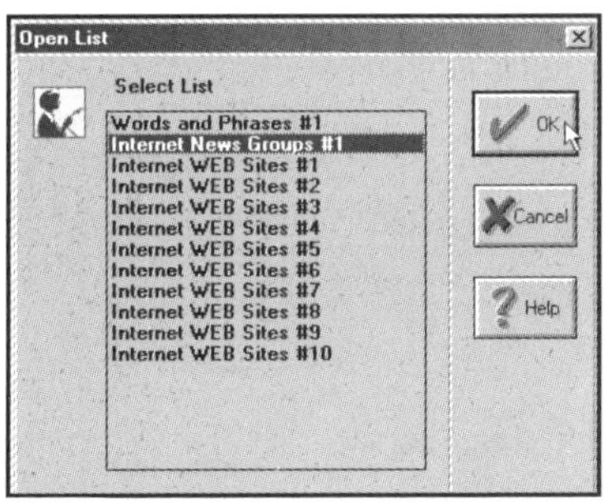

2 Add names of Newsgroups that are banned.

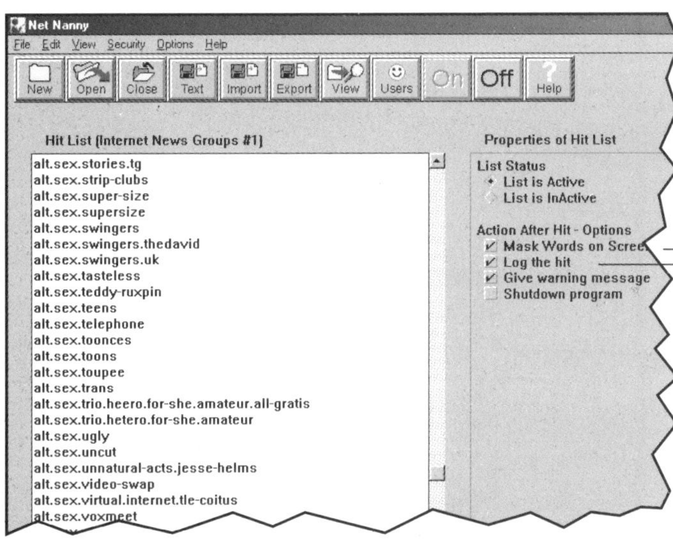

Hide banned words and phrases from the screen.

Save a note of when NetNanny takes action.

Display warning message (further options exists to close program).

INTERNET DIRECTORY

Over the next four pages you will find details of some of Britain's most widely used national Internet Service Providers. If you subscribe to any of these companies you will have access to all of the basic features of the Internet described throughout the book. Beneath each entry you'll find a contact telephone number – they will be only too happy to send you a software starter pack to get you connected. If you already have access to the Internet the addresses of their home pages are also shown – these can give an idea of how reliable or professional a service they operate. The third column indicates the basis on which they charge for access. The final column indicates how you subscribe.

AAPI

0820 4271166	www.aapi.co.uk	Monthly	Telephone

EASYNET

0207 681444	www.easynet.net	Monthly	Telephone

AIRTIME

01254 676921	www.airtime.co.uk	Monthly	Telephone

AOL UK

0800 2791234	www.btinternet.com	Monthly	CD/online

ARSENAL FC

0207 7042020	www.arsenal.co.uk	Free	Online

AVIATORS NETWORK

0700 2842867	www.aviators.net	Monthly	Telephone

BAYNET

01222 256401	www.baynet.co.uk	Monthly	Telephone

BOOTS

01462 743112	www.boots.com	Monthly	Telephone

BT CLICK PLUS

0800 7317887	www.btclickfree.com	Free	Download

BT INTERNET			
0800 800001	www.btinternet.com	Monthly	Online
BT LINEONE			
0800 111210	www.lineone.com	Free	Online
CABLE AND WIRELESS			
0800 0923013	www.cwcom.net	Variable	Online
CABLENET			
01424 830900	www.cablenet.net	Monthly	Online
CIX			
0845 3555050	www.cix.co.uk	Monthly	Online
CLARANET			
0845 3551000	www.clara.net	Monthly	CD/online
COMPUSERVE			
0990 0004000	www.compuserve.co.uk	Monthly	CD/online
CURRANT BUN			
0845 3063636	www.currantbun.com	Free	CD/online
CYBERPHILE			
01543 454840	www.cyberphile.co.uk	Variable	Telephone
DEMON INTERNET			
0208 3711234	www.demon.net	Monthly	Telephone/CD
DIRECT CONNECTION			
0208 2972200	www.dircon.co.uk	Monthly	Online
EASYNET			
0207 681444	www.easynet.net	Monthly	Telephone

THE OFFER OF A LIFETIME?

Sometimes you come across a deal that looks too good to be true. You might get the impression from the directory above that a number of the ISPs listed are operating "free access" services out of the goodness of their hearts. We all know this can't be true, so what's the catch? And why on earth should we pay an ISP every month when we can get the service for nothing? The catch in this instance is the issue of technical support. All of the ISPs that charge a monthly or annual fee, or charge by the amount of time you spend connected to the Internet, offer free down-the-phone advice - no matter how long your problem takes to sort out. The "free" suppliers charge for their technical know-how, usually by the minute. Many of these ISPs have deals with telephone companies so that support fees are calculated and appear on your regular telephone bill. So which way should you go? As a crude benchmark, if you spend more than a total of about 20-30 minutes during the course of a month being aided by your ISP's help-line, then you'll find it far more economical to pay a flat monthly fee. Ironically, although the recent growth of "free" ISPs has brought a whole load of newbies onto the Net, it is the experienced user – who rarely needs technical help – that gains the most.

ENTERPRISE			
0845 6040174	www.enterprise.net	Monthly	Telephone
ENTWEB			
0800 525470	www.entweb.co.uk	Monthly	Telephone
FREEDOTNET			
0208 9383338	www.thefree.net	Free	Online
FREENET			
01329 828000	www.freenet.co.uk	Free	Online
FREESERVE			
0990 50040	www.freeserve.net	Free	CD/online
FRONTIER			
0207 5369090	www.ftech.net	Monthly	Telephone
GATEWAY.NET			
0800 552000	www.gateway.net/free	Free	Online
GLOBAL INTERNET			
0870 9098000	www.global.net.uk	Annual	Online/CD
HIWAY			
01635 573300	www.hiway.co.uk	Monthly	Telephone
HMV			
0906 3021200	hmv.yahoo.co.uk	Free	Online/store
KAROO			
01482 602742	www.karoo.net	Monthly	Telephone
LINEONE			
0800 111210	www.lineone.net	Monthly	Telephone
LUNA			
01782 855655	www.luna.co.uk	Monthly	Telephone
MSN			
0870 601100	www.msn.co.uk	Monthly	Online
NATIONWIDE			
0800 7316860	www.nationwide.co.uk	Monthly	Online
NETCOM			
0800 9809110	www.netcom.net.uk	Monthly	Online
NETKONECT			
01420 542777	www.netkonect.net	Monthly	CD
ONYX			
0345 715715	www.onyxnet.co.uk	Monthly	Telephone
PARADISE			
0125 6414863	www.pins.co.uk	Monthly	Online
PAVILION			
0845 333500	www.pavilion.net	Monthly	Online

PIPEX DIAL
0541 506066 www.uk.uu.net Monthly Online

PLANET ONLINE
0113 2345100 www.theplanet.co.uk Monthly Telephone

EASYNET
0207681444 www.easynet.net Monthly Telephone

POPTEL
0207 9239465 www.poptel.net Monthly Online

PUBLIC ONLINE
0208 6367373 www.publiconline.net Free Online

REDNET
01494 513333 www.red.net Monthly Telephone

SCOTLAND ONLINE
0800 0272027 www.scotland.net Monthly Online

SONNET
0702 8912000 www.sonnet.co.uk Monthly Telephone

TESCONET
0845 6050100 www.tesco.net Free CD

TIMEWARP
01619 508855 www.timewarp.co.uk Monthly Telephone

TINY COMPUTERS
0800 7834575 www.tinyonline.net Free Telephone

UK PEOPLE
0870 7403930 www.ukpeople.net Free Online/CD

U-NET
01925 484444 www.u-net.net Monthly CD

UUNET PIPEX
0500 474739 www.uunet.pipex.com Monthly CD

VIRGIN NET
0500 558800 www.virgin.net Free CD/online

WATERSTONES
0122 5448595 www.waterstones.co.uk Free Visit store

X-STREAM
0207 7716666 www.x-stream.com Free Online

WHICH? ONLINE
0645 830240 www.which.net Monthly Telephone

ZYNET
0139 2209500 www.zynet.co.uk Annual Telephone

GLOSSARY

When you first visit a foreign country, life is always that much more straightforward if you can speak the language. Although English is the principle language of the Internet, the proliferation of technical jargon can sometimes make it seem as coherent as Chinese (to an English speaker, that is). In this section you'll find succinct descriptions for some of the terms that you may find a little daunting when you first get connected.

56K
The speed measured in bauds (bits per second) that most modems currently run at. The higher the speed, the faster the modem will be able to download files and Web pages. Older models operate at 14.4K, 28.8K or 33.6K .

ACCESS PROVIDER
A company that sells (or gives) a connection to the Internet.

ACTIVEX
Microsoft's programming language for use on the World Wide Web that allows Web pages to be more interactive.

ADDRESS
Usually refers to a Web address - the URL code that needs to be typed into the browser to locate the Web site. It can also refer to the unique IP Address given to every computer connected to the Internet.

ANONYMOUS FTP
A method of connecting to a remote computer (without needing special permission or a password) to download publically accessible files or software.

ANONYMOUS REMAIL
A service for forwarding e-mails or newsgroup postings so that your personal details are not included.

APPLET
A tiny computer program written in a language called Java which is designed to add functionality to Web pages. For an applet to work, the browser must be Java-compatible. Some older versions of Internet Explorer or Netscape Navigator require a plug-in to do this.

ARPANET
The Advanced Research Project Agency Network of military computers developed in 1969 from which the Internet evolved.

ARCHIE
A database of publicly accessible files or software that can be downloaded via FTP. It is possible to search Archie by using dedicated client software or a regular Web browser.

ASCII
An acronym for "American Standard Code for Information Interchange". All this really means is that ASCII – pronounced "askey" – is a standardised way of converting text into a format that can be then interpreted by any computer. ASCII is also sometimes referred to as "plain text".

ATTACHMENT
A file of any type or format which is delivered at the same time as an e-mail message.

BACKUP
A safe second copy of a computer file or program. If you're new to using computers, here is the first rule of survival: ALWAYS MAKE BACKUPS OF IMPORTANT DATA. Your computer's hard disk has not been designed to live forever – when it dies make sure your work doesn't go with it.

BANDWIDTH
The amount of data that can be passed through a given connection within a network at one time. The greater the bandwidth, the faster the transfer of data.

BAUD
The speed at which a modem can transfer data, measured in events per second (not, as is often suggested, bits – binary digits – per second).

BOOKMARK
A marker stored by a Web browser that acts as a future shortcut to a Web site. In this way, long and complicated URL addresses can be stored so that users don't have to remember them or retype them when they next want to access the site. Bookmarks are referred to as "Favorites" in Microsoft's Internet Explorer.

BOUNCED MAIL
An e-mail message that is "returned to sender". Usually occurs because the e-mail address had been wrongly entered.

BROWSER
A computer program that lets you view Web pages on the Internet. The two most commonly used browsers by some distance are Microsoft's Internet Explorer and Netscape's Navigator (which now comes as a part of the Communicator package). Browsers can now also handle other areas of Internet activity such as e-mail and newsgroups.

CACHE DIRECTORY
An area on a computer's hard disk in which the browser stores the files downloaded from the Web. If you want to view those pages again, the browser saves downloading time by pulling them from the hard disk rather than reloading them from the Internet. By increasing the cache allocation you can store more Web pages.

CHAT
A "conversation" on the Internet between two or more people. Often takes place using IRC (Internet Relay Chat) but some on-line service providers have their own dedicated chat rooms.

CLIENT PROGRAM
A piece of software designed to exchange specific infomation with a server. For example CuteFTP only works with FTP servers.

COOKIE
A small file left on your hard disk by a web server. These are perfectly safe and are used to identify frequent visitors, but may enable companies to see which sites you have visited for marketing purposes.

CYBERSPACE

A much overused term, originally coined by Sci-fi author William Gibson in his novel "Neuromancer", which is now used to describe all aspects of life on the Internet.

DATA COMPRESSION

A method of reducing the size of a computer file so that it can be sent with greater speed across the Internet. Popular software includes WinZip for PCs and Stuffit for Macs.

DIAL-UP NETWORKING

The TCP/IP program built into Windows 95, Windows 98 and Windows NT that simplifies making an Internet connection on PCs.

DOMAIN NAME

A unique text name that identifies a computer or network of computers on the Internet. The domain name can be used to identify an organisation, nature of business and its location. For example, smithengineering.co.uk would probably signify a British ("uk") company ("co") called Smith Engineering.

DOMAIN NAME SYSTEM

A database that can convert the (theoretically) user-friendly domain names into IP addresses that computers can comprehend.

DOWNLOADING

The process of transferring files or software from a remote computer to your own. The reverse is called uploading – for example, when you create your own Web pages.

E-MAIL

Electronic mail. A system that allows computers connected to the Internet to exchange text messages. The computer equivalent of writing a letter and posting it.

E-MAIL ADDRESS

A unique identifier that allows all e-mails to be delivered to their correct destinations. An example could be fred@smithengineering.co.uk.

EMOTICONS

Sometimes referred to as "smileys", emoticons are standard punctuation symbols that can be used in e-mails, newsgroups and chat rooms to convey an emotion. When viewed from the side they appear to show a facial gesture. The happy :) and sad :(emoticons are the two most commonly used.

ENCRYPTION

The use of specialized software for converting data so that it cannot be read by any other than those intended. The recipients require the same software to decode the data. Encryption is commonly used for security within online shopping sites.

FAQ

Acronym for "frequently asked questions". Simply a list of amswers to the most common questions relating to various aspects of the Internet – from newsgroups to software queries. This avoids newcomers repeatedly asking the same questions.

FAVORITES

An alternative term for bookmarks used by Microsoft's Internet Explorer Web browser.

FLAMING

An offensive or abusive e-mail or newsgroup posting. Usually served as a response rather than to initiate an argument.

FRAMES

Found on more sophisticated Web pages, frames allow some parts of the page to alter while other parts remain still.

FREEWARE

Software often distributed via the Internet that you can download free of charge.

FTP

Abbreviation for "File Transfer Protocol", the most common way of transferring files across the Internet. Information can be downloaded by using an FTP client program or, more commonly nowadays, a Web browser.

GIF

Acronym standing for "Graphics Interchange Format", one of the two most commonly used formats on the Internet (the other is JPEG). Popular for Web sites because they are smaller in size than JPEGs, but can only hold a maximum of 256 colours. In the PC world, GIF files are usually suffixed with ".gif".

GIGABYTE

Measurement of file size or disk space being approximately equal to one billion bytes. Abbreviated to "Gb".

GOPHER

The forerunner of the World Wide Web, a menu-based system for browsing and retrieving documents.

HARD DISK

The vital part of your computer that permanently stores programs and files that can be written to and read. Data remains secure when switched off, although backups are ALWAYS advisable. Hard disk capacity is measured in megabytes (Mb) or gigabytes (Gb).

HIT RATE

The number of occasions that a Web site has been viewed by another Internet user. The sites with the highest hit rates can sometimes attract advertising sponsors.

HTML

Acronym for "Hypertext Markup Language", the standard language used to turn ASCII text into Web pages.

HTTP

"Hypertext Transfer Protocol" is the standard for which Web pages are transferred and identified around the Internet.

HYPERLINK

A part of a Web page - usually a piece of text or image - that, when clicked on, automatically transfers the reader to a different point within the same page, a different page or an entirely different Web site.

HYPERTEXT

A system developed by scientist Tim Berners-Lee where text can contain links to other parts of the same document or documents held on a different computer. HTML is a hypertext language used by the World Wide Web.

INTERNET

A massive network of computers and sub-networks all linked together making it possible to exchange information. Often abbreviated as "the Net".

INTRANET

A private network within an organization that uses the same protocols as the Internet but is not necessarily connected directly to the Internet.

INTERNET SERVICE PROVIDER (ISP)

A company that sells the facility to connect to the Internet. Most ISPs also provide the software necessary to access the Net.

IP ADDRESS

A unique address assigned to every site on the Internet so that information can be routed to the correct destination. The address consists of four numbers separated by dots, for example, 131.156.4.23 and they correspond directly to the domain name. Although the IP address may change, the DNS server maintains the correct link to the domain name.

IRC

Internet Relay Chat. A commonly used system for "chatting" over the Internet. Chat networks are accessed by special client programs (which are usually freeware). Different chat room are usually described as "channels".

ISDN

An acronym for "Integrated Services Digital Network", or more simply a high-speed digital phone line. An ISDN connection can achieve speeds of up to 128,000 bits per second, much faster than a standard telephone line but is only useful for Internet connection if your ISP can match such speeds.

ISP

An "Internet Service Provider" is quite simply the company that provides you with your Internet conncection.

JAVA

An "object-oriented" programming language used to create Applets - tiny programs that give additional functionality to web pages. A simpler, plain-English derivative called JavaScript can be inserted directly into an HTML script.

JPEG

Short for "Joint Photographic Experts Group", an alternative image file format to GIFs. JPEGs can store over 16 million colours and so it is an excellent format for storing photographic images, although they take up more space than GIFs which makes them less ideal for simpler forms of artwork.

LAN

Acronym for Local Area Network. This usually describes a small network of computers linked together within an office for the purposes of file sharing or communication.

LEASED LINE

A line hired from a telecommunications company that provides a permanent link to an Internet service provider. Leased lines are extremely fast and extremely expensive.

LIST SERVER

An automatic system used to send the same e-mail message to a large number of addresses simultaneously. See Mailing List.

LOGGING ON AND OFF

Connecting to and disconnecting from the Internet from your computer via a dial-up line and modem.

LURKING

The act of reading newsgroup postings or chat room conversations without participating. There is nothing sinister about lurking in this sense

MAILING LIST

This can refer to a list of e-mails that are sent to the same address at the same time by a List Server, or a discussion group in which the messages are distributed via e-mail rather than in a newsgroup.

MAIL SERVER
A computer whose whose only task is to distribute e-mails around the Internet.

MEGABYTE
Approximately one million bytes.

MIME
Acronym for "Multipurpose Internet Mail Extension". A system used to handle attachments in e-mails and newsgroup postings.

MIRROR SITE
A Web site that appears in duplicate on a different computer. Sites with high hit-rates are often found on multiple servers (sometimes located in different countries) so that the pressure is eased on the main computer.

MODEM
A "modulator/demodulator" – a piece of hardware used to transfer data between two computers across a telephone line. The modem converts the data back and forth into formats that can be read and interpreted by each computer. Modems can be external devices or, more commonly, built into the computer.

MP3
A file format that allows very high-quality sound to be played across the Internet. Widely viewed as the future of on-line music.

MPEG
Along with QuickTime, this is the most popular format for movie files on the Internet.

MUD
Acronym for "Multi User Dungeon", a type of text-based game that can be played by multiple users across the Internet.

MULTIMEDIA
Slightly archaic term used to describe text, graphics, sound and video combined within a Web site or on a CD-ROM.

NET
An alternative name for the Internet.

NETIQUETTE
An informal code of conduct developed over the years by Internet users. Formed from the words "Net" and "etiquette", it encourages members of the Net community to be civil to one another and to use the resources of the Internet efficiently. Spamming is one of the most serious transgressions of netiquette.

NETWORK
A group of interconnected computers.

NEWBIE
Slightly derogative term given by experienced users to those who are new to the Internet.

NEWSGROUP
One of approximately 40,000 known Internet discussion groups (sometimes referred to as "USENET groups"). Newsgroups are organized to cater for often very specific interests. Subscribers leave messages on a "notice board" to which other subscribers can respond.

NEWSREADER
Software that allows you to participate in newsgroups. Nowadays the news-reader option in browsers is most commonly used to access newsgroups.

NEWS SERVER
A computer system devoted to the collection and distribution of newsgroup postings.

NNTP
"Network News Transfer Protocol" is a standard for transferring newsgroup data around the Internet.

OFFLINE
A term to describe a computer or user which is not currently connected to the Internet.

ONLINE
The reverse of offline.

ONLINE SERVICE PROVIDER (OSP)
In their original forms, most of the on-line services were miniature versions of the Internet. Paid-up subscribers could communicate with one another via e-mail and discussion groups as well as being able to access specialized databases and other services. When the Internet reached the general public OSPs were forced to add general Internet access to their services. The world's biggest OSPs are AOL (America Online) and Compuserve.

PACKET
A unit of data sent over the Internet. Packet "switching" is used to break information down into these units which are reassembled when they reach your computer.

PING
A "Packet Internet Groper" is a message that tests the connection between two computers. Data is sent from one machine which calculates how long the destination computer takes to make its response (called a "Pong").

PLUG-IN
A tiny add-on program that adds functionality to a Web browser, allowing you to play, for example, animations, videos or sound files.

POP
The "Point Of Presence" is the telephone number that your computer dials via the modem to connect with the ISP and hence the Internet.

POP3
"Post Office Protocol 3" is the most recent standard for receiving e-mails. With POP3, e-mails are stored on a server until the user decides to collect them. POP3 also allows you to download your mail onto any computer anywhere so long as you have a password set up.

POSTING
A message sent to a newsgroup.

PPP
"Point-to-Point Protocol" is the standard data transfer method used to connect computers to the Internet via a modem and telephone line.

PROTOCOL
The rules of communication between two computers designed so that it becomes possible for different types of machine to "talk" to one another.

QUICKTIME
Popular video format developed by Apple and often used in Web sites. A QuickTime viewer or plug-in is needed to see Quicktime files in action.

REALAUDIO
A system that allows the streaming of moderately high-quality audio over the Internet. This means that you can begin to hear the sound file playing as it is downloading.

SEARCH ENGINE
A Web site that can be used to locate other Web sites by performing keyword searches. The most commonly used are Yahoo!, Excite, Lycos and Altavista. Each system uses slightly different search criteria, so it's always worth trying different engines.

SERVER
A general term for any computer or software that allows a computer (or network of computers) to connect to it and share its data.

SHAREWARE
Software, usually developed by an individual or small company, that can be downloaded from the Internet and used free of charge for a trial period.

SIGNATURE
A piece of text that you can set up so that it is pasted onto the end of every e-mail or newsgroup posting you make. Typically, this is used to supply a contact addresses without the need to type it out on each message you send.

SLIP
"Serial Line Internet Protocol" is the predecessor to PPP; it is now used rarely.

SMTP

"Simple Mail Transport Protocol" is an alternative e-mail protocol to POP3. There is little to choose between the two, although POP3 is more flexible in enabling mail to be downloaded onto any computer.

SPAMMING

High treason as far as netiquette is concerned, spamming is the Net term for sending the same message to multiple newsgroups and e-mail addresses. Not only is this form of junk mailing irritating, it also clogs up the Internet, reducing bandwidth for legitimate Internet uses.

STATIC IP ADDRESSING

Some service providers allocate permanent IP addresses to their subscribers. The alternative is dynamic IP addressing, in which Internet users are assigned temporary addresses each time they go online.

STREAMING

A technique for playing audio or video files as they are being downloaded. A browser plug-in decompresses the signal and plays it back immediately meaning that you don't have to wait for the entire file to be downloaded.

SURFING

A term that usually describes aimless browsing of the World Wide Web.

TAG

The HTML codes that create hypertext in Web pages.

TRANSMISSION CONTROL PROTOCOL/INTERNET PROTOCOL (TCP/IP)

These two most important Internet protocols govern communication between your computer and the Internet.

TELNET

A terminal emulation program that allows you to connect to a suitably configured remote computer and use it as if it were your own computer.

UPLOADING

The opposite of downloading – copying files from your own computer to another across the Internet.

UNIFORM RESOURCE LOCATOR
A "URL" is the unique address of a file on the Internet. It can comprise four elements: the protocol; server or domain; path and filename (the latter two may not always be needed). In most cases the URL describes a web address. In this example – http://www.smithengineering.co.uk/products – "http://www" represents the protocol, "smithengineering.co.uk" is the domain and "/products" represents the path below the main page.

USENET
A network of computers which distributes newsgroups and their postings.

UUENCODE/UUDECODE
UUencode is a program that converts binary files so they can be transmitted by e-mail. UUdecode converts the file back when it reaches its destination. Most e-mail and newsgroup readers now do this automatically.

VIRUS
A tiny malicious program deliberately designed to corrupt data. Most are distributed via the Internet so it's always a good idea to run software from the Interent (or from an outside source) through virus-checking software first.

VRML
"Virtual Reality Modelling language" allows three-dimensional images to be displayed and manipulated in Web pages.

WEB PAGE
A single page on the World Wide Web.

WEB SITE
Technically, the server on which a set of Web pages are maintained, though commonly used to describe a complete set of Web pages.

WEB SPACE
The space your ISP allocates for you to create your own Web pages.

WORLD WIDE WEB
A vast collection of Web sites on the Internet that can be navigated using hypertext links.

INDEX

A

B

C